Audrey Hepburn

Also by Warren G. Harris

Lucy & Desi

Gable & Lombard

Cary Grant: A Touch of Elegance

Natalie & R.J.

*The Other Marilyn: A Biography of
Marilyn Miller*

Warren G. Harris

Audrey Hepburn

A Biography

WHEELER
PUBLISHING, INC.

★ AN AMERICAN COMPANY ★

Published in Large Print by arrangement with
Simon & Schuster, Inc. in the United States and
Canada.

Wheeler Large Print Book Series.

Set in 16 pt. Plantin.

Library of Congress Cataloging-in-Publication Data

Harris, Warren G.
    Audrey Hepburn: a biography / Warren G. Harris.
        p.   cm.—(Wheeler large print book series)
    "Published in large print . . ."—Verso t.p.
    Filmography: p.
    Includes bibliographical references and index.
    ISBN 1–56895–156–6 (lg. print) : $24.95
    1. Hepburn, Audrey, 1929–   .   2. Motion picture actors and
actresses—United States—Biography.   3. Large type books.
    I. Title.   II. Series.
    [PN2287.H43H33   1994a]
    791.43'028'092—dc20   94–31165
    [B]   CIP

---

for

EVELYN SEEFF

Contents

chapter one

THE CALL OF FASCISM

"What is needed in order to really become a star is an extra element which God gives you or doesn't give you. You're born with it. You cannot learn it. God kissed Audrey Hepburn on the cheek and there she was," said director Billy Wilder.

When she burst on the world in *Roman Holiday* in 1953, she seemed a total original. Her beauty was more gamine than classic, with large expressive eyes, sculpted cheekbones, lips quick to smile, the graceful neck of a swan.

She seemed to walk on music. She had the gait and carriage of a ballerina, which she had trained to be. Her tallish (five foot seven), slender figure was a designer's dream.

Her speaking voice could melt hearts. Cecil Beaton said it had "a singsong cadence that develops into a flat drawl ending in a childlike query." Director Stanley Donen described it as "extremely cultured, with wonderful pronunciation. Audrey never raised her voice, so you were drawn in, you had to listen carefully, and you wanted to."

She had the aura of a true princess. "She is one of us," the mother of Queen Elizabeth was overheard murmuring in her daughter's ear after

1

they were introduced to Audrey at a Royal Command Film Performance in London.

She also possessed a wistful, fragile quality that reminded her great friend, Hubert de Givenchy, of "a little lost bird," and undoubtedly came from childhood traumas and wartime suffering.

Audrey once told a friend that if she ever got around to writing an autobiography, it would begin: "I was born on May 4th, 1929, and I died three weeks later." She developed such a bad case of whooping cough that her tiny heart stopped beating. Her mother revived her with a wallop on the backside and stayed with her ceaselessly through two days and nights until the crisis passed.

Her name at birth was Andrey Kathleen Ruston, "Andrey" being an uncommon feminine of "Andrew," which would have been her given name if she'd been born a boy. "Kathleen" honored her father's favorite aunt. Inevitably, the tendency of "Andrey" to turn up misspelled as the better known "Audrey" became a constant annoyance, so the quickest solution was for the family to adopt that name instead.

Because Audrey happened to be born in Brussels, her original nationality has often been erroneously cited as Belgian. But being born on Belgian soil does not by itself convey Belgian citizenship. That must come through at least one Belgian parent or through naturalization, neither of which applied in Audrey's case. Though she had a British father and a Dutch-born mother, both were British in the eyes of the law, and she was duly certified as such by the British consulate in Brussels.

Audrey had a multinational ancestry—English, Scottish, Irish, French, and Austrian on her father's side; and Dutch, Hungarian, and more French on her mother's. Her parents first met and were married in the Netherlands East Indies (Indonesia after 1949).

At the time of his daughter's birth in 1929, Joseph Victor Anthony Ruston was nearly forty years old. An experienced world traveler, he'd worked at many things but *never*—as often reported—for the Bank of England or as manager of its Brussels branch. (A good trick, given that the BOE is England's exchequer, not a conventional bank, and has never had branches abroad!)

Born November 21, 1889, in Ouzeg, Slovakia, Ruston had an Austrian mother and a British father with business interests in Central Europe. In his credentials, he claimed to have studied at Trinity College, Cambridge, and to have served in the British Army during the Great War of 1914–18, neither of which can be verified. But archives of the British Foreign Office reveal that after the war he joined the diplomatic service and got posted to the Netherlands East Indies as vice-consul in Semarang, a burgeoning town on Java halfway between the capital, Batavia (now called Djakarta), and Surabaja. Marriage to a European settler named Cornelia Bisschop had already ended in divorce by the time Ruston became romantically involved with Baroness Ella van Heemstra.

Eleven years younger than Ruston, the

Baroness had come out to the East Indies from Holland with her husband, Hendrik Quarles van Ufford, an executive with the Bataafsche Petroleum Company. They had two sons, Alexander and Ian, before the marriage ended in divorce in 1925.

Ruston saw an opportunity for himself and seized it. The Baroness belonged to a wealthy and highly respected family. No doubt Ella had reasons of her own for welcoming his advances. For someone who'd just been rejected by her husband, he made a charming, irresistible companion. They were soon making plans for a future together. Ruston resigned his diplomatic post for a managerial job with Maclaine Watson & Company, a British arbitrage house that handled most of the international trading in East Indian tin. This required moving to Batavia, where the couple were subsequently married in September 1926. Ella's two sons came to live with them.

Along with a ready-made family, Ruston took on an alternate surname, the poshly hyphenated Hepburn-Ruston, which his aristocratic bride concocted and preferred him to use. It made Ruston seem closer to her own social class and also gave her an even more distinguished name for her personal calling card—Baroness Ella van Heemstra Hepburn-Ruston.

Ella picked "Hepburn" because it was the only noble name that she could find in Ruston's family tree. It had been the maiden name of his grandmother, Isabelle Ruston, who was three centuries removed from James Hepburn, Earl of Bothwell. History remembers him as the third husband of

Mary, Queen of Scots. That he may also have murdered Mary's second husband, Lord Darnley, didn't seem to bother the Baroness when she borrowed the name.

Since Joseph Ruston never bothered to legally change his name to Hepburn-Ruston, claims of the latter being Audrey's original surname are false. It was just "Ruston," as her birth certificate proves. She, of course, later took "Hepburn" for a professional name, but that's jumping ahead of the story.

While Joseph Ruston had a bourgeois heritage, the Baroness Ella van Heemstra's noble background can be traced directly back to 1528 in the records of the Dutch peerage. But to bring it into modern times, Ella was the third of six children (all entitled to the rank of baron or baroness) of Baron Aarnoud van Heemstra and the Baroness Elbrig van Asbeck. She was named after her mother, who was called "Ella" within the family.

The van Heemstra wealth came from colonial trading, but Ella's father studied to be a lawyer and devoted his life to government service, including terms as burgomaster of Arnhem in Holland, a chief magistrate in that city's Court of Justice, and governor of Dutch Guiana (now Surinam) in northeastern South America.

Ella's mother's family owned the magnificent Huis Doorn, a fifty-six-room mansion (the Dutch prefer to call them castles) set in acres of gardens and woods near Doorn in central Holland. The van Heemstras and van Asbecks had close ties to Queen Wilhelmina, who'd assumed the Dutch throne in 1898 at the age of eighteen and showed no signs of relinquishing it. Ella's younger sister, Baroness Jacqueline van Heemstra, was a lady-in-waiting to Crown Princess Juliana. Ella's first husband had been a lieutenant in the queen's equerry before the couple moved to the East Indies.

Ruston and Ella made a striking and highly volatile couple. Tall and handsome, he'd grown a mustache to compensate for his receding hairline. An expert horseman, he loved tweeds and casual wear, smoked a pipe, and looked quite the dashing adventurer. Though borderline homely, Ella had a flair for clothes and adornment which, combined with her aristocratic carriage and sparkling personality, made her seem almost beautiful. It's probable that Audrey inherited her good looks from her father and her fashion sense from both parents.

In character, they were both extroverts, with flirtatious and jealous natures. They often fought like hellcats, but not in a destructive way. Some marriages thrive on quarrels as long as they end in kisses. The Rustons' may have been one of those.

Ella was the more dominating and domineering of the pair. A longtime friend, brewery magnate Freddie Heineken, describes her as "a born actress. She was very dramatic, highly emotional, and had a great sense of fun. When Ella was growing up, she wanted to become, of all things, an opera singer! But in those times, a daughter of the nobility was forbidden to work or to have a career. She was expected to marry well and to have lots of children."

Neither Ruston nor Ella wanted to spend the rest of their lives in sweltering, semi-uncivilized Java, so he applied for a transfer to Maclaine Watson's headquarters in England and got it. But after a year in London, the couple, with Ella's boys still in tow, uprooted again when Ruston joined an Anglo-French credit society that was based in Paris and specialized in loans, mortgages, and financial planning. With the title of vice-president and deputy administrator, he was sent to Brussels to open and manage a branch office.

The Rustons settled in a furnished maisonette at 48 rue Keyenveld in the Ixelles district, the most Parisian quarter of Brussels. Their daughter, Andrey Kathleen, was born at home, at three in the morning of May 4, 1929. In what proved typical of her lifelong relationship with her father, he was away on a business trip at the time. Attending the birth was a trusted nurse-midwife sent from Holland by Ella's parents.

Audrey, of course, arrived in the world possessing two half brothers, Alexander and Ian Quarles van Ufford, who were going on nine and five at the time. Ian, closer in age, became her favorite. "Like most newborn babies, Audrey was small, wrinkled, and monkey-faced," he recalls. "But she quickly grew out of it and bewitched us all with her ravishing dancing eyes."

When city life proved too confining for a family of five, Ella went hunting for a place in the country and finally found what she wanted just a few miles from Brussels in the woodsy village of Linkebeek. In January 1932, the Rustons took a lease on a small estate known as "Castel Sainte-Cecile" (again, really a mansion, much smaller but reminiscent of Huis Doorn in Holland, where Ella spent some of her childhood).

Raised in the company of two boisterous males, Audrey developed into a tomboy very quickly. She hated dolls, whose lifelessness she equated with dead babies, playing house, or any of the usual girlish pursuits. "We were very naughty. We did a lot of tree climbing," Ian recalled.

Yet Audrey had a softer side. Whenever Ella took her out strolling or shopping, Audrey wanted to look into every pram and pick up the infant inside it. "My mother would get terribly embarrassed and threaten to disown me," she remembered. "What I've always had, and maybe that I was born with, was an enormous love of people, of children. Love meant not only receiving it but wanting desperately to give it. My mother herself was not a very affectionate person. She was a fabulous mother, but she had a Victorian upbringing of great discipline, of great ethics. She was very strict, very demanding of her children. She had a lot of love *within* her, but she was not always able to show it. I went searching all over the place to find somebody who would cuddle me, and I found it, in my aunts or my nannies."

As time went on, the Baroness realized that her daughter was more perceptive and sensitive than most children. Audrey much preferred her own company to running and playing with others.

She favored her brothers' adventure books by Rudyard Kipling and Robert Louis Stevenson over fairy tales, and often acted out scenes from them, using the household dogs and cats as her supporting cast.

From the beginning, she loved all types of music, especially classical. She would wear out her little arms cranking up the family's Victrola to listen to her favorite records. At age four, she started taking piano lessons and eventually became adept enough to play at birthday parties and other family gatherings.

She was also very artistic. "Audrey made beautiful little sculptures out of colored clay. She also loved to sketch. She used to fill notebooks with delicate drawings of the hands and feet of ballet dancers," cousin Elisabeth van Heemstra recalled.

Given her heritage and surroundings, Audrey was virtually born multilingual, speaking English, French, Flemish, and Dutch from an early age. Her first years were divided between home in Belgium, frequent visits to her maternal grandparents in Holland, and regular trips to London and Paris in conjunction with her father's business activities.

Audrey always remembered her Belgian years with affection. The Rustons' lovely old country house, with its gardens and fruit orchard, inspired her adult cravings for similar dwellings. And it was in Brussels that the future film star saw her first movies. In those days, Belgium had ultrastrict censorship regulating attendance by children under sixteen, so the Baroness decided that the only proper place to take her daughter was the Cinéac Le Soir (named after Brussels's top newspaper). There Audrey could learn something from the newsreels and travelogues and still be entertained by the cartoons and comedy shorts that filled out the programs.

Momentous things were happening around Audrey that couldn't have been understood by a preschooler. The family was traveling more and more to London, but not exclusively for her father's business. Both Ruston and the Baroness had fallen under the spell of economist-politician Sir Oswald Mosley, who in 1931 at age thirty-five had resigned a top place in Ramsay MacDonald's Labor government to form the shortlived New Party, followed by the British Union of Fascists. Disillusioned and frustrated by Labor's failure to make much headway in solving the problems caused by the Depression, Mosley proposed a radical system of government similar to that already showing signs of success under Benito Mussolini's leadership in Italy.

In the decade before World War II, the word "fascism" and the ideology behind it were not considered as evil and loathsome as history later proved them. For people like the Rustons, who had money and/or aristocratic connections, a fascist corporative state seemed preferable to a communistic one in which they would be reduced to the proletariat, à la their counterparts in Russia following the October Revolution of 1917.

In the Rustons' case, the Baroness was the deciding factor in their becoming members of the British Union of Fascists. No doubt Ella was swayed not only by Sir Oswald Mosley's great charisma (ironically, he bore a strong physical resemblance to her husband!) but also by his noble pedigree and claim to the title of Baron Ravensdale. Her own aristocratic connections gave Ella instant access to the BUF's innermost circle, where she also became acquainted with widower Mosley's companion and future wife, Diana, and her sister Unity, who were two of the six celebrated Mitford sisters. The Baroness discovered much in common with Diana, a divorcée with two sons, but less so with Unity, who was totally infatuated with her friend Adolf Hitler and spoke of nothing else.

As the BUF continued to build in size and strength, the Rustons became more and more involved in its recruitment and fund-raising activities. They were spending so much time in London that a permanent move there seemed inevitable. Meanwhile, they stayed at a residential hotel in Chelsea near the Sloane Square headquarters of the BUF. Audrey was now old enough to attend nursery school during the day. Her half brothers remained in Linkebeek under a housekeeper's care, since the Baroness didn't want to interrupt their schooling.

Mosley and the BUF were taking politics into the streets with huge rallies and marches that often erupted into riots. The Blackshirt Brigade, dressed like Mussolini's militia in Italy, became one of the BUF's trademarks, along with the traditional fascist emblem of the ancient Roman fasces (a bundle of rods containing an ax with the blade projecting). The BUF never used the

German-preferred swastika and had yet to behave as rabidly anti-Semitic as Hitler's Nazis, because Mosley wasn't sure how much the British people or the government would tolerate. But the BUF's propaganda reeked of it, and there had also been demonstrations in heavily Jewish-populated districts of London and other cities.

By the spring of 1935, Baroness Ella had become such a devoted Mosleyite that she poured out her feelings in an article published in the April 26 issue of *The Blackshirt*, a weekly newspaper published by the BUF and sold on newsstands and by subscription throughout the English-speaking world. A glamorous photograph of Ella accompanied the piece, which was entitled "The Call of Fascism."

We who have heard the call of Fascism, and have followed the light on the upward road to victory, have been taught to understand what dimly we knew, and now fully realise that only the spirit can cleanse the body, and only the soul of Britain can be the salvation of Britain.

Too long have we been fettered by the fetish of materialism. At last we are breaking the bondage and are on the road to salvation. . . .

And we who follow Sir Oswald Mosley know that in him we have found a Leader whose eyes are not riveted on earthly things, whose inspiration is of a higher plane, and whose idealism will carry Britain along to the bright light of the new dawn of spiritual rebirth.

"Britain dares to be great," said our Leader. Britain dares to have a soul!

Interestingly, the Baroness comes off sounding to the reader like a native-born Englishwoman rather than Dutch. Marriage to an Englishman and their increasingly extended residencies in London had undoubtedly affected her sense of national allegiance. Yet she still chose "By Baroness Ella van Heemstra" for a byline. A rousing endorsement of Mosley and the BUF by a titled aristocrat would have a much greater impact than one signed by "Ella Ruston" or even "Ella Hepburn-Ruston" (by now her husband's surname of choice).

Following publication of the article in *The Blackshirt*, Mosley expressed his appreciation by inviting the Rustons to join a BUF delegation going to Germany to observe conditions under the National Socialist system. Sir Oswald, who'd just returned from Munich and his very first meeting with Adolf Hitler, couldn't say enough about the "miracles" that the Führer and the Nazi party had already accomplished in their promised efforts to cure the nation's economic and social problems.

With Mosley's "We can do it here" still ringing in their ears, the Rustons and the rest of the BUF contingent took off for Germany and received the grand tour of brand-new autobahns, factories, schools, hospitals, and housing developments. During a reception at the Brown House, the ornate Nazi headquarters in Munich, they met Hitler himself, who came down from his upstairs office and stayed just long enough to shake hands and to join in a group photograph. Back in England again, the Rustons soon received a print by mail, which went straight into a silver frame on the mantelpiece.

Looking back from a perspective of more than half a century, one could say that the Rustons were not only keeping bad company but well advanced in becoming dangerous characters themselves. But the bubble was about to burst.

It happened sometime between Audrey's sixth birthday in May and the end of 1935. As Audrey would later remember it, her father simply walked out and never came back. Perhaps that was how it appeared to a young child, but it was far more complicated than that.

"The most traumatic event in my life was when my father left my mother," she said many decades later. "I remember my mother's reaction. She cried day in, day out. I thought that she never would stop. You look into your mother's face, and it's covered with tears, and you're terrified. You say to yourself, 'What's going to happen to me?' The ground has gone out from under you. I'm not afraid to say something of that feeling has stayed with me through my own relationships. When I fell in love and married, I lived in constant fear of being left. I learned that you can't love without the fear of losing."

But why did Joseph Ruston leave? If Audrey ever learned the reason or reasons, she never divulged them publicly. But the answer is almost certainly linked to her parents' involvement in the fascist movement. Friends who knew the couple insist that Ruston's sudden exit was forced by his father-in-law, Baron van Heemstra, who could no longer tolerate the couple's increasing visibility in

14

the BUF or Ruston's management of Ella's family income, which had been going on since they married. In those nine years, considerable sums of money had disappeared, possibly in part into the BUF's campaign chest.

The Baron also allegedly received instructions from his close friend Queen Wilhelmina to silence his daughter's mouthings for the BUF, which could be interpreted as Dutch endorsement of Mosley's platform. The Dutch royals and their cousins in England loathed and feared the prospect of their nations turning into fascist dictatorships and were rabidly opposed to the BUF and Holland's similar NSB.

Exactly how the Baron persuaded Ruston to "disappear" is uncertain, but it could have been through a threat of criminal prosecution for embezzlement of Ella's money. But the Baron was more intent on putting a quick end to the relationship, and he may have put more cash on the line just to get Ruston on his way.

Whatever happened, Ella was kept out of the negotiations, and Ruston's departure came as a tremendous shock. Friends claim Ella was so madly in love with her husband that they feared she would commit suicide if he didn't return. She certainly had the temperament to do so, but common sense and concern for her three children prevailed.

In adult reminiscing about her childhood, Audrey often gave the impression that her father had abandoned his family and that they never saw him again after he left. But that's far from the truth, especially in young Audrey's case. After the shock had subsided, there was the legal process of divorce to be faced, which had to go through a maze of English and Dutch courts and ended up taking several years.

Lest it seem that Ruston was completely heartless, he made it plain through his lawyers that he wanted Audrey to continue her education in England so that he could visit her regularly. Ella consented and suggested a place in Elham, a picturesque village in Kent where the Rustons had often vacationed. Audrey was enrolled in a little private school owned and staffed by the six unmarried Rigden sisters (quaintly called "maiden" in those days). Elham had a good train connection to London and was just five miles from Folkestone, a departure point for the Continent, so Audrey would be easily accessible for both parents.

Ella, meanwhile, wound up affairs in Belgium and moved back to Holland with the two boys to reside with her parents on their estate in Arnhem, where the van Heemstras had settled in 1929 at the completion of the Baron's term as governor of Dutch Guiana. The magnificent Huis Doorn of Ella's youth had been sold by her mother's family to Germany's exiled Kaiser Wilhelm II (he lived there until his death in 1941).

Angelic six-year-old Audrey had not only the split between her parents to contend with but also the severing of the intensely close relationship she'd enjoyed with her mother since birth. Mentally, the two seemed still attached. They knew what the other was thinking without having to ask. They were extremely respectful and

16

protective of each other. That bond lasted a life-time and never weakened.

At school in Elham and deprived of daily contact with her mother, Audrey grew even more shy and withdrawn. She did not want to mix with the other girls and often vanished into the garden, where she would eventually be found hiding in a tree or under a bush. Though it's hard to imagine Audrey Hepburn ever having any bad habits, in that period she became a compulsive nail biter and a chubby overeater. She begged for second portions at mealtimes and binged on the Baroness's frequent shipments of her favorite chocolates and cookies.

At the advice of the teachers, Ella stayed away for six months in the hope that Audrey would snap out of it. But when she returned, she was appalled by the pitiful child she found. By then Audrey was also showing a tendency for migraine headaches, something that would plague her for the rest of her life. It didn't take a psychiatrist to tell that most of Audrey's problems were prob-ably psychosomatic, caused by bottled-up sorrow and rage over the collapse of the united family of parents and half brothers that she'd known since babyhood.

Though an instant solution might have been for Ella to take Audrey back to Holland with her, Ruston and his lawyers didn't want the child leaving England while divorce proceedings were going on. The next best thing was for the Baroness to move to Elham, or at least to spend more time there, since she also had her sons in Arnhem to consider.

Ella being loose again in the stomping grounds of the British Union of Fascists caused great concern to the van Heemstra family, which threatened to disinherit her if she reactivated her BUF membership. If she did, it must have been secretly, because it was not evident to Elham's 1,200 residents. Some still recall her staying there for two or three weeks at a time at Orchard Cottage, a boardinghouse owned by a Mrs. Butcher. The Baroness and her saucer-eyed daughter became familiar sights as they shopped on the High Street or took afternoon tea at the Rose and Crown Hotel.

With her mother much more on the scene, Audrey soon came alive again, and by the end of her second school term she was absolutely blooming. She'd made many friends among the other girls and landed on the honor roll in her studies. She was ecstatic over her progress in what had been her first year of dance instruction. Miss Rigden, her teacher and an ardent disciple of Isadora Duncan, told the Baroness that Audrey had a natural talent and that a career in ballet might be possible if she received the right training and really worked hard at it.

But the world was hurtling toward its second Great War in a bit over twenty years, so planning for Audrey's immediate safety and survival would very soon take priority over dreams for her adulthood. By her tenth birthday on May 4, 1939, the annexations by Germany, Italy, and Japan in Eastern Europe, Africa, and Asia threatened to become global if they weren't stopped.

In June of 1939, the final papers in the Ruston's

divorce proceedings passed through a court in The Hague and the couple were officially unhitched. Though Ella received full-time custody of Audrey, the girl had adjusted so well to her British school that it seemed essential to keep her there, or at least until the resolution of England's efforts to maintain some sort of peace with the fascist aggressors.

Where Ella stood politically is uncertain; friends claim not to know or refuse to discuss it, which suggests that she was still pro-fascist in mind if not in practice. But her ex-husband had become so dissatisfied with the BUF's dillydallying on the Jewish question that he finally quit to join a splinter group that was violently pro-Nazi and anti-Semitic.

When all attempts at appeasing Hitler failed and both England and France declared war against Germany on September 3, 1939, the Baroness happened to be in Holland with her sons. But as soon as she heard the news, she took immediate action toward Audrey's evacuation.

As Audrey later remembered it: "My mother became desperate to get me out of England, because Holland was neutral. There were still a few Dutch planes that were allowed to fly. Somehow she contacted my father and asked him to make the arrangements. Gatwick Airport was closed for some reason, so we had to drive to an airfield down in Sussex. They put me on this bright orange plane, which is the national color of Holland. It flew very low. It really was one of the last planes out. That was the last time I saw my father for many, many years."

That separation proved to be one of the few genuine tragedies of Audrey Hepburn's life. "I worshiped my father," she recalled. "Having him cut off from me was terribly awful. If I could have just seen him regularly, I would have felt he loved me. I would have felt I had a father."

chapter two

LIFE UNDER THE NEW ORDER

The ten-year-old Audrey Hepburn might have been safer remaining in England instead of being evacuated to Holland. She'd gone from the frying pan into the fire. But who knew then that except for being heavily bombed, England would never be conquered or occupied by Nazi Germany? Holland would not be so lucky.

During the five years of World War I, Holland had remained neutral. The small but densely populated trading nation intended keeping that stance because Germany and England were the biggest customers for its agricultural, manufacturing, and East Indian rubber and petroleum industries. But it didn't take much brainpower to realize that Nazi Germany would become covetous of Holland's resources and its close proximity to England's shores. At the end of August 1939, the Dutch government ordered the mobilization of its armed forces to fend off a possible invasion. Troops were stationed up and down the eastern frontier with Germany. Barbed wire fences and searchlights became the visible part of the heavily mined terrain.

Reunited with her mother in Arnhem, Audrey adjusted quickly to her new surroundings, although she missed Grandma van Heemstra, who'd died in March while Audrey was still in England. Nineteen-year-old Alexander van Ufford, the eldest of Audrey's two half brothers, had just been called up for the army, so there was only fifteen-year-old Ian sharing quarters with them. Since arriving in Arnhem, Ella and the boys had left the van Heemstra mansion for a spacious garden apartment of their own in the Sonsbeek district, a woodsy area reminiscent of Linkebeek in Belgium, where Audrey spent her first years.

While Holland is famed for its flat and often below-sea-level landscapes, Arnhem is an exception, with hilly terrain that seems absolutely mountainous to the Dutch. In 1939, it was a fairly modern town that started as a health resort and had become a retirement mecca for wealthy returnees from the overseas colonies. Few foreign tourists were attracted there, but the Dutch considered Arnhem an earthly paradise because of its knolls, forests and gateway to the river IJssel. With war clouds on the horizon, its main drawback was being only twelve miles from the German border.

Audrey traded her British girls' school for the municipal coeducational Tamboersbosje (Drummer's Wood) School. Since ballet wasn't part of the curriculum, the Baroness also enrolled her in classes at Arnhem's Conservatory of Music. Immediately Audrey suffered cultural paralysis, since all of her previous schooling had been in English or French. Her Dutch was deplorable.

"That first morning in school," she remembered, "I sat at my little bench, completely baffled. I went home at the end of the day weeping. For several days I went home weeping. But I knew I couldn't just give up. I was forced to learn the language quickly. And I did. Considering what was to happen to me later, it was a useful basic experience."

Audrey was alluding, of course, to Holland's involvement in the war. Christmas 1939 came and happily passed with peace still in the air. It held into the spring of 1940, although in April Germany's seizures of Denmark and Norway suggested that Holland might be next. While Hitler could tolerate a neutral Sweden in Scandinavia, he needed Holland as well as Belgium and France as bases for his planned invasion of England.

On May 4, Audrey turned eleven and wished for peace when she blew out the candles on her birthday cake. For five days her wish seemed to have come true, but on the night of May 9 she discovered otherwise. Ironically, it was supposed to be a happy evening for Audrey, with a visit to the municipal theater for a recital by the Sadler's Wells Ballet Company of London, including such eminent dancers as Margot Fonteyn and Robert Helpmann. The troupe had been traveling around Holland to encourage British-Dutch solidarity. As president of the local arts council, Baroness Ella had been instrumental in persuading them to add Arnhem to their tour as the final stop.

About an hour before curtain time, there were rumbles of cannon fire and explosions from the direction of the German border, but in the hallowed tradition, the show went on anyway. The Britishers wouldn't let possible capture by their Nazi enemy stand in the way of their art. Audrey watched enthralled from a front-row seat as they performed choice bits from their repertoire of classical and contemporary pieces.

"I had this tremendous love of ballet," Audrey remembered. "For the occasion, my mother had our little dressmaker make me a long taffeta dress. I'd never had a long dress in my life, obviously. All the way to the ground, and it rustled, you know. The reason she got me this, at great expense—we couldn't afford this sort of thing— was that I was to present flowers to two very important ladies at the end of the performance."

By the final curtain, the distant battle noises had intensified, and the Britishers were desperate to board their chartered bus to head back to England via plane from The Hague. But Baroness Ella swept on the stage, delivered a long thank-you speech, and then summoned Audrey out from the wings to hand bouquets of red tulips to Margot Fonteyn and director Ninette de Valois. Appearing remarkably poised for a child of eleven, Audrey curtsied, said a few admiring words, and confessed to dreams of becoming a dancer herself when she grew up.

The Baroness had also arranged a backstage reception and buffet, which further delayed the ballet troupe's departure. Finally, the loudest detonations yet forced them to disregard etiquette and to flee in their bus, leaving almost everything behind but the clothes they were wearing.

The Sadler's Wells group got back to England safely, but not very easily because of the delays caused by the Baroness's excessive hospitality. By the time they reached The Hague, all plane flights had been canceled, so they had to take an even more perilous route by ship through heavily mined areas of the North Sea.

Many years later, Audrey would describe the Baroness's behavior that night as part of a scheme to create a pro-Nazi cover for herself as an agent in the Dutch resistance movement. Seemingly the German sympathizers in the audience that night would guess that Ella was deliberately delaying the Britishers so that the advancing Nazis could arrest them. But would a once devout fascist need to *pretend* to be pro-Nazi? Perhaps she really was.

After spending a sleepless night, Audrey and her family rose the next morning, May 10, to a roar of aircraft engines that continued overhead for several hours. The Baroness tried to calm everybody by suggesting that they were German planes headed for an attack on England, but that proved to be only half correct. After grouping in the skies over the North Sea, the armada of bombers and fighters turned around and launched a blitzkrieg on Rotterdam, Holland's most important seaport and warehousing center.

Nazi bombs, either by direct hit or through the fires ignited by them, completely destroyed Rotterdam's Centrum, leaving about a thousand people dead and tens of thousands more wounded and homeless. Meanwhile, seventy-six miles east in Arnhem, German troops that had been crossing the border through the night marched into the city late that morning.

"We were told not to open the curtains and not to look out the windows, that we might be shot at," Audrey recalled. "The Germans came to our town with armored cars and tanks, with machine guns trained on the roofs."

While the Germans may have taken Arnhem, they still had the rest of Holland to conquer and it wouldn't prove as easy as Hitler believed. The comparatively tiny Dutch Army and Navy fought back so fiercely that the invaders suffered heavy casualties. Combat was especially bloody in the vicinity of The Hague, the seat of government, where Nazi paratroop squadrons were under orders to capture Queen Wilhelmina and her cabinet ministers. The nearly sixty-year-old monarch had instructed her secretary to shoot her dead if that became the only way of preventing her from falling into Hitler's hands.

The Dutch forces held out for five days, finally surrendering to defuse Hitler's promise to bomb the city of Amsterdam as well as The Hague. But while the fighting was still going on, a special task force secretly moved the royal family and the top cabinet ministers to England. Crown Princess Juliana and her two children were then sent to Canada for even safer keeping, but her husband, Prince Bernhard, remained in London to help Queen Wilhelmina set up a no longer neutral government-in-exile.

On May 14, 1940, Germany officially seized

the Netherlands and appointed an Austrian, Artur von Seyss-Inquart, as Nazi High Commissioner, headquartered in The Hague. In his inaugural speech, the new *Reichskommissar* described Germany's designs on Holland as exclusively military and promised to return to "normal" life if the people obeyed his rules and regulations. But it would rapidly become plain that the Nazis had additional plans for Holland: to turn it into a National Socialist state that would eventually be absorbed into Germany itself when Hitler won the war, to make maximum use of its industries and labor force, and to expel its Jewish population.

From that time on, Audrey would live in a tight little world consisting of Arnhem and not much more. Like all Hollanders, she and her family would have only the vaguest idea of what was really happening in their country or in the war generally. The Germans took control of the radio and the press, reporting only the Nazi view of things and either ridiculing or ignoring any progress made by the Allied enemy. The people's only alternate sources of news, if that's the word, were the rumor grapevine and illegal radio broadcasts from abroad.

In July 1940, the Dutch government-in-exile in London started a nightly service known as "Radio Orange," using the facilities of the British Broadcasting Corporation, whose English-speaking programs could also be received in Holland. But the Germans immediately retaliated by confiscating thousands of radio sets from homes, sending people to jail for listening, and frequently shutting off electrical power for the night in the most heavily populated cities and regions. Those tactics didn't last long. Depriving people of their radios also meant they wouldn't be able to hear the Nazi broadcasts, which were essential to Propaganda Minister Goebbels's efforts to brainwash the Dutch citizenry.

At age eleven, Audrey was exempt from a new German edict requiring an identity card for everybody fifteen or older. The *persoonsbewijs* bore the photograph, signature, and fingerprints of the registrant, and was stamped with a large "J" if the person happened to be Jewish. That was obviously done to make it easy for the Nazis to round up the Dutch Jews when the time came. Many started looking for hiding places, which was just about their only means of escaping arrest. By this time Germany had also taken France, Belgium, and Luxembourg; the Dutch Jews really had no way to flee except across the North Sea to England, which was virtually impossible because of war conditions.

Although the van Heemstra family had some Jewish ancestry several centuries back, the Nazis were too busy to delve that deeply, so Audrey's mother and other eligible members of the clan avoided having "J" stamped on their identity cards. But the van Heemstras were not so lucky when it came to financial matters. As members of the wealthy elite, they naturally stood to lose more than people lower down the scale. Everybody had to surrender any gold in their possession, and also to exchange their Dutch money for a new everyday currency using zinc coins instead of silver. But the van Heemstras also saw their property confiscated, including real estate, bank accounts, investments, jewelry, and antiques.

Surprisingly, that wasn't as disastrous for the van Heemstras as it might seem. For the time being, much of it was a paper transaction; ownership was transferred to the new German regime, which couldn't really do much with it until victory came. Also, Audrey's grandfather, Baron Aarnoud van Heemstra, was one of Arnhem's most respected citizens. Since the Nazis were trying to create a benevolent image for themselves in Holland, it would be inappropriate to evict the Baron from his home, so he was allowed to continue living there, but under drastically reduced circumstances.

For starters, the Baron had to turn part of the mansion into a billet for Nazi officers. To make room for them, several relatives living with him were ordered to leave. Eventually even the Baron's quarters were taken over, but the Nazis gave him permission to live in another of his seized properties, a weekend house in the nearby town of Velp.

The Nazi takeover put Baroness Ella and children in a bind because *Opa* (Grandpa) could no longer afford to support them. They were forced to move to a small flat above some shops on the fringe of Arnhem's business center. It was all they could manage on the living allowance that they were now entitled to under the German regime's new social welfare scheme.

Audrey's immediate family unit still consisted

of just her mother and the younger of her two half brothers, Ian van Ufford. The older one, Alexander, had just entered the Dutch Army when the Germans invaded. Like the majority of soldiers who survived the fighting, he went into hiding to avoid the alternatives of serving in the German Army or landing in a slave labor camp.

The Dutch had a new word for such people: *"onderduiker,"* or someone who dives under. Between the military, Jews, and other enemies of the Third Reich, there were increasing thousands of "divers" concealed all over Holland. In Alexander's case, Audrey learned to never ask where. Even if her mother knew, she couldn't burden a child with such a dangerous secret. If caught, Alexander, as well as the person or persons hiding him, could be executed.

In her own way, Audrey was also in peril. The occupation turned Holland into an ally of Germany, but England remained an enemy, and Audrey's British citizenship qualified her for internment. Her mother warned her to *never* speak English in public, because one never knew who was listening. They made up the Dutch name of Edda van Heemstra for her to use for herself in case she was ever stopped for questioning. Living in mortal dread of betraying herself through a slip of the tongue, she became even more shy and timid whenever she ventured out by herself to school or ballet classes.

Ironically, a fate similar to the one feared for Audrey had already struck her father, though neither she nor her mother had any way of knowing about it. But in June 1940, a month after Holland fell to the Germans, Joseph Ruston was among about nine hundred people jailed by the British government as security risks because of their pro-fascist activities. The imprisonments without trial had been attempted the previous September at the outbreak of the war, but got delayed by a parliamentary uproar over their legality. Needless to say, Sir Oswald Mosley and Lady Diana headed the list, but after three years in London prisons the couple would be permitted to sit out the war under house arrest instead.

Audrey's father, however, was one of the more severely treated of the so-called Churchill's Guests. In 1941, Ruston's "hostile associations" would cause him to be moved from a London jail cell to a new offshore detention camp on the Isle of Man, which is in the Irish Sea halfway between England and Northern Ireland. The British government became absolutely phobic about the pro-Nazis getting loose in the event of a German invasion of the mainland, so Ruston and hundreds of others were evacuated for the duration.

But that was all unknown to Audrey then. She still missed her father terribly, but her main worries about him were that he might be killed in the German blitzkreigs on London, which were always gleefully reported on the Nazi-controlled radio. Audrey hated listening to it, especially when Hitler or Goebbels gave a long speech and then an announcer repeated the whole thing in Dutch. But there were compensations in the musical programs. New records were becoming scarce, Audrey's precious old ones kept breaking or getting scratched, so radio was her main contact with the classical composers she loved, or at least some of them. Mendelssohn, Offenbach, and Chopin were banned from the pure German-Aryan playlist.

Despite Nazi warnings to the contrary, the family listened at low volume to Radio Orange and the BBC whenever it seemed safe. Audrey had the job of making sure that the dial was always turned back to the setting for the approved Nazi station when they finished. If the police came around on one of their frequent spot checks and found anything suspicious, they would arrest the head of the household.

It might seem that daily life in Holland had been reduced to trying to avoid falling into the hands of the *Moffen* (a new Dutch expletive for the Nazis), but once the initial shock of occupation wore off, people began to adjust and continued much as before. For as long as the Germans seemed to be winning the war, the conquerors would try to be as pleasant as possible. The most noticeable difference was a midnight to 4 A.M. curfew. Despite exportations to Germany, food was still plentiful, especially in rural areas like the one around Arnhem, where everybody lived close to farms and dairies.

The future movie star had never been a frequent filmgoer, but Audrey's choices now became restricted to those produced in Germany, Nazi-controlled France, or fascist Italy (Dutch studios were closed, with equipment dispatched to UFA in Berlin). American and British movies, which used to occupy about 70 percent of the screening time in Holland, were banned, though the latest product couldn't get in anyway. Theaters also had to start their programs with a half-hour selection of German propaganda shorts and newsreels, with patrons forbidden to leave their seats while they were being shown.

For Audrey directly, the most obvious and immediate changes were at school. Several Jewish teachers were dismissed. The curriculum turned pro-German; old history and geography books were replaced by new ones reflecting the official Nazi ideology. As in music, literature study excluded Jewish as well as pro-Jewish or anti-Nazi writers. *Jud Süss* and other anti-Semitic works became required reading. What influence that all had on the minds of the students is impossible to know, but in Audrey's case it seems to have gone in one ear and straight out the other.

The reason being that Audrey's thoughts were always elsewhere. She just couldn't wait for the day's closing bell to ring so that she could rush to her dance classes at the Conservatory of Music, the one place where the Nazi influence had yet to be heavily felt. Probably without her fully understanding why, ballet had become her bridge to the future, provided that the rapidly disintegrating world still had one.

"I had decided to become a dancer. I was very serious about it, and I wanted to dance solo roles," Audrey recalled. "Pavlova was my ideal. I had started collecting books and magazines on dancing long before the war started. I loved music and I was fantastically dedicated and I desperately wanted to do those solo roles because they would allow me to express myself. I couldn't express myself while conforming to a line of twelve girls. I didn't want to conform. I was going to hit my mark and I was working very hard."

Audrey's favorite teacher was ballerina Winja Marova (born Winnie Koopmans!), who became her idol as well. "I'd admired many dancers from afar," Audrey remembered, "but Winja was the first one that I really got to know and could call a friend. She was a beautiful world-class dancer. I think that her being Dutch helped this very young girl in Arnhem to believe that she could become one too."

Meanwhile, the war raged on. No one knew how much longer it would continue, although Hitler kept promising on the radio that it would soon end in victory for Germany and the other Axis powers. But Audrey's twelfth birthday came and passed with no end in sight. In December 1941, there was a glimmer of hope when Radio Orange announced that America had finally entered the war. Audrey's mother told her that when the same thing happened in the last one, it was all over within a year. But circumstances were hardly the same; the United States stood in danger of being wiped out by Japan before ever getting a chance to come to Europe's rescue.

It had become plain that Holland's liberation might have to come from inside its own borders rather than with Allied help. Yet a Resistance movement was late developing because the government, before escaping to London, had always intended remaining neutral in the war and never gave much consideration to forming the nucleus for an underground network that would be responsible for sabotage, espionage, rescue work, and communication with the citizenry. Consequently, the Dutch Resistance movement didn't get started until occupation took place and grew into a number of groups that never became an effectively unified whole.

The first evidence of it was Radio Orange, which immediately gave Queen Wilhelmina a direct link to her subjects and would also become a conduit for sending coded messages to the underground. The Order Service, or *Orde Dienst* (O.D.), had the optimistic mission of preparing for an orderly return of the legal government when Germany was defeated. The Council of Resistance (R.v.V. in the Dutch initials) specialized in sabotage and espionage. The L.K.P. and the L.O. encompassed a multitude of local action groups that published clandestine newspapers and provided *onderduikers* with hiding places and forged documents.

Ironically, in Arnhem, one of the hubs of secret activity became the Conservatory of Music, the cavernous old building where Audrey took her ballet lessons. In time, like many other students, she would be conscripted into service, but it was going to be a long war and that didn't happen for several years.

In the decades since World War II, a cottage industry in movies and novels about that period has created the impression that the Nazi-occupied countries were seething from start to finish with violent repression and Resistance heroism, but in Holland, at least, that was the exception rather than the rule, especially in the first years. The majority of the population came to terms with the reality of occupation and went on with their lives as best they could. In the summer of 1941, Audrey and her mother had even managed a two-week holiday at the coastal resort of Noordwijk aan Zee, though the Baroness had to sell a bit of jewelry she'd been hiding to pay for it.

One can only guess where Baroness Ella stood politically by this time. There's no evidence that the ex-BUF member had joined Holland's similar National Socialistische Beweging (NSB), which by 1940 had a membership amounting to about 8 percent of the population. The Dutch Nazis saw the occupation as their golden opportunity to rule Holland, but the Germans didn't quite trust them, reducing their role to mere enforcers of laws made by the Third Reich. The general populace loathed the NSB and considered them traitors, so what would Ella have gained by joining them, even though she might have agreed with some of their fascist principles?

More likely, Ella was trying to keep an open mind or at least an open escape hatch to being on the right side when the war ended. If she became identified with the Germans or the NSB and the Nazis happened to lose the war, she knew it wouldn't be pleasant for her. It also wouldn't be pleasant for her—right then or after a German total victory—if she did anything that might be considered anti-Nazi.

By the beginning of 1942, the Germans were starting to turn nasty. If Ella did have any pro-

Nazi sentiments, she certainly received good reason to change them, based on what she learned or experienced personally. It must be remembered that news always came to the Dutch people highly slanted in favor of the sender, regardless of whether it was the Germans, Radio Orange, or the underground. There was no truth, only their version of it. Many things never got reported because they were too horrible, too demoralizing, too dangerous to security, or whatever.

But it was becoming gradually though sketchily known that Jews were being arrested and deported, that a work stoppage by the citizenry of Amsterdam in protest had been instantly crushed by the Germans, and that the Resistance had started a campaign of murder and terrorism against the Nazis. To halt the latter, Holland's chief SS officer, Lieutenant General Hanns Rauter, decreed that three Dutch nationals would be executed for each German killed and that there would be similar reprisals for acts of sabotage.

In August 1942, Rauter's edict struck at the heart of the van Heemstra family when Audrey's uncle, magistrate Otto van Limburg Stirum (husband of Ella's eldest sister, Wilhelmina), was among five prominent men selected from different parts of Holland to pay the price for the Resistance's blowing up of a German freight train. Shot by a firing squad along with forty-nine-year-old Uncle Otto were a retired Rotterdam police chief and three businessmen, including a member of the Schimmelpenninck cigar family. If any were actually members of the Resistance, they took that secret to their graves.

If her brother-in-law's execution wasn't enough to end Baroness Ella's romance with fascism (or at least Hitler's version of it), another outrage must have done it. Two weeks later, Audrey's younger half brother, Ian van Ufford, turned eighteen and faced conscription by the Third Reich. Although Ian could have dived under like brother Alexander, he felt guilty about leaving Audrey and Ella on their own without a man to protect them, so he stayed on and eventually suffered the consequences. In the summer of 1943, the dreaded Green Police began rounding up men between ages sixteen and forty for labor service in Germany, and Ian was one of many thousands selected from throughout Holland.

The Nazis would never have called it slave labor, but that's what it amounted to. In Ian's case, he ended up working fourteen hours a day in a factory in Berlin. But at that time all he knew was that he had a train ticket to Germany for the next morning. Audrey and her mother saw him off at the railroad station, where they were joined by Alexander, who'd been notified by the Baroness and was risking arrest himself by coming out of hiding. In the mass confusion on the station platform, nobody bothered him.

It was the last time the family would be together during the war. Though Alexander was at least reachable in his hideout, Ian's fate would be a mystery. Audrey and her mother could never shake their feelings of loss, or the nagging question of whether he was alive or dead.

chapter three

WINTER OF DESOLATION

Now more dependent upon each other than ever, Audrey and her mother carried on as best they could, taking comfort and courage from the fireside chats that Queen Wilhelmina delivered nightly on the forbidden Radio Orange. While growing up among the nobility, Ella had always found Wilhelmina to be cold and overly dignified, so she was amazed to suddenly hear her sounding like everybody's doting mother or grandmother. At times, Ella and Audrey couldn't help smiling when the old girl used the rude *Moffen* for Germans, called the Dutch Nazis *lummels* (nitwits), or urged her loyal subjects to "Beat them on their heads."

Audrey and the Baroness never went to that extreme, but they were gradually becoming involved with the underground movement, though no deeper than as accomplices. The Baroness might have desired a more important role for herself, but the Resistance leaders in Arnhem knew of her pro-fascist history and didn't trust her. It's doubtful that she even knew who the actual leaders were. All her contacts were with minions whose possible betrayal would not undermine the organization. She passed on information that she sometimes picked up in social contacts with the Nazi elite and occasionally helped to raise money for the Resistance. There wasn't much of that around, but just a few guilders paid for the mimeographing of a two-page newspaper that would be distributed by high school kids on their bicycles.

Delivery was one of the riskiest sides to clandestine publishing; sooner or later many of the students got caught and sent to work camps. That was one danger Audrey never faced, because her mother didn't want her bike riding for fear she'd have a crippling accident that would prevent her from becoming a ballerina. So Audrey sort of danced her way into helping the Resistance, performing with some of her conservatory classmates at fund-raisers that the Baroness arranged in private homes. The little soirees fell into a category known as "black," with all the window coverings drawn to keep the *Moffen* from peering in. Because of wartime shortages, Audrey's ballet slippers were now well patched, her costumes made from materials in her mother's rag bin.

"We danced to scratchy old recordings of highlights from *Swan Lake*, *The Nutcracker*, and *Giselle*, which has always been my favorite among the classical ballets," Audrey remembered. "Alas, I always had to be the boy in a pas de deux because I was too tall to play the girl."

In March 1944, she also danced in a recital of Conservatory of Music students at Arnhem's municipal theater that was attended by the usual mixed audience of locals and German occupiers. A critic for the weekly magazine *Cinema & Theater* singled Audrey out as "no doubt the best

40

of Winja Marova's pupils. A girl of barely fifteen, she seems obsessed by a real dance rage and already has a respectable technical proficiency."

Although Audrey was now officially a woman (she started menstruating just before her thirteenth birthday), she still looked such an innocent babe that the Resistance put her into a pool of students who worked as couriers for the local cell of L.O., which assisted "divers" and operated out of the Conservatory of Music. For their own protection, the youngsters couldn't be used too often or the Nazis might begin noticing their movements, so Audrey's turn came maybe two or three times a month tops.

Those were probably Audrey Hepburn's first performances as an actress, as a juvenile Mata Hari delivering forged identity papers and counterfeit ration cards to "divers" in the vicinity (actually to go-betweens, because it would be too dangerous for her to know where they were actually hiding). The documents were always concealed in her bookbag or in her lunch box. That way, if stopped and searched, she could claim that someone must have slipped them in without her knowledge. If things were found stashed in her clothing or in her shoes, it would be harder to explain and she might be arrested. Still too young to be sent to a labor camp, she *could* be quarantined at home except during normal school hours, which would mean the end of her ballet lessons at the conservatory.

By 1944, many of the "divers" came from outside Holland—Allied paratroopers on reconnaissance missions, pilots and crew members of downed Allied aircraft, and escapees from POW camps in Germany. Since the majority of them spoke only English, Audrey, with her excellent command of the language, would sometimes be sent to help new arrivals in the area to get to their havens. Once, while bringing a message to a British pilot hiding in the forest outside town, she suddenly saw two German sentinels heading toward her. Dropping to her knees, Audrey pretended to be picking wild flowers and smilingly handed the Nazis a handful as they passed.

Instead of stopping to question the girl's reason for being there, the soldiers were so charmed that they just patted her on the head and walked on. Proceeding to her specified rendezvous point, Audrey spoke a few reassuring words in English to a man concealed from her view behind rocks, slipped him instructions through the gaps, and headed home. That meant having to pass the *Moffen* again, so she presented them with a few more posies and they were even more pleased. One told the other that he wished all Dutch youngsters could be as friendly to their German protectors.

On another mission, Audrey took a shortcut through Arnhem's railway station and happened upon a scene she would never forget. "I saw German soldiers herding Jewish families with little children, with babies, into meat wagons—train cars like big wooden vans with just a little slat open at the top for air to get in. They were separating them, saying, 'The men go there and the women go there.' Then they would take the babies and put them in another van. All the night-

42

mares I've ever had are mingled with moments from that day," she recalled. (Though she couldn't have known it at the time, the human freight was almost certainly being taken to Transit Camp Westerbork, about seventy-five miles northeast of Arnhem, which was the processing center for Dutch Jews being deported to Auschwitz or other death camps.)

In her movie star fame, Audrey always scoffed at press coverage that depicted her as a youthful heroine of the Resistance: "Every loyal Dutch schoolgirl and boy did their little bit to help. I'm sure that many young people were much more courageous and daring than I was. I'll never forget a secret society of university students called 'Les Gueux' [The Beggars], which killed Nazi soldiers one by one and dumped their bodies in the canals. Now that took real bravery, and many of them were caught and executed by the Germans. They're the type who deserve the memorials and the medals."

As Holland headed toward its fourth full year under German occupation, simply surviving and trying to avoid starvation became the main concerns for Audrey and her mother. Food rationing, which started in 1942, had turned into a joke because store shelves were practically bare. The Nazi regime consumed most of the food supply, with the surplus shipped to the Fatherland to replenish its own drastically depleted resources. People living in an agricultural zone like the one around Arnhem felt the deprivations later than those in big cities like Amsterdam or bomb-devastated Rotterdam. For a long time there were black-market farmers selling milk, cheese, eggs, pork, vegetables, and grain; but when the Nazis began sending even cows and other livestock to Germany, the resultant drop in production depleted supplies.

Audrey's fifteenth birthday celebration in May 1944 was her first without a cake. Her mother couldn't get any of the ingredients needed to bake one, so she improvised by filling a bowl with wild strawberries and sticking a candle in the middle. Sugar had been scarcer than gold since 1940, but the dessert still made a fairly sweet ending to Audrey's spartan birthday dinner, which started with leaves of endive for an appetizer, followed by some watered-down vegetable soup and a quarter-loaf of ersatz bread made from dried pea flour.

Most meals weren't even that grand, so small wonder that Audrey's natural slenderness had started to look as if she had more bones than flesh. She was anemic, suffered from asthma as well as chronic migraine headaches, and frequently missed school and ballet classes because she didn't have the strength. Along with her mother, she was also having problems with colitis and missed menstrual periods, so both women were feeling pretty miserable most of the time.

During the morning of June 6, 1944, there came a ray of hope when the BBC carried news of an Allied landing in Normandy. Audrey and her mother pulled out a map and started guessing how long it would take for the forces to get from the French Coast to the Netherlands. Later in the afternoon, they were introduced to the flat American voice of General Dwight Eisenhower, who officially proclaimed D-Day and predicted a total Allied victory before the end of the year.

In the days and weeks that followed, the BBC and Radio Orange continued to report Allied advances, but in Holland living conditions were getting worse. Besides the food shortages, there were no essentials of any kind and no way of repairing what wore out. There was no soap, no darning thread, no tire tubes. A permanent look of dingy poverty took over.

And on the official radio, Hitler sounded more hysterical than ever, ranting about new miracle weapons that would turn the war back in Germany's favor and guarantee total victory. In July, Audrey and her mother rejoiced over a flash bulletin of an attempt to assassinate the Führer. They sat glued to their radio waiting for more news, but it wasn't what they were praying for. Later that afternoon, Hitler himself spoke on German radio to prove to the world that he'd escaped.

Finally, in the early days of September, Audrey's birthplace of Brussels was liberated as the Allies advanced into Belgium. On the evening of Monday, September 4, Radio Orange reported them in Breda, on Dutch soil at last. The next day became remembered as *"Dolle Dinsdag"* ("Crazy Tuesday") as everybody went wild with anticipation and took their orange flags out of hiding to welcome the liberators. But as the week progressed and nothing dramatic happened, depression and disappointment set in. The reports about Breda were later proven untrue, broadcast simply to boost public morale.

Audrey and her mother weren't deeply enough involved with the Resistance to know that Arnhem would soon be the focus of a massive Allied offensive with the code name "Market-Garden," masterminded by Field Marshal Bernard Law Montgomery. Just after ten in the morning on Sunday, September 17, 1944, the greatest armada of bombers, fighters, and troop-carrying aircraft ever assembled for a single operation took to the skies from bases all over southern England and headed for Arnhem to wipe out the Nazi defenses and to secure the bridge across the Rhine into Germany itself.

Luckily, Audrey and the Baroness lived far enough from the center of Arnhem to be away from the main targets. But they heard the roar of approaching aircraft and rushed outside to see what was happening. Moments later, there were terrific explosions as the first bombs were dropped. Mother and daughter panicked and dashed for shelter with other tenants in the basement of the building. Time seemed to stand still as the ear-shattering bombardment continued. By nightfall it had subsided enough for them to return to their apartment and tune to Radio Orange for news of what was happening.

Finally, Queen Wilhelmina and son-in-law Prince Bernhard, her appointed commander-in-chief of the Netherlands Forces, came on the air announcing that an Allied attack on Arnhem had begun and predicting a swift victory. In support of the invasion, the queen instructed all employees of the Dutch railways to immediately go on strike in order to stop Nazi troop and supply trains from rolling and to prevent the Germans and their sympathizers from fleeing the country.

But by a fantastic stroke of luck, the Germans had drawn a winning hand. In the debris of an Allied glider shot down in the first hours of the invasion, they found an undamaged briefcase containing the complete plans for Market-Garden! At first, Nazi Field Marshal Walther Model guessed that they were deliberately planted there to mislead, but he couldn't risk disregarding them, because there were details of an even more massive onslaught for the next day. If that took place, the Germans would be defeated for lack of sufficient ground and air strength in the Arnhem area to retaliate.

So overnight, Germany's nearly depleted Luftwaffe mounted an allout effort and managed to get 190 planes to gather over Holland to attack an Allied drop scheduled for ten o'clock on Monday morning. But neither side counted on fog back in England, which forced the Allies to delay takeoff and to reschedule the drop for two in the afternoon. That also worked in Germany's favor, giving it four more hours to rush additional troops, artillery, and tanks into Arnhem and vicinity.

Audrey, her mother, and most of their neighbors rushed to the basement again at the first sound of plane engines, but a few brave souls went up on the roof and gawked at the approaching Allied armada. It was a spectacle they'd never forget: an immense column of over

47

three thousand aircraft—fighters, bombers, troop and cargo carriers, gliders—extending seemingly from infinity and flying no higher than 2,500 feet because of the inclement weather.

Needless to say, the Allies were an easy target for the waiting Germans, but their staggering numbers guaranteed that many would land safely and attempt to carry out their missions. The battle dragged on for ten long days that seemed, to Audrey living in a basement with hardly anything to eat, more like a hundred. Historians later claimed that the Allies suffered nearly twice as many casualties as the D-Day invasion of Normandy, with at least 7,500 killed and another 10,000 missing or wounded. The victorious Germans may have lost as many as 13,000, of which perhaps 4,000 were killed.

At the end, the Germans were so enraged over the Dutch Resistance's participation in the combat that Arnhem had to be sacrificed. People were given twenty-four hours to evacuate the city. Afterwards, hundreds of abandoned buildings and houses were looted of their contents and either dynamited or burned to the ground. Previously destroyed in the combat were landmarks like the Conservatory of Music, site of Audrey's ballet classes, and the age-old Town Hall, where her grandfather had once served as burgomaster.

The Germans had dubbed the sea of devastation *"der Hexenkessel"* (the witches' cauldron). Streets were littered with everything from burned-out cars to bathtubs and pianos. Thousands of corpses, Allied, German, and townspeople alike, were being stacked like sand-bags in long rows, with the heads and feet placed alternately for balance.

At the evacuation order, Audrey and her mother fled on foot to Grandpa van Heemstra's house in Velp, about five miles to the north of Arnhem. "I still feel sick when I remember the scenes," Audrey said decades later. "It was human misery at its starkest—masses of refugees on the move, some carrying their dead, babies born on the roadside, hundreds collapsing of hunger."

In Velp, Audrey and the Baroness would be sharing very close quarters with Grandpa, Aunt "Miesje" (widow of the executed Uncle Otto), additional relatives and friends, and a contingent of Germans who'd taken over the attic with a radio transmitter. "Not counting our uninvited guests upstairs, we eventually had thirty-seven people sleeping in our house as evacuees continued to arrive," Audrey recalled.

An entire house next door was being used by the Nazis as a temporary cage for Allied prisoners being processed for shipment to POW camps. Fifty-five German guards were assigned to more than five hundred Allied detainees, so some of the more determined among the latter managed to escape. One of them, British Major Anthony Deane-Drummond, discovered a small closet with a concealed door and hid inside, with a tiny cache of bread crusts and water, for thirteen days before getting away.

The much-emaciated major finally got back to Allied lines with help from some of the local people, including Baroness Ella van Heemstra. Through someone in the neighborhood who happened to be harboring Deane-Drummond at the time, she heard how much weight he'd lost and sent him a gift basket in behalf of Audrey and herself, addressed "To the poor British officer who is so thin."

Years later, in his wartime memoir *Return Ticket*, Deane-Drummond recalled: "On opening up the basket, I found a bottle of vintage Krug champagne, a jar full of beef tea and some coffee. Straightaway I wrote a note of thanks to go back by hand, little knowing that my unknown admirers were living in the next-door house to where I had hid in the cupboard. I would have been even more incredulous if someone had told me that the daughter would one day grow up into the beautiful stage and film actress Audrey Hepburn.

"The delicacies that they had sent round were literally more valuable than gold in wartime Holland, and were freely given to a complete stranger. I later heard that the Heemstra family were themselves suffering shortages of food and that little Audrey was even too weak to dance. Such was true generosity which I will always remember."

Lest it appear that the Baroness had some secret access to precious goodies, the coffee happened to be of the ersatz variety, while the Krug champagne was a bottle she'd been hoarding since 1940 toward that great day when Queen Wilhelmina returned from exile. No doubt beef bouillon seemed like filet mignon to

50

the major after thirteen days of starving in a closet, but it had been one of the last things to be rationed, and Ella had managed to stockpile a few jars before they disappeared from sale.

By the time of the German victory in Arnhem, Audrey and her mother had survived 1,603 days of war, but the worst was yet to come. Besides demolishing most of Arnhem, the Nazis also reversed Queen Wilhelmina's call for a national railway strike by closing the trains to all civilian transport. Nature seemingly conspired by bringing Holland's severest winter in years, which virtually stopped all shipments of food and heating fuel because barges couldn't get through the frozen rivers and canals. Thousands would die from starvation and/or exposure to the cold.

By Christmas, the Germans had reduced the Dutch food ration to five hundred calories per day. Like everybody else, Audrey and her mother began to depend on endive and wild mushrooms as their main sources of nourishment. To appease their empty stomachs, they often read aloud to each other from cookbooks, planning stupendous meals for after the war. Audrey craved her beloved chocolate so much that her taste buds would ache whenever the word was mentioned.

The new year of 1945 brought an epidemic of tuberculosis. Funeral processions, traditionally led by undertakers in tall black hats and black coats, became a dawn-to-dusk sight. Coffins were so scarce that they were restricted to ceremonial use only; corpses had to be transferred to a sack or wrapped in rags or cardboard for the actual burial.

Not surprisingly, Arnhem's schools (or what remained of them after the September conflagration) were closed for the foreseeable future, but the Baroness tried to give Audrey some tutoring early each morning before the overcrowded household got too noisy. There was no wood or coal to heat the place with, the few candles left for illumination had to be saved for extreme emergencies. Electricity came on briefly in the evenings or not at all. By necessity, everybody turned in early, not in their beds but huddled together on the floor in heaps to keep warm.

Every day, Audrey and the other kids in the household went out scrounging for anything that could be used as fuel for a little portable stove that everybody used for cooking and heating water. For lack of soap, clothing never got clean, nor did the people who wore it. The whole house reeked of boiled vegetables, drying laundry, and body odor.

The straitened German occupiers were so desperate for manpower that they started seizing teenagers as young as thirteen for menial labor. Males, of course, were taken first, but when the supply ran out, females became equal game. The Nazis drove around the streets in trucks, literally snatching them off the sidewalks in herds. The captives were then parceled off to local military bases and hospitals to serve as resident cleaners, kitchen help, laundresses, and nursing assistants.

Audrey's turn came one day while she was doing an errand for her mother in Arnhem's center, where a few of the less damaged shops had reopened, though with hardly anything to sell. Just as she was turning a corner, Audrey collided with a machine-gun-wielding German soldier who had five girls lined up a few feet away and ordered her to join them. He said that a truck would soon come to take them all to headquarters.

In a flash, the quaking Audrey realized that her only chance for escape was now, before additional soldiers arrived. When her captor put down his gun for a moment to smoke a cigarette, she ran like hell back around the corner, down a long alley and into an intersecting one that finally landed her in the cellar of a bombed-out building.

Once Audrey calmed down and no Germans came after her, she fell asleep exhausted. When she woke up she didn't know the hour or how long she'd been there. She built herself a little nest from some of the debris around her and decided to stay until it seemed safe to leave. Fortunately, she'd left home that morning with a snack of bread crusts and apple juice in her knapsack, so she knew she wouldn't starve.

In the perpetual darkness of the cellar, Audrey quickly lost track of time. She may have spent several days there, alternating between deep sleep and feverish delirium. Finally, stabbing hunger took over. Edging her way upstairs, she discovered night outside and sneaked home to Velp via every back road she knew.

No words can describe the welcome that Audrey received from her mother, who'd been searching everywhere and thought that she was either dead or, like half brother Ian, sent to the nether world of slave laborers. That fate seemed unlikely now, since Audrey had developed jaundice and swollen joints while in hiding. With almost no medications left because of the war, the family doctor could only prescribe bed rest and lots of leafy green vegetables. There weren't many of those around either, so Audrey made a very slow recovery.

The malnutrition that Audrey suffered throughout the war also permanently affected her metabolism. In future years, she would almost never have to worry about excess poundage. Dieting would usually be to gain weight, not to lose it. Just keeping herself from becoming too thin was a lifelong struggle.

One of many lessons that the long war taught Audrey was that the human body and mind can endure much more deprivation than might seem possible. As the spring of 1945 approached, the winter-ravaged Holland seemed doomed, despite reports on Radio Orange that Allied bombers were pounding Germany to dust and that General Eisenhower's land forces were nearing the Rhine.

Ironically, bits of rural southern Holland were liberated in late January when the Allies swept up from the Ardennes after the Battle of the Bulge, but the Germans still occupied most of the country and were using it as a base for some of their V-2 rocket firings on England. In western Holland, which included the cities of Amsterdam, Rotterdam, and The Hague, people had become as thin as skeletons and were literally perishing in the streets. Thousands headed for the countryside scrounging for food, but few got very far. Besides shutting down the railways to civilian use, the Nazis were seizing everything on wheels, including bicycles and baby carriages, to replace their nearly exhausted fleet of transport vehicles.

In Arnhem, living conditions were still a bit better than in the heavily populated cities, but not much. "We reached a point where there was no food whatsoever," Audrey remembered. "My aunt said to us, 'Tomorrow we'll have nothing to eat, so we'd better stay in bed and conserve our energy.' That very night, a member of the underground brought us food—flour, jam, oatmeal, even butter. I believe that my prayers had something to do with it. I don't want to sound pompous, but from childhood I always had this faith that things somehow work out. I've had black moments, but when I hit rock-bottom, there's always something there for me."

The spring thaw brought Holland a new threat of plague from a frozen winter's worth of uncollected garbage. A glimmer of hope came when Radio Orange reported that the Allies were pressuring the Germans to permit some supplies of food and medicine to come in. If the Dutch were allowed to starve to death, the Germans would have yet another charge of genocide to add to their list of war crimes.

On April 29, American planes started parachuting bundles of necessities on Amsterdam and Rotterdam. While people were devouring canned meats and biscuits, Canadian and British air and ground forces began the task of liberation, pushing the German occupiers eastward and back into the homeland where they belonged. Audrey, her mother, and the rest of the household stayed tuned to the radio for the latest news. Everybody cheered over a Radio Orange bulletin that Queen Wilhelmina had re-entered the kingdom and was sequestered in one of the liberated zones until she could safely return to her palace in The Hague.

On May 1, the German radio made the astonishing announcement that the Reichsführer had died the previous evening in the line of duty and that Admiral Karl Doenitz would succeed him as chancellor. The BBC soon carried a more accurate report that Hitler had committed suicide.

Three days later, on May 4, 1945, Audrey had more than her sixteenth birthday to celebrate as the liberation of Holland became complete. From that time on, May 4 also became Holland's official day of mourning for those who died in the war, so Audrey's future birthday observances would always have that sorrowful specter hanging over them.

Fortunately, the German troops in the area had retreated, so Arnhem was spared further devastation when Canadian forces marched in to take over as temporary guardians and to dismantle any mines or booby traps the Nazis might have left behind. Audrey, her mother, and the entire household were among thousands who rushed to the center of the ghost city to welcome the liberators.

"We whooped and hollered and danced for joy," Audrey remembered. "I wanted to kiss every one of them. The incredible relief of being free—it's something that's hard to verbalize. Freedom is more like something in the air. For me, it was hearing soldiers speaking English instead of German, and smelling real tobacco smoke again from their cigarettes."

Celebrations continued for several days, reaching a crescendo on May 7, when the war in Europe finally ended with Germany's unconditional surrender. By that time, Audrey and her mother had additional reason for rejoicing. Ella's eldest son, Alexander van Ufford, emerged from five years as an *onderduiker*, bringing with him a pregnant wife who would soon make the Baroness a grandmother. Younger brother Ian remained among the silent missing, but it seemed much too early to give up hope for his return.

While World War II wouldn't be over for Holland until Japan was defeated and surrendered the occupied Dutch colonies in the East Indies, the worst was behind Audrey and her family, but her memories of the Nazi terror would haunt her forever. "The war left me with a deep knowledge of human suffering, which I expect many young people of later generations never know about," she once said. "The things I saw during the occupation made me very realistic about life, and I've been that way ever since. Don't ever discount anything awful you hear or read about the Nazis. It's worse than you could ever imagine. I came out of the war thankful to be alive, aware that human relationships are the most important thing of all, far more than wealth, food, luxury, careers, or anything you can mention."

chapter four

BALLERINA TO SHOWGIRL

"I finished the war highly anemic, and asthmatic, and all the things that come with malnutrition," Audrey Hepburn remembered. "I had a bad case of edema, which also comes with malnutrition. It's a swelling of the limbs. It's all lack of vitamins."

The Allied liberators were immediately followed by personnel and supply trucks from the United Nations Relief Agency and the International Red Cross. "They filled the local churches and schools with food, medications, and blankets. And I was one of the lucky recipients. Then CARE packages started coming in, and I got a little bit tubby. I'd just sit down with a spoon and eat a whole jar of jam and drink a whole can of condensed milk. Obviously I'd be very ill afterwards, but I put on about ten pounds," Audrey said.

While Arnhem struggled back to life, Audrey did volunteer work at the Deaconess Hospital, visiting wounded Allied soldiers who'd been left behind by their German captors. The men were delighted to meet someone who spoke English and often shared their food and goodies with her. One day she ended up with seven chocolate bars and got violently sick when she gobbled up the lot in less than two minutes.

Unintentionally, the generosity of the hospital patients also got Audrey started on a lifelong addiction to smoking cigarettes, which were unavailable during the war and became more irresistible than chocolate to a strictly reared teenager who would have been forbidden them. In later, more health-conscious decades, her chain-smoking would often shock those who expected Audrey Hepburn to be perfect. "The only bad thing I can say about Audrey—the *only* thing— is that she smoked," designer friend Jeffrey Banks recalls.

On July 17, 1945, Audrey became a *tante* for the first time with the birth of Michael Quarles van Ufford, the son of ex- "diver" Alexander and his wife, Maria. With her love of children, Audrey was overjoyed, though the event soon became overshadowed by what seemed a miracle to everyone in the family. Audrey's younger half brother, Ian, came knocking at their door one morning, having walked nearly all of the 325 miles between Arnhem and Berlin.

During his two years of forced labor in an armaments factory, Ian had been severely punished for joining in a failed rebellion by the workers, but at least he survived to tell about it. Historian Louis de Jong later estimated that over 5,000 of the Dutch sent to work in Germany died there, which was still a low figure considering that about 400,000 were taken.

But Audrey's family circle wouldn't be complete until she at least knew what had happened to her father, with whom she'd had no contact since he put her on a plane back to Holland in September 1939. Perhaps in anticipation of distressing news, the Baroness didn't seem interested in tracking down her ex-husband, but when Audrey persisted they applied to the International Red Cross for assistance.

"I had to find out if my father was still alive," Audrey recalled. "In due course, we found out that he was living in Ireland, and that was that. I didn't try to reach him. By then the war had been over for months and he had never tried to reach *me*, nor had I ever heard from him in the ten months between my leaving England and Holland's occupation. So the feelings of rejection were very strong, and I thought he didn't want to see me anymore."

Had she been aware of the details of her father's situation, Audrey might have reacted differently. Because Joseph Ruston's pro-fascist activities had landed him in prison soon after she left England, there was no way he could have contacted her, even if he'd wanted to. His detention on the Isle of Man ended when the European war did, by which time Ruston was nearly fifty-six and in miserable health (prisoners got even less to eat than England's heavily rationed populace). Also flat broke, he sought refuge at a Trappist monastery in County Waterford, Ireland, where the pro-Mosley abbot was helping ex-detainees to find jobs and housing.

But all that was unknown to Audrey and her mother, who were then caught in a similar predicament. The devastated city of Arnhem had

61

nothing to offer them but sad memories and more frustrations. Audrey had already lost too many precious years in her ballet training to wait around for facilities to be restored, so they would have to move. Desiring only the best for her daughter, the Baroness wanted to send her to the Sadler's Wells school in London but lacked the money to do it. She had none of her own, and the van Heemstra family holdings seized by the Germans were in a legal limbo that might take years to resolve.

The Baroness would also have to get a job just to support them. Fortunately, Ella no longer had to provide for her two grown sons, who were talking about returning to their native East Indies to strike it rich in one of the industries newly reclaimed from the Japanese. Hopefully, Alexander and Ian would be able to help their mother financially, but not now while she needed it.

The capital city of Amsterdam, which escaped heavy war damage and had always been a major cultural center, was the only logical place for Audrey and the Baroness to go. But thousands of other displaced Hollanders had the same idea, and housing was scarcer than rubber tires or silk stockings. Finally, in October 1945, the Baroness got around it by landing employment in Amsterdam as a live-in housekeeper and taking Audrey with her, though not under the same roof. For the time being, she would stay with her new ballet teacher, Sonia Gaskell, who was a friend of Winja Marova and had agreed to lodge Audrey until her mother could find them a place of their own.

"The girl wanted to be a dancer, but had no money to pay for the lessons. Yet I thought she deserved a chance," Gaskell recalled. "In the two floors of studio space below my apartment, I found her a tiny room in which she barely could move, but she loved it and became a very serious pupil."

The living arrangement lasted only a month. The Baroness was obviously not born to be someone else's housekeeper and she soon quit to take a more suitable job managing a flower shop. In a stroke of good luck (for her anyway), Ella also landed an apartment when a customer recommended her for one just vacated by a relative's death. The flat was small and not in Amsterdam's ancient canal-ringed Centrum, but it was near the Beatrixpark in the Nieuw Zuid and carried a low rent that would leave enough for Audrey's ballet lessons if they pinched their guilders and cents.

Audrey couldn't have found a better teacher than forty-one-year-old Sonia Gaskell, who'd studied with the great Russian ballerina Ljoebov Egorova and danced and choreographed for the Ballets de Paris and other European companies before the war. Though Gaskell was a Lithuanian-born Jew, her marriage to Dutch gentile Heinrich Bauchhenss got her through the Nazi purge (about 70,000 of Amsterdam's 80,000 Jews died in concentration camps).

Audrey became a charter member of Gaskell's newly formed Balletstudio '45, which, over several decades and with input from additional choreographers, evolved into the world-acclaimed Het Nederlands Danstheater. Declaring that "the classic dance is dead," Gaskell used traditional training methods but aimed for a modern repertoire with music by contemporary jazz and avant-garde composers.

When she started working with Gaskell, Audrey was still so thin that her arms and legs were like sticks. Her teacher tried going easy on her for fear she'd collapse, but Audrey was determined to make up for lost time and rejected any special treatment.

"I would train for two or three hours at a time, and even if I were purple in the face and covered with sweat, Sonia would shout: 'Stand up, *lieveling*—don't slouch!' That gave me strength," Audrey recalled. "My one fear was my height. I was growing too tall for a ballerina. Sonia tried everything to make it an asset. Instead of a lot of allegro—little small tight movements—we worked extra hard on adagio, so that I could make the most of my long legs and long back."

Another of Gaskell's pupils, Anneke van Wijk Koppen, recalls that "Audrey's expression was fabulous. The way she used her hands and eyes showed she also had talent for acting. Her enormous eyes were not to be believed. I asked her once, 'What are you doing to make them seem so wide?' She said, 'Nothing. They've always been this way.' "

In May 1946, Audrey was among several others chosen to dance with Gaskell's prize student, Beatrix Leoni, in a matinee recital at the Hortus

Theatre. She hardly stole the show from Leoni that day, but her three solo dances won her an encouraging though brief mention from the ballet critic for the daily newspaper *Algemeen Handelsblad*: "A true appraisal of 17-year-old Andrey Hepburn will have to wait until she's older. She performed *Grillen*, *Paysanne*, and *Danseuse de Delphes*, with Louis Born at the piano. She does not yet have much technique, but she is undoubtedly talented."

"Andrey Hepburn" was the first of several professional names that she tried out. To complicate matters, in personal life she was using the name Audrey Hepburn-Ruston. Now that Audrey had reached debutante age, her mother wanted to launch her into high society. Unfortunately, Baroness Ella's title could not be passed on to her daughter, so "Hepburn-Ruston" was dragged out of the family closet to denote highborn background.

Ballet became Audrey's whole life. Except for dance classes, her formal education had ended. She never went back to school after the ordeal of Arnhem, but her mother encouraged her to take advantage of Amsterdam's rich cultural resources. Audrey loved to visit the massive Rijksmuseum with its Rembrandts and other early Dutch and Flemish masters, as well as the Stedelijk, which had a magnificent collection of Van Gogh and later painters.

For Christmas 1946, the Baroness saved up to buy Audrey a season pass to the Concertgebouw, home for Holland's world-famous symphony orchestra and Amsterdam's number-one stage for the performing arts. Audrey's ticket was only for one of the cheapest seats in the rear balcony, but she rarely missed an event, walking nearly two miles each way because she couldn't afford the tram fare.

Though going on eighteen, Audrey had yet to develop any romantic attachments. She had reached mating age during wartime, when the only men around were young boys or old-timers and it would have been easy to be attracted to someone of her own sex. But more likely the malnutrition and mental trauma that she suffered during the war set back a "normal" development. She had the outlook of a thirteen-year-old, still a girl more interested in deciding what to do with her life than in finding someone to spend it with.

"Somehow my world remained closed shut to everything but music. The sublime joy that I derived from it was all that mattered," Audrey remembered.

Yet the past had a way of intruding. One day, a friend who worked for a publishing firm in Amsterdam loaned Audrey some galley proofs to read: "They were for a book entitled *Het Achterhuis*, or *The Secret Annex*. The whole world would know it as *The Diary of Anne Frank*. I was not only touched, I was devastated. Anne Frank and I were the same age—she was born less than six weeks after I was—so I felt very drawn to her. I must have been one of the first pilgrims to the office building on the Prinsengracht where she had lived in hiding, which later was converted to a museum in her memory."

Eventually, there would be offers for Audrey

Hepburn to portray Anne Frank on stage and screen, but she always declined. "I knew I would have cried too much," she once said.

Ironically, Audrey herself had been struggling against starvation in Arnhem when Anne Frank died, probably from typhus, in the Bergen-Belsen concentration camp in March 1945. Was it a matter of chance or providence that the aspiring ballerina survived and the fledgling writer didn't?

For Audrey, time danced on. By the summer of 1947, the war had been over for two years, but Europe's recovery was lagging badly and being pumped up by billions of Marshal Plan dollars to halt the expanding net of the Soviet Iron Curtain. Holland, which still had rationing and critical shortages of food and consumer goods, seemed headed toward a new socialistic government.

Baroness Ella was now doing facials and make-up for a beauty salon in the fashionable P. C. Hoofstraat. To help pay for her ballet lessons, Audrey came up with the bright idea of making hats and selling them to her mother's clients. "Audrey had exquisite taste," her friend Loekie van Oven recalled. "She bought ordinary hats in the big stores and then remade them to look like they came out of a designer's shop. She was really quite ingenious. In those days ballet costumes were impossible to buy. Audrey used to make tights from medical gauze and then dye them by soaking them in water colored by red crepe paper."

Audrey's ballet skills had not yet developed to a professional level, though that was hardly a wide-open job market at the moment anyway.

In fact, Sonia Gaskell lost a promised municipal subsidy and had to shut down her studio. Audrey was left temporarily high and dry when Gaskell took off for the United States to raise money by working as a consultant to choreographer friends George Balanchine and Martha Graham. Meanwhile, Audrey transferred to a traditional ballet school run by an elderly Russian emigré, but she also started considering alternatives in case Gaskell stayed longer than expected in America.

Through a renewed correspondence with one of her prewar school friends in England, Audrey discovered that she might be eligible for a scholarship to the London academy of Marie Rambert, the celebrated Polish ballerina who'd coached the likes of Nijinsky, Markova, and Fonteyn. But "might" became the crucial word, because there was a mountain of qualifying conditions, including the question of whether Audrey and her mother would be able to visit England, let alone stay there for an extended period of time. The duo had lived through too much together to want to be separated now. For Audrey, the move should be possible once she brought her British citizenship papers up to date, but the Baroness had to confront strict Dutch emigration laws designed to keep the nation's labor force and bank deposits from being drained.

While they were filing applications and waiting for answers, Audrey had a lucky break which other young women might have killed for, though the dedicated ballerina saw it only as a means of paying for her next lesson. But for a time, two

Dutch film makers thought she could become Holland's first contender in Europe's postwar race to develop new movie stars. Since Holland is a small country, her discoverers can perhaps be excused for believing that a bit part in a thirty-nine-minute black-and-white travelogue could do it.

The project entitled *Nederlands in 7 Lessen* (*Dutch in 7 Easy Lessons*, aka *Dutch on the Double*) started out as a short subject commissioned by Britain's financially troubled Rank Organisation, which suddenly canceled its order, leaving producer Hein Josephson and director C. H. van der Linden stuck with thousands of feet of unedited views of Holland photographed from the cockpit of a low-flying plane. Hoping to recoup their losses in the export market, the partners decided to make a supporting feature (those were the days of double bills!) by attaching scenes of the sightseers' paradise to a skeletal plot that mixed in some typically Dutch folk customs. Borrowing from Jules Verne and Buster Keaton, van der Linden created a film within a film about a travelogue cameraman given only seven days to crisscross Holland to capture all its sights.

To save money, the movie would have very little dialogue and only one professional actor, a radio comedian named Wam Heskes, who would portray the cameraman and also be the voice of the offscreen narrator. The rest of the cast would be ordinary people selected along the way, but when KLM couldn't spare a ground hostess for a scene coming up at Schiphol airport, the director turned to friends and begged them to send over any pretty girl they knew for an audition.

Among those arriving at van der Linden's office were Audrey and her mother, who'd apparently dragged her there. "If you're expecting an actress, Mr. van der Linden, you'll be disappointed," Audrey blurted out before giving an account of her training as a dancer.

"I stared at her while she was chirping away about her ballet work," van der Linden remembered. "Then I picked up the telephone and told my partner to stop looking for a girl. I said, 'Did you ever see a dream walking? Well, I just did.' Audrey was bright, cheerful, chummy, and just emanated style, breeding, intelligence, and good manners."

Just to be on the safe side, van der Linden sent for his cinematographer to make a quick camera test of Audrey outside on the street. She'd come fetchingly dressed in her best Sunday outfit—a short-sleeved print dress with puffed shoulders, long gloves, and a frilly little hat—so there was no need to doll her up.

Van der Linden directed Audrey across the road and told her to walk back toward the camera. When she reached close-up range, he asked her if she'd like to appear in a Dutch movie, and she nodded delightedly. The test turned out so well that van der Linden used it for one of his opening scenes to establish the film-within-a-film structure, with the offscreen narrator posing the question to Audrey.

Audrey's actual performance came a week after the test, when she donned a KLM uniform for a scene in which she escorted the cameraman hero to a waiting plane and waved to him as he took off on his assignment over Holland. For her brief moment of glory, Audrey received fifty guilders and not much else. Since the film makers couldn't afford the traditional opening parade of on-screen credits, the narrator thanked everybody individually by name at the end. Anyone not listening attentively would have missed Audrey's as the names rattled by.

By coincidence, *Nederlands in 7 Lessen* had its first press screening on May 7, 1948, three days after Audrey's nineteenth birthday. Not surprisingly, she wasn't mentioned in any of the reviews, but critics were divided on the movie itself, some calling it pretentious nonsense and others finding it appealingly different from the usual run of travel films. Dutch moviegoers, however, displayed no interest, and for lack of box-office success the film makers were never able to get distribution outside Holland.

Seemingly the only one impressed by Audrey's contribution to *Nederlands in 7 Lessen* was its director. "I definitely thought she had something special—she radiated sunshine," van der Linden remembered. "I wanted to make a starring film with her, but I couldn't raise the financing, and we both moved on to other things. It turned out to be one of the Dutch film industry's greatest losses. Audrey Hepburn was the superstar who got away."

Slight as it was, Audrey's film experience gained her a part-time job as a mannequin for Tonny Waagemans in his ritzy fashion salon on

Amsterdam's Keizersgracht (Emperor's Canal). "Audrey had a natural elegance," Waagemans's widow recalls. "She was a real personality, and she walked beautifully. Tonny used her especially for evening dresses and wedding gowns. She was a vision as a bride. When we had our mode shows, Audrey was always the model who got the most applause."

Although she now seemed to have other options, Audrey was still passionately and totally dedicated to ballet, though at nineteen she seemed to be pushing the age limit for trainees. The ambition was there, but the body and the muscles were growing less flexible in the aging process. She might never become a solo dancer, but she would happily settle for anything, even if it meant a non-performing career as a teacher or choreographer.

Yet time appeared to be conspiring against her. The planned transfer to London for study with Marie Rambert developed into a bureaucratic nightmare and took a full year to arrange. The long delay was for the usual reasons—essential documents lost, destroyed, or expired during the war; thousands of people with the same problem; and restrictive immigration laws. In the case of Baroness Ella van Heemstra, the English government also may have considered her a security risk because of her pro-fascist activities before the war.

Ironically, while Audrey and her mother were arranging to leave Holland, the tumultuous era through which they'd lived came to an official end in September 1948 with the abdication of sixty-eight-year-old Queen Wilhelmina in favor of her daughter, Juliana. Having inherited the throne at age ten in 1890 and kept the empire intact after two world wars, Wilhelmina reportedly did not want to go down in history as the reigning monarch when Holland lost its precious crown colony in the East Indies. That development seemed imminent as a bloody three-year war for Indonesian independence intensified. Audrey and her mother were plenty worried because Ella's sons, Alexander and Ian, had resettled there.

One of the first official portraits of the new queen was being painted by the eminent Dutch artist Max Nauta. Ella's spinster sister, Baroness Jacqueline van Heemstra, a former lady-in-waiting to Juliana and still an intimate friend, ran into Nauta one day and mentioned that she had a niece who would make a lovely model for him. Nauta agreed to meet Audrey and became so enchanted that he did two studies of her wearing a bare-shouldered evening dress she borrowed from Tonny Waagemanns. The portraits, one a full-body in watercolor and the other a head-and-shoulders in wash crayon, reveal an unexpected voluptuousness in the nineteen-year-old Audrey, who wore her hair long in those days and still had a typically Dutch face with full cheeks. When Nauta learned that Audrey and her mother were leaving Holland, he insisted on giving the Baroness the larger of the two pictures to keep within the family for future generations. No one knew, of course, that Nauta's model would turn out to be one of the most famous beauties of the twentieth century.

After getting all the necessary visas and clearances, mother and daughter finally departed for England on December 18, 1948, traveling by boat-train from The Hague across the North Sea to London. Because of British currency restrictions, the duo couldn't bring in more than fifty pounds between them, but they managed to put together the maximum from Ella's savings and a gift from Grandfather van Heemstra, who was finally starting to receive some compensation for his war losses. In those days even a shilling (twenty to the pound) went far, so the new arrivals had enough to sustain them awhile if they economized.

Straight off the train, they checked into the first cheap bed-and-breakfast they could find and headed by bus to Marie Rambert's School of Ballet in Notting Hill Gate. The pair, of course, had become familiar with London before the war, but after residing for three years in unscarred Amsterdam, they were totally unprepared for the many damaged buildings and flattened tracts of rubble that still testified to the Nazi blitzkriegs.

Audrey also had a bit of a shock when she met the sixtyish Marie Rambert, a petite dynamo who wore a pink ruffled smock, black tights with knee protectors, and a little veiled hat. Having read about the celebrated *monstre sacré* in some of her ballet books, she'd been expecting a cross between witch and bitch. "Madame," as she wanted to be called by her pupils and teaching staff, immediately put Audrey and the Baroness

74

at ease by sending for tea and biscuits when they told her that they'd just arrived from abroad.

Afterwards, Rambert showed them around her premises in the Mercury Theatre, a converted nineteenth-century church hall containing studios and a 150-seat recital space. Then came the crucial test as Madame asked Audrey to change into practice clothes and to demonstrate her skills at the barre. Rambert kept her opinions to herself, but her offer of only a partial scholarship suggests that she was mainly impressed by Audrey's radiant beauty, spritelike grace, and iron determination to amount to something. Perhaps she also felt a bit sorry for the girl after listening to some of her mother's memories of Arnhem. In any case, Audrey would get free tuition, but not the living allowance that some pupils received as part of their grants (all funded by Madame's dance company, Ballet Rambert).

Since new classes wouldn't be opening until after New Year's, Audrey and the Baroness didn't want to be stuck on their own in London over Christmas and arranged to stay with their old friend Mrs. Butcher, at Orchard Cottage in Elham, Kent. Audrey had a joyful reunion with some of her former schoolmates and their teachers, the Rigden sisters, reminiscing and comparing war experiences. By a bizarre coincidence, following Audrey's evacuation to Holland, Elham and vicinity had been one of the main sites for the aerial Battle of Britain. Fate seems to have destined her to be personally involved in one or another of World War II's epic confrontations. Too bad it had to be in Arnhem rather than in Elham, where life returned to comparative normal after British Spitfires and bombers quelled the Nazi invasion attempt.

Marie Rambert turned out to be the strictest and most demanding of Audrey's dancing teachers, not averse to swatting her with a stick for sloppy posture or faulty technique. But Rambert realized from the beginning that she could never turn her into a solo ballerina. "Audrey had lovely long limbs and beautiful eyes, but her tragedy was being too tall," Rambert recalled. "I tried to do whatever I could for her. She was a good worker, a wonderful learner. I always knew she would amount to something, but there was no future for her in my company of dancers. Even in classes it was always a struggle to find partners who were tall enough for her."

Meanwhile, the move to England wasn't proving as happy as Audrey and her mother had hoped. London then still had winter fogs thicker than Dutch pea soup. They were sharing a one-room bed-sitter in a tatty street in Bayswater. Thanks to an austere Labor government, food was scarcer and more stringently rationed than in Holland. A week's ration per person consisted of one egg, a small loaf of bread, two ounces of meat and similarly stingy amounts of sugar, tea, and butter. There was a brisk black market in everything from bananas to American Hershey bars, but they couldn't afford the exorbitant prices.

Making matters worse, the non-British Baroness Ella couldn't get a work permit, so funds were running low. She was doing a little work off the books for a new friend in the decorating trade, but seemed to be steering clear of pals made through her prewar membership in the British Union of Fascists. By this time, Sir Oswald Mosley and Lady Diana had moved to an eleven-hundred-acre farm in Wiltshire and were organizing a new crusade known as the Union Movement. His opponents compared it to giving Hitler a second chance, but Mosley failed to gain any support, and he and his wife eventually took a self-imposed exile in France.

Though Audrey's father might have been expected to assist her financially, the total severance between them continued. Surely at least the Baroness knew by this time of Ruston's imprisonment during the war, though she may have considered it too disturbing to tell Audrey. Joseph Ruston's present circumstances were unknown to both of them, but he was now almost sixty and working for an insurance broker in Dublin. Rumor has it that he also had a connection with the illegal Irish Republican Army. Given Ruston's hatred of England for nearly six years of harsh detention, that could be true.

Life improved a bit for Audrey and her mother when the Baroness skirted the labor laws by prevailing on a wealthy friend to appoint her resident manager of an apartment building that he owned. That the married man had a mistress whom Ella knew about may have entered into the negotiations. In any case, she wouldn't be drawing a salary but would get tenancy of one of the less desirable flats above some ground-floor shops. Yet the posh address of South Audley

Street, Mayfair, would make up for any inconvenience.

That still didn't solve their financial problems. To help out, Audrey started working after ballet classes as a part-time filing clerk or office receptionist.

As a pupil of Marie Rambert, Audrey began receiving modeling bids from fashion and advertising photographers who often dropped by the school. At nineteen, she resembled a long-stemmed Peter Pan, a beguiling pixie who also had the elegance to not look silly in designer clothes. In those days, commercial modeling paid only a few shillings per hour, so she would never get rich. But Audrey learned fashion fundamentals that served her well in subsequent years.

One of the most important was that she looked best in black, white, or subtle tones like beige, primrose, or mauve. "Bright colors overpower me and wash me out," she once said. "Paler ones bring out my eyes and make my hair seem darker."

She also got wise to ways of getting around what she considered her two main flaws—her five-foot-seven height and her scrawny, angular figure. She would never wear high heels, only flat shoes or preferably ballet slippers durable enough for street wear. Any frills or accessories that directed attention to her wide shoulders or long neck were to be avoided.

Ironically, the British first got to know Audrey Hepburn just from the chin up as an unnamed face in newspaper and magazine ads for Lacto-Calamine, a beauty preparation recommended for use as "a powder base by day, a skin food by night." Whether she used the product herself is doubtful. She had too much of the dew of youth to need it.

Acceptance as a model caused Audrey to reconsider her goals for the future. Nearly twenty, she knew that becoming a solo ballerina was a next to impossible dream. "Besides being too tall, I still needed five more years of training before I could qualify for dancing in the chorus. I hadn't a penny to my name. I couldn't afford to put in all those years to end up earning five pounds a week, which was the going rate then," she recalled.

Together with some of her Rambert classmates, Audrey started going to auditions and casting calls listed in *The Stage*, a trade weekly covering theater, nightclub, and vaudeville activity in London and the rest of the U.K. Early one morning, they took the underground to the Leicester Square station, located directly beneath their targeted Hippodrome Theatre. Alas, there were already about a hundred hopefuls lined up outside the stage door to apply for ten openings in the dancing chorus of the next production, *High Button Shoes*, the London edition of a current New York success.

After a decade of hardship, perhaps it was high time for Audrey's luck to change. But beauty and talent also entered into it, though she herself wouldn't remember it that way: "I knew nothing about modern dance steps, and my ear wasn't attuned to the rhythms. I don't know how I even had the nerve to try for the job in the first place."

But director Archie Thomson admired

Audrey's high-kicking energy and the way she rolled her expressive eyes when he asked her to pretend to be acting in a silent movie. He also needed ballet-trained dancers who could execute a lengthy and highly intricate production number choreographed by Jerome Robbins. How could he go wrong for the pittance that went with the job: eight pounds per week, with a schedule of twelve performances.

Featuring a musical score by Jule Styne and Sammy Cahn, *High Button Shoes* was created as a Broadway vehicle for the fast-talking former burlesque clown Phil Silvers, who portrayed a 1913 con man selling worthless Florida swampland to unsuspecting New Jerseyans dreaming of moving south. American comedian Lew Parker starred in the West End production. Needless to say, chorister Audrey Hepburn got the barest listing in the cast credits, but she was onstage throughout, either dancing in musical numbers or blending into the backgrounds of other scenes as a dress extra.

The uproarious "Mack Sennett Ballet," with virtually the whole cast involved in a Keystone Kops chase on the beach at Atlantic City, never failed to stop the show with its split-second timing. Audrey was one of the bathing beauties who helped to keep things moving as everybody popped in and out of the doors of a row of individual changing huts.

Sitting in a front-row seat at the Hippodrome one evening, impresario Cecil Landeau was captivated by Audrey's high jinks and inquired about her name on the way out. "The first impression was made by a pair of big dark eyes and a fringe [bangs]flitting across the stage," Landeau remembered. "Something exciting projected over the footlights. I marked her down in my book as someone to consider when I started casting my next production."

During the run of *High Button Shoes*, Audrey became friendly with two of the other chorus girls, none of them ever dreaming that all three would end up major stars. One was twenty-two-year-old Kay Kendall, who became a luminous film comedienne as well as the wife and acting partner of Rex Harrison. The other was sixteen-year-old singer Alma Cogan, who blossomed into England's beloved "Miss Show Business." Tragically, all three would fall victim to cancer, though Audrey would be the luckiest of the trio. The others died while still in their prime, Kendall at age thirty-three and Cogan at thirty-four.

When *High Button Shoes* failed to grow box-office legs and closed unexpectedly (probably because the humor was too American for Londoners to appreciate), Audrey decided to stay in show business rather than continue her studies with Marie Rambert.

"I was finally earning money as a dancer," she recalled. "Maybe it wasn't the kind of dancing I dreamed of, but I was out of the classroom and into the real world. I loved being in a musical show. I needed music in my life very badly. I loved sharing a dressing room with other girls. That brought me back to normal. From a young age, I was very aware of suffering and fear. For the first time, I felt the pure joy of living."

chapter five
STARDOM BECKONS

Later in the spring of 1949, Cecil Landeau remembered the dancing sprite he'd seen in *High Button Shoes* and hired her for the chorus of his international revue *Sauce Tartare*, which opened on May 18 at London's Cambridge Theatre. Like the show's title, Audrey Hepburn would only be savory dressing, adding long-legged loveliness to a menu of musical numbers and satirical sketches. The black American singer Muriel Smith, Broadway's original Carmen Jones, headed the cast, which included comic actors and performers from England, Scotland, Belgium, South Africa, Russia, Norway, Portugal, Spain, and Argentina, as well as a Trinidad calypso band.

Audrey amounted to a dancing and parading mannequin, never speaking any lines but looking scrumptious in costumes designed by Honoria Plesch. Trying to restore the dazzle that London revues lost during the war, Landeau splurged £25,000 (a huge sum for those times) on the production, and most press reviews expressed pleasure over the results. "Gay, topical and tuneful," said the *Daily Telegraph*. Audrey found herself in a hit, assured of a steady job for as long as business held up.

Now earning ten pounds a week, two more

than for *High Button Shoes*, Audrey decided that if she wanted to advance any further she would have to learn the basics of acting. An actor friend advised her to start with movement, which should be a snap, given her ballet training. She enrolled in Saturday morning classes at the Buchell Studio, where stage and film actor Robert Flemyng, who would later work with Audrey in *Funny Face*, met her for the first time.

"I arrived for my movement class as usual and there, exercising at the barre, was one of the most enchanting creatures I had ever seen," Flemyng recalled. "She was very shy, but over the weeks, everybody got to know her, and love her. We all realized that beneath that shy little elfin exterior lay a strong will and determination, and we felt that she would *do* something when she put it all together."

Sauce Tartare sparked new interest in Audrey as a model. Noted magazine photographer Antony Beauchamp attended the revue one evening and got bewitched. "I kept looking again and again at the startling eyes which were never still. I'd been searching for someone fresh for a fashion assignment, and there she was on the stage, at the right-hand side of the chorus. After the show, I went backstage and asked to see 'the chorus girl with the eyes.' They led me straight to Audrey," Beauchamp remembered.

Beauchamp's photographs of Audrey landed her in British *Vogue* and some of the society magazines for the first time. Beauchamp also thought she had potential as a film actress and sent her to meet a friend who worked as a talent scout for

Metro-Goldwyn-Mayer. It turned out to be the first of many rejections.

But Audrey still had a booster in Sidney Landeau. When *Sauce Tartare* went sour at the box office and closed after six months, the producer changed the recipe and came up with *Sauce Piquante*, which relighted the Cambridge Theatre on April 27, 1950. This time Audrey would continue in the chorus but also step out on her own to introduce some of the comedy sketches. For speaking lines, her salary was raised from ten to twelve pounds per week.

Tarted up like a "saucy French waitress" in skimpy costume and black fishnet stockings, Audrey would stroll onstage to wryly set up the fun to follow, which might be Moira Lister and Norman Wisdom spoofing *A Streetcar Named Desire* or drag star Douglas Byng's rendition of "I'm One of the Queens of England." Audrey always got as much applause as the performers—at least from the men in the audience.

A highly developed showgirl from Scandinavia named Aud Johanssen came offstage one night cursing, "I can't stand it! I know I've got the biggest tits in London, and yet they're all staring at a girl who hasn't got any!"

Principal dancer Diana Monks was also constantly complaining to the other girls. "They're always looking at bloody Audrey," she once shouted. "We don't stand a chance when she's onstage. We might just as well stay in our dressing rooms."

Featured comedian Bob Monkhouse recalled, "The standard of dancing in *Sauce Piquante* was of such a superior quality that I honestly have to say that Audrey's was the worst in the show. If she'd been a good dancer, the other girls wouldn't have minded the reactions she got, but everyone knew she was the least talented among them. They all loved her offstage, but hated her on, because they knew that even if she just jumped up and down, the audience would still be attracted to her.

"What Audrey had," Monkhouse continued, "was an enormous, exaggerated feeling of 'I need you.' Judy Garland always had that; the message was urgent: 'I'm helpless—I need you.' When people sense this, they respond to it immediately, perhaps not realizing why they're doing so. And Audrey had it in abundance, that same air of defenselessness, helplessness. I think everybody in the audience thought, I want to look after little Audrey. She seemed to be too pretty, too unaware of the dangers of life."

Based on the audience reactions, producer Landeau started visualizing Audrey as one of the leads in his next *Sauce*, but strictly as a farceur and not as a dancer. When he told her that, she giggled in disbelief. In her obsession with ballet, she'd seen very few plays or even movies in her entire lifetime (the war hadn't helped). She wasn't even sure if she had what it takes to be an actress, but she was willing to learn.

When Landeau offered to pay for some coaching, he may have had more than a professional interest in Audrey Hepburn's future. But to begin with, he sent her for elocution lessons with sixtyish character actor Felix Aylmer, who turned out to be someone Audrey *had* seen perform, portraying the Archbishop of Canterbury alongside her ballet idol Robert Helpmann's Bishop of Ely in Laurence Olivier's film of *Henry V*.

The young Vivien Leigh and Charles Laughton had studied with Felix Aylmer, so Audrey couldn't have found a more skilled instructor. After their first meeting, Aylmer realized that teaching her too much technique might mean the death of her natural grace and sparkle, and he concentrated on polishing some of her rough edges.

Audrey's voice was pitched too high and she had diction that wobbled between English, Dutch, and French, the three languages she'd grown up with. Since this was England, Aylmer strove to make it perfect English diction, but it would always roll from Audrey Hepburn's tongue with a hint of foreignness. That voice, suggesting a princess of mysterious nationality, became one of her most endearing qualities.

Since Audrey turned twenty-one a week after *Sauce Piquante* opened, it seemed about time that some romance entered her life. Why it hadn't happened up to then was anybody's guess, but the Baroness's daughter had been very properly reared and wasn't the type to chase men.

Given the fact that Audrey was working six nights a week at the Cambridge Theatre, it wasn't surprising that love finally ignited with one of the cast's headliners. French singer Marcel Le Bon, who fancied himself another Maurice Chevalier and was certainly much younger and handsomer, fell first, making his interest known by leaving red roses for Audrey at the stage door prior to her arrival. Had he known she preferred lilies of the valley he might have scored faster, but an affair developed, soon followed by rumors of an imminent wedding.

Whether out of jealously or just to create publicity for *Sauce Piquante*, Cecil Landeau threatened to sue Audrey for breach of contract if she married Le Bon. Whether a producer could oversee the private life of a chorine is doubtful, but Landeau claimed that the punters who bought tickets to gawk at showgirls expected them to be single. His argument may have been loony, but it engaged the gossip columnists of the daily and Sunday tabloids for the better part of a week.

Audrey and Le Bon carried on regardless, though neither was marriage-minded. But *Sauce Piquante* closed after only six weeks, the victim of an unusual summer heat wave. To cut his losses, Landeau prepared a condensed version (minus Marcel Le Bon) for staging as a floor show called *Summer Nights* at swanky Ciro's nightclub. It was there, performing practically in the laps of showbiz celebrities and London high society, that Audrey Hepburn made her greatest impact to date. In later years, many influential people would claim to have "discovered" the doe-eyed gamine at Ciro's and to have touted her to some agent or talent scout of their acquaintance.

But the true credit should go to Robert Lennard, casting director of Associated British

Pictures Corporation, who was so captivated by Audrey at Ciro's that he recommended her to director Mario Zampi for the ingenue role in an upcoming comedy entitled *Laughter in Paradise*. After catching the show, Zampi also fell under Audrey's spell and wanted to hire her, but she turned him down for reasons of the heart.

Audrey had already promised Marcel Le Bon that she would organize a cabaret troupe with him as soon as *Summer Nights* closed. Several other performers from the *Sauce* revues were also involved, and Audrey didn't want to disappoint them. Le Bon had started negotiating bookings at nightclubs in the provinces, with plans to eventually bring the unit to Ciro's or one of the other glitzy London spots.

Audrey's mother wasn't too pleased by any of these developments. While she'd always encouraged Audrey's ballet ambitions, Baroness Ella was a woman of culture and refinement. She tolerated Audrey's employment in vulgar show business because they needed the money, but she didn't want it to become her daughter's life endeavor. Ella also disapproved of showbiz people generally and Marcel Le Bon in particular. She thought he was mainly interested in capitalizing on her daughter's talent and bright future.

Unluckily for the romance, Le Bon couldn't secure the necessary bookings for a nightclub tour and the whole project collapsed. Audrey was brokenhearted but also flew into a rage because she'd turned down a film job to accommodate her lover's plans. A battle royal ensued, ending with the hot-blooded Frenchman severing the relationship by signing up for a nitery revue being sent to the United States and Canada.

Audrey prayed that the role in *Laughter in Paradise* would still be vacant, but in the meantime it had gone to rising star Beatrice Campbell (and whatever happened to her?). All that director Mario Zampi could offer Audrey now was a bit part as a scantily dressed cigarette girl wandering around a nightclub purring "Who wants a ciggy?" It amounted to a day's work (at six pounds), and a brief scene with leading man Guy Middleton portraying a playboy who stands to inherit a fortune if he stays away from women for a month. He makes a date with Audrey for later in the evening, then shoos her away, claiming that someone might be watching and he's not supposed to talk to women. "Don't I count as a woman?" she asks.

Audrey made the most of it, landing more small film parts through her first agent, Jack Dunfee of Linnit and Dunfee, an affiliate of the American MCA. In the bedroom farce *One Wild Oat*, she portrayed a hotel receptionist. *Young Wives' Tale* found Audrey as a lodger in an overcrowded boardinghouse during England's postwar housing shortage. Associated British Pictures Corporation (abbreviated ABC) was encouraged enough to sign her to a seven-year contract, hardly risking much, because the deal started at fifty-five dollars per week and came up for review every six months.

The early 1950s weren't the best time to be getting started in movies, but at least war-retarded England had yet to feel the impact of television, which was shaking up Hollywood. ABC, British Lion, and the Rank Organisation were the Big Three producing companies, followed by many smaller entities ranging from Ealing Studios to Alexander Korda's London Films. Most of the American majors had token representation, and MGM even owned a studio, but none was a significant factor, though some co-produced with British companies.

Though production was organized along Hollywood lines, the British industry had never achieved a lasting grip on the American or European markets, so budgets had to be kept lean if costs were to be recouped domestically. About 125 features were made annually, the majority ending up on double bills in support of glossier Hollywood pictures.

In the autumn of 1950, Audrey had the good luck to be loaned to Ealing Studios for a tiny part as Chiquita in the opening scene of *The Lavender Hill Mob*, where she bumps into former flame Alec Guinness while he's waiting to catch a flight out of the Rio de Janeiro airport. When he unexpectedly hands her some money as a parting gift, she gives him a delighted cuddle, murmuring, "Oh, but how sweet of you." The droll comedy about a timid bank clerk turned criminal mastermind was one of Guinness's first box-office hits, both in England and on the so-called art circuit in the United States, winning Audrey Hepburn more public exposure than any of her previous work.

Audrey also made a vivid impression on Alec Guinness, who later remembered: "She only had half a line to say, and I don't think she even said it in any particular or interesting way. But her faunlike beauty and presence were remarkable." A few weeks after they worked together, Guinness recommended Audrey to Hollywood director Mervyn LeRoy, who was in London casting for MGM's multimillion-dollar epic *Quo Vadis*. She made a camera test in ancient Roman costume but did not get called back for anything more.

It's doubtful that Audrey would have passed a major Hollywood studio screen test anyway. Despite such supporters as Guinness, there were many who thought she should stick to dancing and forget about acting. Years later she said, "I probably hold the distinction of being one movie star who, by all laws of logic, should never have made it. At each stage of my career I lacked the experience. But at least I never pretended to be able to do the things that were being offered."

On the recommendation of Marie Rambert alumnus Andrée Howard, she got her first movie role of any consequence in *The Secret People*, for which Howard had already been hired to do the choreography. While hardly a musical, the melodrama about European political refugees in pre-World War II London would feature interludes of dance to support Audrey's characterization of a promising ballerina. Stars of the film were Italy's Valentina Cortese and French-Italian Serge Reggiani, with Audrey portraying Cortese's younger sister.

Though Audrey's lifelong immersion in ballet won her the part, she had to contend with the fact that she'd always been much better at toe dancing than at half-point (on the balls of her feet). "The ballet scenes were a great strain for her—far greater a challenge, in a way, than the scenes calling for acting and spoken dialogue," producer Sidney Cole recalled. "She was a little fraught. She was very critical of the fact that she wasn't the greatest dancer in the world. She'd been trained as a classical dancer, she certainly knew the ropes, but we all noticed it was a great effort for her to do it."

John Field, a leading dancer with the Royal Ballet, was retained to partner Audrey in one number, more than a bit unfair for her because she was hardly of Covent Garden caliber. It took them nine days to rehearse and perfect the scene, literally working step-by-step while technicians figured out the lighting and camera movements. In the finished movie, it would run about three minutes, but the actual filming—from the stage of a rented theater, before a simulated audience of dress extras—took two full days, working from eight in the morning until midnight. Though every muscle throbbed with pain, Audrey had to laugh. None of her experiences in the actual world of ballet had been so punishing. She'd left it for this?

Surprisingly, the acting side of the work came easier. Director Thorold Dickinson was impressed by Audrey's natural charm and intelligence. Her expressive eyes reminded him of silent movie stars like Lillian Gish and Greta Garbo; she hardly needed to speak. He didn't want her to worry about technique. "Don't bother about how you're going to play the scene or recite the lines," he told her. "Think of the emotion behind the words. Try connecting them to something you've felt in your own life. If you get the feeling right, everything else will take care of itself."

Prior to shooting a scene where Audrey had to tell older sister Valentina Cortese about a gory terrorist bombing she'd just witnessed, Dickinson sent her to a corner of the set with instructions to spend half an hour concentrating on similar horrors from her own experiences during the war. Sadistic though it might seem, the order did the trick. Audrey went through the scene in one take, trembling with emotion and breaking down in the required tears at the end.

During production of *The Secret People*, the studio publicity department took Audrey in hand and started giving her the traditional star buildup. At times when she wasn't filming, her contract required her to be available for interviews, photo sessions, personal appearances, or whatever else might grab space in the news media. She drew the line when they wanted her to pose for cheesecake art. She may have had the shapely legs, but she was no Diana Dors and refused to wear bust pads to create that impression.

But huckstering had its perks. Audrey got invited to all the best parties and film premieres, where she was usually escorted by her agent, Jack Dunfee, since she'd yet to fill the romantic void left by Marcel Le Bon. But that changed one evening during a cocktail reception at Les Ambassadeurs Club, when Audrey locked eyes with James Hanson, a captivating six-footer who resembled a blend of James Stewart and Gary

Cooper. The attraction being mutual, he invited her to have lunch with him the next day. They started keeping company and fell madly in love.

Seven years older than Audrey, Hanson came from a rich Yorkshire family, served in the Army's Duke of Wellington Regiment during World War II, and currently ranked as one of London's most eligible bachelor playboys. He collected expensive cars, piloted his own plane, and excelled at yachting, golf, and horsemanship. On the face of it, he had nothing at all in common with Audrey Hepburn, but that's probably why she was so attracted to him. At twenty-two, with very little experience at love, she needed to be swept off her feet, and a dynamo like James Hanson seemed the man to do it.

Soon they were considering marriage, though there was never any doubt about Audrey's place in it. She wanted to give up whatever amounted to her career and have oodles and oodles of babies. It must be remembered that she'd been dreaming of that ever since she was a child herself, so it wasn't a sudden lovestruck decision. But it was all just pillow talk for the moment. The lovers were very happy as they were.

Contrary to what's been reported in the past, Audrey's mother liked Hanson and did not try to discourage the relationship. Although she'd always been supportive of Audrey's ballet ambitions, the Baroness didn't care for the crasser world of show business or the people connected with it. She regarded Hanson as an ideal husband for Audrey. While he didn't belong to the aristocracy, his family had wealth and social prestige, not to mention a fabulous Yorkshire estate which he stood to inherit. He promised a secure and happy future for Audrey. Who knew whether her "career" would ever amount to anything?

Audrey delivered such an impressive performance in *The Secret People* that the studio gave her billing above the title, though in lettering only a quarter of the size for Valentina Cortese and Serge Reggiani (then both major stars of international cinema). The film, however, did little to raise Audrey Hepburn's public recognition factor. "We never disguised the fact that the movie was what you would call 'art house' fare, not for the general public so much as for a smaller audience," director Thorold Dickinson recalled. "It wasn't expected to earn all its money back just in England. But when the film failed here, the distributors in Europe and America weren't much interested in buying it."

Producer and scriptwriter Alfred Shaughnessy admired Audrey's work in *The Secret People* and wanted to hire her for one of the leads in a frisky caper based on Geoffrey Household's best-selling novel *Brandy for the Parson*. But while negotiations were going on, ABC assigned Audrey to a musical comedy confection entitled *Monte Carlo Baby*.

Her bilingual abilities were the main reason for Audrey landing in the British-French co-production, which would be filmed on location with a separate version for each language, the French one to be entitled *Nous Irons à Monte Carlo*. The minor role of a French movie star was a comedown from *The Secret People*, but at least she'd get a free trip to Monaco and the chance to wear several outfits designed by Christian Dior. Since her daughter had never visited the Riviera before, Baroness van Heemstra offered to come along as guide/companion, but ended up having to pay her own way because of Audrey's lowly status in the project.

With a screwball plot revolving around a misplaced infant, *Monte Carlo Baby* starred a mixed bag of international talent including the French singing bandleader Ray Ventura and Hollywood funnyman Jules Munshin. One afternoon while Audrey was involved in a scene being photographed in the Hotel de Paris, the Riviera's most splendid example of Belle Epoque architecture, she couldn't help noticing an elderly woman with hennaed hair and heavily rouged face being taken across the lobby in a wheelchair. Inquiring around, Audrey discovered her to be Colette, the legendary French writer and novelist, who was staying there as the guest of Prince Rainier and the royal family.

That day and the next, Audrey could spot Colette watching some of the filming, but she never guessed it had anything to do with her. Then she received a phone call from Colette's husband, Maurice Goudeket, inviting her to an audience in their suite. Audrey had never set eyes on Goudeket, who sounded considerably younger than his seventy-eight-year-old wife. To make sure he wasn't attempting to seduce her, she wanted to know what it was about. He said that Madame Colette thought she might be the right person to act the leading role in a play based on one of her books.

By the time Audrey arrived, Colette had already convinced herself that the young woman was the personification of one of her most famous characters. She'd also taken the liberty of writing to playwright Anita Loos in New York, prefacing the recommendation with a cablegram teaser reading, "Don't cast your Gigi until you receive my letter."

As Colette jabbered away in French, Audrey thought she'd met the Madwoman of Chaillot. She listened in total bewilderment to a tale of a fruitless two-year search for an actress to play Gigi on Broadway. "And then, my dear, I saw you filming in the lobby," Colette said. "I could not take my eyes off you. You are my Gigi! You have that piquant quality so essential to the part. Would you not like to do it?"

Audrey thought for a moment and answered as honestly as she could: "I'm sorry, Madame, but I wouldn't be able to, because I can't act. I'm not equipped to play a leading role. I've never said more than one or two lines on stage in my life. I've done bits in films, of course, but I don't consider that acting. I trained for the ballet for many years, but I'm too tall, and I had to give it up to earn a living some other way."

But Colette pressed on. "Well, if you've been a dancer, you must have worked hard, and if you work hard you can do this, too," she said. "I have faith in you, my dear."

Audrey knew it was useless to resist. After giving Colette's husband the name of her agent in London, she thanked the couple, made a deep curtsy before the literary royal herself, and left. She rushed back to tell her mother what had happened. Needless to say, the Baroness couldn't take it all in either. Only time would tell whether it was a genuine opportunity or just an old woman's pipe dream. Meanwhile, neither had ever read *Gigi*, so they purchased a copy the next day. It was so short that they sat down and read it aloud, taking turns with the chapters.

Set in fin de siècle Paris, the story concerned a sixteen-year-old schoolgirl being raised by a family of courtesans to assume her rightful place as mistress to a wealthy libertine. The starry-eyed Gigi rebels against the unromantic tradition, but ends up finding true love and marriage with the very man whom her relatives had picked to be her "protector." At age twenty-two, Audrey doubted she could pass for sixteen, but if it hadn't bothered Colette, why worry? She had a feeling that it would all come to nothing in the end anyway.

When *Monte Carlo Baby* finished, Audrey and her mother returned to London to await further developments. In 1951, life moved at a leisurely pace. There were no jet airliners or fax machines. Even by airmail, Colette's letter from Monte Carlo took a week to reach Anita Loos in New York. While it contained a glowing recommendation of Audrey Hepburn, Loos and producer Gilbert Miller decided that they could wait until July to meet her. Miller spent every summer in London, and Loos was due to vacation in Europe with her movie star pal Paulette Goddard. Everybody who was anybody crossed the Atlantic by luxury liner in those days, so Audrey would just have to be patient until things fell into place.

By this time, sixty-year-old Anita Loos had been involved with *Gigi* for several years. As a Hollywood scriptwriter and author of the bestselling *Gentlemen Prefer Blondes*, she was almost as much of a legend in America as Colette was in France. Both specialized in boudoir sex and kept women, and Colette had personally selected Loos to adapt *Gigi* into a play. The novella was written as a diversion by the author during the Nazi occupation of France and was first published in neutral Switzerland in 1944. It became a bestseller in France right after the Liberation, had a successful English translation in 1946, and in 1948 was turned into a French movie with Daniele Delorme in the title role.

Prior to Anita Loos, a French playwright had tried adapting *Gigi* but couldn't boil it down to less than a cast of thirty-eight actors and twenty scenery changes, which would have cost too much to produce. Loos's version needed only eight players and four sets. For a time she considered turning it into a musical, with a score by her friend Frank Loesser, but they soon realized it would be difficult enough finding a suitable actress for Gigi, let alone one who could also sing and dance.

"It's a Cinderella story told in terms of sex," Loos said in an interview at the time. "The play loses everything unless the actress looks like an absolute child. Yet she has to have the kind of charm that would make a worldly man fall in love with a sixteen-year-old girl."

In Loos's hands, Colette's story had been transformed into a play of two hours running time, which is just about as long as it would take to read the original novella. Gigi's Great Aunt Alicia and grandmother, Madame Alvarez, are determined to find a wealthy protector (or, better still, several) for the lovely teenager. For generations, the family of women, none of whom ever married, have been raised to be courtesans, though Gigi's mother moved on to an acting-singing career that has left her destitute and being supported by her relatives. Aunt Alicia, who collected a fortune in jewels from her liaisons with kings and dukes, doesn't want Gigi ending up like her mother, so she's targeted for a rich playboy whose mistress has just left him. Gigi has known Gaston Lachaille, the son of one of her grandmother's former lovers, since childhood and adores him. She always welcomed his gifts and enjoyed playing card games with him, but she balks at the idea of becoming his kept woman. In the end, the unprepared and then beguiled Gaston proposes an honorable marriage, which shocks Gigi's elderly guardians.

This was pretty hot stuff for Broadway in the early 1950s. With producers anticipating another gold mine like Loos's *Gentlemen Prefer Blondes*, a bidding war developed. The exalted Gilbert Miller ended up buying the play, but—astonishingly—just to prevent it from being acquired by his hated rival, the Theatre Guild. Personally, Miller didn't care much for Anita Loos or *Gigi*, so he put the script in a drawer and kept finding excuses not to produce it.

Finally, while Miller was away on one of his frequent trips abroad, his twenty-nine-year-old general manager, Morton Gottlieb, happened upon the play and, with nothing else to do, started sounding out ticket brokers and theater-party groups. The combination of Anita Loos and the risqué reputation of Colette excited great interest, so Gottlieb boldly announced a fall opening to the press and began soliciting the list of playgoers who subscribed to all of Gilbert Miller's productions. Miller was furious when he found out, but things had gone too far to cancel. He dubbed the project "Gottlieb's folly" until proven otherwise.

Rotund, sixtyish Gilbert Miller was one of the most powerful moguls in the American and British theater, a millionaire producer even before he married super-rich Kitty Bache, heiress to the stockbrokerage empire of Bache & Company. The two were treated as a royal couple on their frequent trips to London, where they resided in great luxury at the Savoy Hotel in a permanent suite overlooking the Thames. At the time he got saddled with *Gigi*, Miller was in London preparing for one of the most colossal Broadway undertakings of his forty-year career, Laurence Olivier and wife Vivien Leigh starring in alternating performances of the Cleopatra plays by William Shakespeare and George Bernard Shaw.

When the moment finally arrived for Audrey to meet Miller and Loos, the producer didn't want to waste any time interviewing a possible zero, so he gave his playwright the first look. Arriving at Loos's suite in the Savoy Hotel,

101

Audrey found not only Loos but also her more glamorous traveling companion, Paulette Goddard. Both women were fixtures of the international social set. Audrey couldn't have had two tougher judges.

As Anita Loos remembered it: "This girl wafted in, dressed in a simple white shirt with the tails tied around her waist, a flaring black skirt, and flat shoes. It wasn't the sort of getup that you would expect in a bastion of formality like the Savoy, but Paulette and I were bowled over by Audrey's unusual type of beauty. After talking with her a few minutes, I phoned Gilbert's secretary and arranged for her to come back the next day to read for him. I gave her a couple of scenes from the play to study overnight.

"After Audrey left, Paulette said to me, 'There's got to be something wrong with that girl!' I asked 'What?' Paulette replied, 'Anyone who looks like that would have been discovered before she was ten years old. Something must be radically wrong with her.' It turned out that there was nothing wrong, except the strange fact that perfection is almost impossible for the ordinary eye to see. On the stage and in movies, she had been in full view of the British public for two years. She had been seen by thousands, but a vision so lovely was blocked out by the average person's sight. It had taken Colette to *see* Audrey Hepburn."

In the next day's meeting with Gilbert Miller, with his elegant wife Kitty and Anita Loos also present, Audrey became nervous and blew most of the lines she had to read. But the Millers were captivated by her anyway. She might not have been a young Sarah Bernhardt, but she definitely had nymphlike charisma, which, in Gigi's case, seemed more important than acting skill. Audrey's European upbringing, her fluency in French, her ability to *sound* like a Parisian, also gave her a distinct advantage over American and British actresses who'd been considered for the role.

Before he would commit himself, Gilbert Miller insisted on another reading, this time on a theater stage to test the carrying power of Audrey's voice (in those days, no sound amplification was used in either straight plays or musicals). The judge would be Miller's close friend Cathleen Nesbitt, now a mellowing character actress but once a luminous leading lady who'd been the sweetheart and muse of poet Rupert Brooke.

At sixty-two, Nesbitt could still hear a pin drop, but sitting in the back row of the stalls at the empty Savoy Theatre one morning, she could barely make out what Audrey Hepburn was reciting on the stage. But even from that distance Nesbitt could feel the pull of Audrey's magnetism, and she urged Miller to sign her to a contract. What Audrey didn't know, she could learn. Since Nesbitt was winding up a stint in a London play and would soon be returning to her home in New York, she offered to coach Audrey for the Broadway opening. Of course, Nesbitt also expected Miller to hire her for one of the other major roles in *Gigi*, but that's what friends are for, isn't it?

Wheels began turning. Before Audrey could be confirmed for *Gigi*, Gilbert Miller and his representatives needed to hammer out deals with her agent, Jack Dunfee, and with Associated British Pictures, which had her under contract for movies but could prevent her from doing any stage work that conflicted with her studio assignments.

Meanwhile, Audrey's spirits flew over the moon and back. She'd never been happier or more incredulous either. Acting a leading role on Broadway, and the first trip to America that went with it, were the sort of things that happened to sweet young things in novels or movies but never in real life. But it wasn't a dream.

While the negotiations for *Gigi* were going on, Hollywood director William Wyler came to London to confer with Richard Mealand, the head of Paramount Pictures production activities in England and Europe, about his next project, *Roman Holiday*. Wyler was going on to Rome to scout locations, but while staying at the Dorchester Hotel he met a batch of young actresses whom Mealand had suggested as candidates for one of the leading roles in the movie. The enchanting Jean Simmons had been all but signed for it, but she had a contract with RKO, whose owner, Howard Hughes, happened to be madly in love with her and wouldn't agree to a loan-out to Paramount.

Mealand had been impressed by Audrey's performance in *The Secret People*, so she was one of those sent over for Wyler's appraisal. "I had no idea of who William Wyler was, nor was I aware of the significance of doing a picture for him," Audrey recalled. "I was four years out of Holland and the war and all that, when we hadn't been able to keep up at all with Hollywood films. I was very behind, so I had no sense of what Mr. Wyler could do for my career. I had no sense, period. I was awfully new, and awfully young, and thrilled just to be going out on auditions and meeting people who seemed to like me."

Audrey turned out to be one of five actresses that Wyler selected for screen tests. Since he was about to leave for Italy and had neither the time nor the wish to direct any of them himself, Paramount assigned Audrey's test to Thorold Dickinson, who'd squeezed a convincing performance out of her in *The Secret People*. Her newfound friend Cathleen Nesbitt volunteered to assist in the filming, which was done hurriedly in black and white at Pinewood Studios outside London.

"We did some scenes out of the script of *Roman Holiday*," Thorold Dickinson recalled. "Paramount also wanted to see what Audrey was actually like not acting a part, so I did an interview with her. We loaded a thousand feet of film into the camera and every foot of it went on this conversation. Audrey talked about her experiences during the war, the Allied raid on Arnhem, and hiding out in a cellar. A deeply moving thing."

For the scenes from *Roman Holiday*, in which Audrey had to portray a Ruritanian princess on an official visit to the Italian capital, Dickinson took many demanding close-ups, starting with one where she had her back to the camera and slowly turned around to face it. When she did, Audrey gave an impudent wink that wasn't called for in the script. "The minute you saw it, you knew she would get the part," Dickinson said.

In another bit, Audrey had to pretend to be testing the plushly upholstered mattress of the bed in her hotel suite. Since she was obviously enjoying herself, the director kept the camera grinding past the point when he shouted, "Cut!"

"Oh, is it over now? Oh, good." Audrey smiled, releasing a school-girlish giggle and not realizing that her spontaneous reaction had been captured on film. Dickinson made sure it was included in the test reel that he prepared for William Wyler and the Paramount studio brass in Hollywood. Needless to say, they offered Audrey the role in *Roman Holiday*, but for a while it looked like she would not be available.

By this time, she had a fully executed contract with Gilbert Miller for *Gigi* that contained the standard run-of-the-play clause. No one, of course, could predict how long *Gigi* would last. If clobbered by the critics, it could close after one performance. But should it continue, Audrey was obligated to stay with it for up to eighteen months, which the stage unions figured as the maximum life expectancy of a nonmusical play.

Once again, luck smiled on Audrey when Gregory Peck, who was to be the star of *Roman Holiday*, requested a postponement because of production delays on his current film, *The Snows of Kilimanjaro*. To be on the safe side, William Wyler set back the start of *Roman Holiday* from the spring of 1952 to the summer. That decided

106

Paramount to risk hiring Audrey after all. Even if *Gigi* became a hit, New York playhouses had a tradition of recessing for the summer. Furthermore, if *Gigi* made a star of Audrey Hepburn, Paramount would have to pay considerably more for her services than if it signed her up now.

It should be noted that nobody was tossing big bucks around for the moment. Audrey Hepburn was still a comparative nobody in the showbiz scale of things. Her contract with Gilbert Miller called for five hundred dollars per week, but out of that she would have to give her agent 10 percent and also pay for her living expenses in New York. Paramount's first offer for *Roman Holiday* was a flat fee of $10,000, but agent Jack Dunfee succeeded in jacking it up to $12,500, with an option for a second picture at $25,000. Associated British, which still had Audrey under contract, sanctioned everything in the hope that their featured player would come back to them a major international star.

Since "Audrey Hepburn" had not yet become a famous name on either side of the Atlantic, Paramount proposed changing it to avoid confusion and conflict with the inimitable Katharine Hepburn. But Audrey refused, claiming that she was at least twenty years younger than the other Hepburn and that they would hardly be competing for the same roles. (A case might be made for the two Hepburns being very distantly related; Katharine's family tree allegedly springs from the same Scottish James Hepburn as Audrey's paternal great-grandmother.)

Audrey's work commitments raised questions about the future of her romance with James Hanson, but the couple were still very much together. As head of his family's trucking and air freight business, Hanson had a demanding career in his own right and frequently traveled to Canada and Europe. The lovers had no hesitations about their disparate worlds and even considered it a bonus for a more rounded married life. Friends claim that Audrey was still very intent on having babies and becoming a homemaker. She thought she could manage that and still have a career if she stuck to doing one play or movie a year.

In late September, Audrey started packing for the trip to America to begin rehearsals for *Gigi*. Saying goodbye to Jimmy Hanson would be difficult enough, but Audrey also had to face up to being separated from her mother for the first time since her boarding school days in England before the war. The women were closer than close, so it would be a traumatic break for both. They lacked the money to support two people in expensive New York, though Ella couldn't leave London for long anyway if she wanted to keep her building manager's job and the apartment that went with it. Happily, James Hanson cured everybody's blues by promising to fly to New York for *Gigi's* opening night—and to take Ella with him.

To prepare Audrey for the exhausting ordeal ahead, Gilbert Miller splurged on her travel arrangements with a first-class ticket on the *Queen Mary*, an Art Deco floating palace and the most beloved British liner among the celebrity set. For five and a half days, Audrey could enjoy a vacation equal to the best that any resort or health spa could offer.

At daybreak on October 4, 1951, she stood on the top deck of the *Queen Mary* and watched the Statue of Liberty and the skyline of Manhattan coming into view. Audrey had stayed up all night in her stateroom, peering from the porthole every few minutes to make sure she didn't miss anything. Of course, she'd seen it all before in movies or photographs, but what could compare to actually experiencing it with an autumnal breeze kissing her cheeks? For a girl who'd been on the verge of starvation and Nazi servitude in bombed-out Arnhem exactly seven years before, the tears in her eyes were understandable.

chapter six
BROADWAY AND ROME

Audrey Hepburn marched down the gangplank from the *Queen Mary* in New York weighing quite a bit more than she did when she boarded in Southampton. "She gained about ten pounds gorging on the ship's cordon bleu cuisine, which included all sorts of goodies that she couldn't get in England because they still had food rationing," Anita Loos recalled. "When Gilbert Miller saw her, he was appalled. He'd engaged a sprite who had suddenly turned into a dumpling."

Since Miller was a rotund gourmand himself, he couldn't believe that Audrey would be able to reduce by the opening night of *Gigi*, which was only seven weeks away. But Miller's general manager, Morton Gottlieb, put her on a crash diet devised by the chef at Dinty Moore's, a favored showbiz hangout near their rehearsal place. "Audrey took all her meals there for a week, eating nothing but steak tartare, salad greens, and Ry-Krisp," Gottlieb remembers. "I knew that she loved chocolates, so I also made her promise to swear off and to cross to the other side of the street whenever she saw a candy store coming up. She was very good about it all and dropped back to normal weight in no time."

While in New York, Audrey was living at the

Blackstone Hotel on Fifty-eighth street between Madison and Park Avenues, which offered discount rates for extended stopovers and had a sizable clientele of visiting actors who were working on Broadway. For $125 per week, she had a small suite consisting of parlor, bedroom, kitchenette, and bath, with full hotel services provided. Also included was a television set, the first she'd ever had access to because of manufacturing shortages in England. She often watched it until the wee hours of the morning, catching up on old movies she probably would have missed even if there hadn't been a war. (Hollywood had yet to release any of its major product to the rival medium.)

As luck would have it, Audrey's next-door neighbors at the Blackstone were David Niven and his wife, Hjordis, but it took a stupefying incident to make her aware of that. "A body crashed down from the eighteenth floor of the hotel and bounced off Audrey's windowsill on its way to the ground," Niven recollected. "She came pounding on our door and we thought the bug-eyed girl might be hallucinating or something. But I phoned the front desk and it turned out that some poor man had committed suicide.

"However, that grisly beginning ripened into a long, enduring friendship. My wife and I were newly married at the time and didn't know that many people in New York. Audrey was a girl alone and in that big city for the first time, so we all wound up having many jolly times together."

With his screen career in the doldrums, Niven had come to town to co-star on Broadway in a

111

boudoir farce entitled *Nina*, with the seemingly indestructible silent movie queen Gloria Swanson (fresh from an Oscar nomination for *Sunset Boulevard*). Ironically, *Gigi* and *Nina* were due to open within a week of each other, causing endless confusion of the two titles in the news media.

Although the Broadway stage industry was another victim of television's power to keep people at home, the 1951–52 season that included *Gigi* and *Nina* would still end up with a total of fifty-three premieres of new works, forty-four plays and nine musicals. Gilbert Miller had set the opening of *Gigi* for November 24 at the Fulton Theatre (later renamed the Helen Hayes and demolished in 1982).

Because of Audrey's inexperience, Anita Loos wanted her great friend George Cukor, who'd worked extensively on Broadway before becoming Hollywood's foremost director of women, to direct *Gigi*. After viewing Audrey's screen test for *Roman Holiday*, Cukor thought she had as much potential as the other Hepburn, whom he'd directed in her first movie and six after that. He told Anita Loos he'd do it, but while contracts were being drawn up, Columbia Pictures advanced the starting date of his next Judy Holliday project, *The Marrying Kind*, and he had to turn down the *Gigi* offer.

Since all the top Broadway and London West End directors were already committed to other productions, Loos and Gilbert Miller sought help from Colette, who checked around Paris and came up with Raymond Rouleau. The thirty-seven-year-old stage director had a broad range—everything from the original French production of *A Streetcar Named Desire* to Edith Piaf's debut in a book musical. He'd also been a film star in the Cary Grant mold and hailed from Brussels, Audrey's own birthplace, so he would seem to have a natural affinity with both his lead actress and the play's ultra-French milieu.

Unfortunately, Rouleau could barely speak English, so rehearsals would be *difficile*, to say the least. To make it easier on everybody, Anita Loos came up with the idea of working only in French while they blocked out the staging. Crazy though it might seem, she translated her script into French and they went on from there. Helping matters, of course, was the fact that Audrey and the rest of the cast were bilingual. In those days, many American and British stage actors had training in French; it was the most widely used language after their own and also the mark of a chic and sophisticated thespian.

But without meaning to, the rehearsals in French made things even harder for Audrey in her very first full-length acting role in any language. After mastering the part in French, she would have to learn it all over again in English, with its different vocabulary and accents. She became terrified of lapsing into French on opening night and being booed off the stage.

Before Rouleau arrived from Paris, Gilbert Miller again prevailed on Cathleen Nesbitt to coach Audrey. Thanks to the withdrawal of George Cukor, who had intended hiring his formidable dowager friend Constance Collier for the part, Nesbitt would be portraying Gigi's Great Aunt Alicia, so she had more than a casual interest in making sure that Audrey did not disappoint.

"Audrey didn't have much idea of phrasing, and even less of how to project. But she had that rare thing—audience authority—that makes everybody look at you," Nesbitt recalled. On weekends she brought her protégée to her house in Westchester County and they would go out in the garden to practice. Audrey had to learn how to deliver everything from a whisper to a scream. Needless to say, the whisper was the hardest to master because it needed to be heard all the way up to the last row of the second balcony. Nesbitt warned Audrey that the Fulton Theatre, where they would be performing, had some of the worst acoustics in New York, having been built before World War I as a theater-restaurant similar to the Folies Bergère in Paris.

When Raymond Rouleau took over his directorial chores, all hell broke loose (*en Français, naturellement*). Audrey could do nothing right. She declaimed her lines like a kid in a school pageant, showed slight comprehension of the text, and made her entrances and exits like a hyperactive gazelle.

Audrey's only real experience at "acting" had been in the few films she'd worked in, which consisted of memorizing and shooting a few sentences or paragraphs of dialogue in a day. But in *Gigi*, which was her first leading role, she had to have the whole script in her head and act it out every night on stage for two hours. And not only once, as in a movie, but six nights a week plus two matinees. It was a discipline that took years to master, but she had to attempt it in six weeks.

"Audrey seemed to have no idea of what she was doing," Morton Gottlieb recalled. "After five days of rehearsals, Gilbert Miller fired her. By the next morning, he realized it was too late to replace her, so he gave her another chance, and then he fired her again a few days later. This went on right up to opening night. Poor Audrey was on the verge of a nervous collapse. They were working her eighteen hours a day, sneaking into the theater at night because Gilbert didn't want to pay the union technicians overtime."

But if she could get through World War II in one piece, Audrey Hepburn could take whatever Gilbert Miller and crew doled out, because it was obviously for her benefit. "What Audrey had going for her was youth, freshness, and tomboy charm," Anita Loos said. "That would have been enough if Gigi had been a petulant teenager, but she was also a young woman in the throes of her first serious love affair. The role of Gigi, like that of Juliet, required the technique of a seasoned actress.

"What saved Audrey in the end was Raymond Rouleau, who seized on her training as a dancer and in working with her stressed movement rather than the spoken text. He staged the play practically like a ballet. He counted on her natural charm and grace blinding the audience to her deficiencies, and it worked."

Also helping Audrey tremendously were the

period costumes designed by Lila de Nobilli of the Paris theater and opera, whom Rouleau was forced to employ secretly because of Broadway labor union restrictions. Audrey had only two outfits, the traditional French matelot school dress in navy blue with white stripes at the neckline, which she wore through most of the play, and a white chiffon and lace boudoir gown for Gigi's courtship scene with Gaston.

"Since I didn't have much technique to bring to the part, knowing that I at least *looked* like Colette's Gigi gave me great confidence, and the rest didn't seem so tough anymore," Audrey recalled. "Once you're in a three-quarter-length dress, with a rustling petticoat underneath and with high button shoes on your feet, you feel something. You walk differently, you sit differently. My hair was styled beautifully, extended by a long fall that streamed down around my shoulders. I truly felt like sixteen, so I was halfway there."

It's a pity that Audrey Hepburn's first starring performance is lost to history. But it wasn't until many years later that the theater industry began to preserve its endeavors, even though a complete technology became available with the introduction of sound film and later video tape. Like several thousand other Broadway plays and musicals, *Gigi* exists only in still photographs and the memories of those who saw it at the time.

In what was then standard procedure for most Broadway productions, Gilbert Miller took *Gigi* for out-of-town try-outs as soon as rehearsals ended. After the opening night performance of a week's engagement at the venerable Walnut Street Theatre in Philadelphia, Miller once again fired Audrey, this time for faulty enunciation. The producer couldn't decide whether to fold the show or to take a chance on replacing Audrey with her understudy, a similarly inexperienced newcomer named Jill Kraft. Anita Loos persuaded him to refrain from anything drastic until the next day when the Philadelphia newspapers published their reviews.

The Philadelphia stage critics had a reputation for being among the toughest in the nation. They were divided on the merits of *Gigi* as a play but flipped for Audrey Hepburn, two calling her "the acting find of the year." The *Inquirer*'s Henry Murdoch went even further, writing, "She gives a wonderfully buoyant performance which establishes her as an actress of the first rank." *Variety*'s local stringer said, "Miss Hepburn has real talent as well as a magnetic personality. Furthermore, in a wholesome and youthful way, she exudes sex."

Gilbert Miller wasn't a fool. Audrey remained in *Gigi*, receiving more rave reviews when the play moved to the Shubert Theatre in New Haven, Connecticut, for a final three-day tune-up. Somewhere along the way she also caught the flu, but she had recovered enough by November 24 for the Broadway opening to be held as scheduled. Still, she started off in a weakened condition and by the final scene didn't have much strength left.

"I forgot my lines and everything stopped. I missed a whole speech, but somehow I backtracked and the audience didn't seem to notice. I prayed for a miracle before I went on that night, and I think that I got it," she remembered.

As promised, James Hanson and Baroness Ella came over from London for the opening, so Audrey had her own cheering section out front. Not that she needed one. Three solo curtain calls were not enough at the end. The audience called her back for a standing ovation (something still rare in the 1950s).

In 1951, instant reviews of plays and movies on television or radio were almost nonexistent. Since *Gigi* opened on a Saturday night, when newspapers had an early deadline for their Sunday editions, the first reviews wouldn't be published until Monday, when the eight dailies had their say. Producers considered them the determining factor of box-office success or failure, followed by the weekly magazines like *The New Yorker*, the *Saturday Review of Literature*, *Time*, and *Newsweek*, which were more selective in their coverage and didn't review every play that opened.

Monday brought both joy and gloom to the Gilbert Miller office. *Gigi* received three favorable notices (John Chapman, *Daily News*; Robert Garland, *Journal-American*; Walter Kerr, *Herald Tribune*); and five negative (Brooks Atkinson, *Times*; Robert Coleman, *Mirror*; William Hawkins, *World-Telegram and Sun*; Richard Watts, *Post*; Arthur Pollock, *Compass*). Fortunately, even the pans contained praise for Audrey Hepburn.

Brooks Atkinson, whose *New York Times* byline

made him the most influential critic covering the American theater industry, described *Gigi* as "very trivial and old-fashioned," but called Audrey "a young actress of charm, honesty, and talent who ought to be interned in America and trapped into appearing in a fine play." Walter Kerr described her "as fresh and frisky as a puppy out of a tub. She brings a candid innocence and a tomboy intelligence to a part that might have gone sticky, and her performance comes as a breath of fresh air in a stifling season."

One of Audrey's few detractors was George Jean Nathan, the caustic co-founder of *American Mercury* and now at nearly seventy writing syndicated reviews for King Features. Nathan called Audrey "haplessly a baby of some five feet eight or so. Though factually young in years, she acts an innocence and lack of sophistication with such an excess of calculated purpose that she gives off less an air of any such attributes then of a Topsy in white-face putting the bite on Sacha Guitry."

Up to now, *Gigi* had been a play without a star. Everybody in the cast of seven received featured and equal-sized billing on separate lines below the title, starting with Cathleen Nesbitt and ending with Audrey Hepburn, separated from the rest by an "and" above her name.

Overnight, Gilbert Miller raised her to star billing above the title. It would now be "AUDREY HEPBURN in *GIGI*." Suddenly, Broadway seemed to have a new star, though its chroniclers had once again been manipulated by Miller and his master press agent, Richard Maney. "It was all planned in advance," Morton

Gottlieb recalls. "Audrey would have been made the star regardless of how the reviews turned out. Happily, it turned out that she deserved it, though it wouldn't have been the first or last time that a star was created just for the publicity value."

AUDREY HEPBURN also joined *GIGI* in lights on the electrical display sign atop the Fulton Theatre's marquee. Telegrams were sent to the press advising of a photo opportunity in which she would help to set the letters of her name in place. When the big moment came, the obese Gilbert Miller provided ballast for a ladder while Audrey climbed up a few rungs and a tall electrician lifted a bulb-encrusted "A" for her to latch on to as photographers snapped away.

To save time, the other twelve letters had already been installed. While the work was being finished, Gilbert Miller walked Audrey to the opposite side of Forty-sixth Street to watch the lights being switched on. The excitement could have gone to her head, but either modesty or insecurity caused Audrey to sigh, "Oh, dear, and I still have to learn how to act."

Thanks to the rave reviews for Audrey's performance and favorable audience reactions, *Gigi* quickly became one of the biggest hits on Broadway, with the 1,164-seat Fulton Theatre selling out at all performances and grossing $23,228 per week (equivalent to about $279,000 in 1994). *Variety* predicted that Gilbert Miller would earn back his production costs—$88,000!—in about six months.

Miller and Anita Loos were trying to swing a movie deal, with Audrey of course starring. But the combination of Colette's risqué reputation and the play's focus on the system of kept women frightened all the Hollywood studios away from making bids. The industry's self-imposed censorship code of that time had strict prohibitions against themes of illicit sex, which if permitted at all, could not be treated humorously or sympathetically.

Once the excitement of opening night subsided, Audrey had to face up to the fact that she would be stuck in New York for a considerable time on the other side of the Atlantic Ocean from her steady beau. But love is often blinding and they saw no reason for concern. James Hanson traveled frequently to Canada on business, so he could always detour through New York, or Audrey could meet him in Toronto during her Sunday to Monday evening breaks between performances.

While he visited for the premiere of *Gigi*, the couple were inseparable (given the limits of Audrey's work schedule, of course). One night, in a zebra-striped corner of the El Morocco supper club, Hanson pulled a diamond ring from his pocket and proposed getting married as soon as Audrey finished her run in *Gigi*. How could she not accept? The engagement was duly announced in the "Forthcoming Marriages" column of the London *Times*. No date was specified for the wedding, but high society had at least been put on alert.

Stardom in *Gigi* gave Audrey her first taste of celebrity, and she hated it. She could no longer go walking or shopping around Manhattan without people stopping her or pointing her out. Most of all, she loathed doing press interviews, which meant answering personal and often intimate questions from complete strangers. As soon as her marital engagement became known, reporters kept pestering her for information about her fiancé and their plans for the future. Rather than telling them to mind their own business, she would just clam up, which amounted to the same thing.

As a consequence, the public read a lot about Audrey Hepburn's "luminous eyes" and "lily petal skin of unusual transparency," but not much about the twenty-two-year-old woman behind them. During a luncheon interview with columnist Earl Wilson at Dinty Moore's restaurant, she confessed to be still suffering from wartime anemia, then promptly dug into a meal consisting of corned beef hash with two poached eggs on top, a platter of mixed green vegetables, several rolls, and a big dish of coffee ice cream. "You can't appreciate liberty as it's enjoyed in your great country until it has been taken completely away from you," she told Wilson.

Between performances of *Gigi*, Audrey continued to take coaching from Cathleen Nesbitt and also enrolled at a theatrical dance studio to keep in shape. "I'm halfway between a dancer and an actress," she said at the time. "I still have a lot to learn, but I think I've improved in my stage work. Ballet is the most completely exhausting thing I've ever done, but if I hadn't been trained to push myself that hard, I could never have managed to act the leading role in a play eight times a week."

As the spring of 1952 rolled around, Audrey found herself swept up in Broadway's annual Tony Awards (named after actress-producer-director Antoinette Perry), a comparatively new tradition that had been started in 1947 as the theater industry's version of Hollywood's Academy Awards. Unlike the Oscars, there were only Tony *winners* in those days. The finalists in each category were kept secret and known only to the panel of judges. But based on her raves for *Gigi*, Audrey Hepburn's name was being bandied about in the gossip columns as one of the top contenders for Best Dramatic Actress. Among others mentioned were Helen Hayes for *Mrs. McThing*, Judith Evelyn for *The Shrike*, and Jessica Tandy for *The Fourposter*, but the winner turned out to be Julie Harris for her portrayal of Sally Bowles in *I am a Camera*, which had opened three days after *Gigi*. Ironically, before signing Audrey, Gilbert Miller had considered Harris for the part, but she'd already committed herself to the John Van Druten play (later the basis for the musical *Cabaret*.)

Winner or loser, Audrey continued to draw crowds to *Gigi*, causing Paramount Pictures to wonder if it shouldn't turn her deal for *Roman Holiday* into a full-fledged seven-year contract before some other studio grabbed her. But Audrey's MCA agents, who now included the shrewd Kay Brown in New York, refused to discuss it, because they were trying to put an end to the system of long-term servitude that caused so much misery for actors during Hollywood's so-called Golden Age.

Audrey's contract with Gilbert Miller presented a more urgent problem to Paramount because the producer was talking about extending the run of *Gigi* into the summer, which would mean either delaying *Roman Holiday* again or finding another leading lady for the film. To expedite matters, Paramount offered to pay Miller $50,000 if he would release Audrey at the end of May. Since Miller would have just about earned back his $88,000 investment by that time, he agreed; it gave him a chance to make a tidy profit without the hassle of keeping the show on the boards. Miller would not agree, however, to releasing Audrey from her obligation to go on a road tour with *Gigi*, which he scheduled for later in the year after the completion of *Roman Holiday*.

Gigi finally closed at the Fulton Theatre on May 24, 1952, having given 217 performances. By that time, Audrey and James Hanson had decided to postpone their wedding until she finished *Roman Holiday*. They planned to honeymoon in the United States while she was touring with *Gigi*.

"When I marry Jimmy, I want to give up at least a year to just being a wife to him," she said at the time. "I can't do that while I'm working. Jimmy is being wonderfully understanding about it. He knows it would be impossible for me to give up my career completely. I just can't. I've worked too long to achieve something. And so many people have helped me along the way, I don't want to let them down."

Before leaving New York, Audrey had meetings with Edith Head, Paramount's chief costume designer, who flew in from Los Angeles to select her wardrobe for *Roman Holiday*. Head remembered: "Audrey came to see me wearing a little dark suit with white collar and cuffs, very simple, very elegant, with a sprig of lily-of-the-valley in her buttonhole, fresh white gloves, her whole person clean and shining—a little girl with the poise of the Duchess of Windsor. Her figure and flair told me, at once, that here was a girl who'd been born to make designers happy. If she hadn't been an actress, she would have been a model or a designer. She turned out to be all three: a girl way ahead of high fashion, who deliberately looked different from other women, who dramatized her own slenderness into her chief asset."

A good model's figure, according to Edith Head, was at most 34-22-34. "It's a figure seldom seen in the movie business," she said. "During a 'bust' season, you'll have actress after actress boasting a 38 or 39; and during any season, your major dramatic stars are likely to be short and not necessarily symmetrical. Audrey had the perfect model figure: very slim and tall at a shade under five feet seven. She didn't wear pads; she accentuated her slimness; and she had the cultivated taste so dear to a designer."

Head, who started designing for films in the silent era and had worked with most of the great stars, claimed that Audrey had a better understanding of fashion than any actress except Marlene Dietrich. "Like Dietrich, Audrey's fittings became the ten-hour not the ten-minute variety," Head said. "To my sketches for *Roman Holiday*, Audrey added a few of her own preferences: simpler necklines, wider belts. She knew exactly how she wanted to look and what worked best for her, yet she was never arrogant or demanding. She had an adorable sweetness that made you feel like a mother getting her only daughter ready for her first prom."

In that era of right-wing politics and communist witch-hunts, it had taken five years for *Roman Holiday* to reach production. The contemporary fairy tale about a princess and an American journalist was written by Dalton Trumbo, a blacklisted member of the Hollywood Ten who could only sell the script by using the pseudonym of John Dighton and sharing authorship credit with writer friend Ian McLellan Hunter, who was really no more than front man for the project. Producer-director Frank Capra purchased it in 1948 for his Liberty Films unit at Paramount, but when that partnership dissolved the script remained at Paramount, where it sat on the shelf until William Wyler expressed interest. After three decades of working within the confines of Hollywood studios, the fifty-five-year-old director yearned to make a film on location in Europe, which had become quite the vogue since the rehabilitation of the war-torn countries. Paramount encouraged him because *Roman Holiday* could be financed by frozen funds— monies that the studio's movies had earned in Italy but couldn't be taken out because of government restrictions.

Roman Holiday may have been the first

romantic comedy with an unhappy ending. After a tenderly chaste interlude, Crown Princess Anne must return to her royal obligations and try to get over her proletarian prince, American journalist Joe Bradley.

While on the Rome portion of an official visit to Italy from her kingdom (its name is never given), the princess slips out incognito to experience real life. But one of her chaperones had already drugged her bedtime milk to prevent that. When she starts feeling woozy, she luckily runs into a kindly American who offers to let her bed down in his apartment for the night with no sexual strings attached. By the next morning, Joe Bradley has learned his guest's true identity, but pretends not to know so that he can earn some much-needed cash writing a magazine article about her. He offers to take her sightseeing, not mentioning, of course, that he's arranged for a photographer to trail after them to snap candids. During the course of their one-day expedition, Anne and Joe start to fall in love, but the idyll ends when some of her royal entourage discover them out dancing that evening. The next day, at a farewell press conference for Princess Anne, she spots Joe in the throng of reporters and photographers. Though prevented by protocol from approaching him, she finds a chance to express her feelings when an Italian reporter asks which of his country's cities she liked the best. "Rome," she answers. "By all means, Rome. I will cherish my visit here in memory as long as I live."

Audrey again had a very lucky break in getting

William Wyler as director of her first starring role in films. Winner of two Academy Awards, he'd directed such classics as *Wuthering Heights, The Little Foxes, Mrs. Miniver,* and *The Best Years of Our Lives.* A perfectionist and a self-confessed slave driver, he had a special knack for working with actresses and was responsible for some of the best performances of stars like Bette Davis, Greer Garson, Myrna Loy, Jennifer Jones, Olivia de Havilland, and Margaret Sullavan (to whom he'd once been married). Like Audrey, the German-born Wyler had had a European upbringing, so they had a definite affinity, even though he'd been working in Hollywood since the end of the silent era.

Despite the rave reviews she'd received for *Gigi,* Audrey knew she'd need all the help she could get to make an impact in *Roman Holiday.* She was sensitive about her looks and the way she photographed. On the stage, where she didn't have to worry about camera close-ups, she could get away with her crooked teeth, prominent nose and bony construction. She was extremely relieved when Wyler told her that he'd selected the Czech-born cinematographer Franz Planer, who'd filmed Max Ophuls's masterful *Letter from an Unknown Woman,* and had a magical touch for lighting and camera movement.

Audrey also hit the jackpot with her leading man, thirty-six-year-old Gregory Peck. *Roman Holiday* was, in fact, intended to be *his* movie, with sole star billing above the title, beneath which there would be a smaller-sized "introducing Audrey Hepburn." Peck was then one of the hottest of the male stars developed by Hollywood in the post—World War II era. His rugged handsomeness and soft-spoken likability made him a favorite of both men and women in hits like *Spellbound, The Yearling, Duel in the Sun, Gentleman's Agreement, The Gunfighter,* and *David and Bathsheba.*

Strangely enough, Peck rejected *Roman Holiday* when he first read the script, realizing that Princess Anne was really the major character and would dominate the movie. Wyler finally shamed him into accepting: "You surprise me, Greg. If you didn't like the story, okay, but because somebody's part is a little better than yours, well, that's no reason to turn down a film. I didn't think you were the kind of actor who measures the size of the roles."

Since Audrey flew to Rome only days after the closing of *Gigi*, her first meeting with Gregory Peck took place during a cocktail party that Paramount held at the Excelsior Hotel for the international press corps. The six-footer's welcoming handshake so overpowered Audrey that she was literally left speechless. It was a reaction that Peck expected from a swooning fan, but not from a co-actor, and he was greatly amused and charmed. As they began rehearsing and then working together, Peck quickly realized that Audrey would steal the movie, reducing him to nothing more than a foil.

"Everybody on the set fell in love with her. She never put a foot wrong," Peck recalled. "I got on the phone to Hollywood and spoke to my agent. I told him, 'George, it's gotta be Audrey

129

Hepburn above the title.' He said, 'You can't do that. You've worked years to get top billing. You can't give it away like that.' I said, 'Oh yes I can. And if I don't, I'm gonna make a fool out of myself, because this girl is going to win the Oscar in her very first performance.' "

Paramount production head Y. Frank Freeman was flabbergasted when Peck's agent contacted him. But Paramount finally agreed to give Audrey equal billing, because the matching of her name with Gregory Peck's would give her instant status as a major star rather than a promising newcomer.

Audrey Hepburn and *Roman Holiday* seemed to be made for each other. Had she started her Hollywood career portraying a scullery maid instead of a princess, she might not have made a dent, but she had the breeding and the look of the genuine article.

"You could *believe* Audrey as a princess," William Wyler said. "Even if you had never seen her before, and she walked into a room, you would have assumed that she was one."

Audrey also benefited from the timeliness of the story about a princess involved with a commoner. The English-speaking world had gone gaga over royalty in recent years, starting with the marriage of Britain's Princess Elizabeth and continuing through her coronation as queen. During the filming of *Roman Holiday*, the queen's sister, Princess Margaret, was making headlines with a sizzling romance with an equerry officer, Group Captain Peter Townsend. Paramount's publicity machine had a field day making parallels between fantasy and reality.

Filming *Roman Holiday* in the middle of summer turned out to be hell, not only because of Rome's sweltering humidity and lack of air conditioning, but also because of the volatile political situation, with demonstrations and street battles between the ruling Christian Democrats and the opposing communists and fascists. Audrey often thought she was back in war-torn Arnhem as schedules were constantly changed to avoid involvement in some terrorist incident. One day, five bundles of explosives were discovered under a bridge over the Tiber River where filming was due to take place several hours later.

After he'd seen the first week's rushes, William Wyler regretted the decision to photograph the movie in black and white. The Eternal City seemed to have been built with Technicolor in mind, but Paramount said it was too late to change over. To accommodate the different film stock and lighting conditions, the entire production would have to be reorganized, which meant losing precious time, hiring more personnel, and adding a bundle to the $1.5 million budget.

The filming moved slowly anyway. Rome's heat was so intense that makeup melted; Audrey bathed or showered every chance she got to avoid collapsing. The combination of the weather and William Wyler's inexperience at working on location drove his perfectionism to new heights of tyranny. He ordered take after take of the same scene, never less than three and often a dozen or more, until he was satisfied.

Work was further complicated by hordes of Roman gawkers. "One of the first scenes we shot was at the Piazza di Spagna," Gregory Peck remembered. "There were at least ten thousand people assembled at the foot of the Spanish Steps and in the street. The police couldn't stop them from whistling and heckling. For Audrey and me, it was like acting in a huge amphitheater before a packed house of rowdies. I asked her if she didn't find it very intimidating. Ah, no, not at all. She lived her role. She took it as calmly and serenely as a real princess would have."

That day, an unexpected thing happened which continued through all the outdoor locations. "Whenever William Wyler didn't like something and said 'Let's try it again, it wasn't quite right,' people in the crowd would cry, 'No, that went well, it's very good.' They were satisfied. And when Wyler said 'That's fine, we can print that,' there was usually someone who would shout 'No, no, one more time.' Willie learned to listen, because they were usually right," Peck said.

Margaret Rawlings, a British actress working in the film, was surprised that Audrey didn't rebel against Wyler's perfectionism. "During the meal breaks, we were usually served a weird sort of boxed lunch of sandwiches, antipasto, and a sparkling Italian wine similar to champagne. Audrey barely touched anything or spoke, and just sat conserving her energy for the next take. I very much admired the way she disciplined herself and controlled her emotions," Rawlings recalled.

Audrey gave blind obedience to Wyler because

she was a perfectionist herself and considered him the key to becoming an accomplished actress. But unfortunately, Wyler was one of those directors who did not offer a lot of advice and instruction to his actors. He knew exactly what he wanted from them, but preferred that they find their own way through a scene. The blunt command to do it again, which he always barked with a mischievous grin on his face, was usually the extent of Wyler's direction.

In Audrey's case, Wyler bent a bit because she lacked the experience of hardened veterans like Bette Davis or Barbara Stanwyck. He did everything he could to strengthen Audrey's confidence in herself and to bring out her natural strengths. "Audrey needed to forget to 'act' and to learn how to just 'be,'" Wyler said later. "The first lesson in movie acting is to respond with inner feeling and not to play 'at' the camera, which is a very sensitive instrument that picks up every nuance. The exaggerated techniques that an actor must use on the stage seem false and ridiculous when magnified a hundred times on the movie screen."

The most difficult scene for Audrey was one in a parked car where Princess Anne and her gallant American share their last private moment before parting. "I was supposed to cry," Audrey recalled. "It was late at night, and I was tired from working all day. I played the first part of the scene very nicely, but tears didn't come and I didn't know how to turn them on. Unless they came naturally, I hadn't ever tried or learned. Nothing was happening, so Willie Wyler finally came over and gave me *hell*! He'd always been so adorable and very gentle with me, always bringing out the best in me and everything. He really let me have it, and I burst into tears and they shot the scene."

Wyler kept springing surprises on Audrey to make her performance more spontaneous. In cahoots with Gregory Peck, he borrowed one of comedian Red Skelton's classic shticks for a scene in which Peck introduces Audrey to the Mouth of Truth, an ancient relic sculpted on a wall of the Colosseum. "The legend goes that a monster lurking inside will bite off the hand of anyone who isn't telling the truth," Peck recalled. "I was supposed to stick my hand in and pretend to be eaten up. But what Audrey wasn't prepared for was my breaking loose with the hand hidden up my sleeve. She was so startled that she just exploded with fright and then merriment when she realized what I'd done."

Always sniffing for scandal, the ferocious Roman press corps and paparazzi tried to create a real-life romance between Audrey and Peck when his Finnish-born wife, Greta, suddenly packed up their three children and flew home to California. But the Pecks had been having marital problems long before *Roman Holiday*, and if Audrey did cause their latest difficulties, there's no evidence of an intimate relationship between the two stars.

The rapport between them, however, seemed more than just professional. "I'm enchanted with Greg," Audrey said at the time. "He's so marvelously normal, so genuine, so downright *real*!

There's nothing of the 'behaving-like-a-star' routine, no phoniness. He's a dear!"

Similarly, Peck said that "Audrey is not the type who, bit by bit, turns to granite and becomes a walking career. She's modest and as lovable as an overstrung tennis racquet."

Roman Holiday took five months to film, finishing in October 1952. Audrey had no time to rest afterwards, since she needed to fly back to New York to prepare for the road tour of *Gigi*, which would continue into the spring of 1953 and include bookings in Boston, Cleveland, Chicago, Detroit, Washington, D.C., Los Angeles, and San Francisco.

Her plans to wed James Hanson remained in limbo, but she'd already purchased a wedding dress that she carried with her luggage just in case they decided to marry on the spur of the moment. During Audrey's stay in Rome, Hanson had visited only once, but they kept up a steady stream of letters and telephone calls. In press interviews, Audrey still talked of settling down on the Hanson family estate in Yorkshire and having babies. But as her career continued to burgeon, that seemed more and more unlikely to happen.

After Audrey started the *Gigi* tour, Hanson flew over during the Chicago run so they could celebrate the Christmas holidays together. What happened during that visit is known only to the two involved, but soon after Hanson returned to England, another announcement appeared in the matrimonial column of the London *Times*, this one stating that "The engagement between Mr.

James Hanson and Miss Audrey Hepburn has been broken."

When queried by reporters, both insisted that there had been no violent quarrel or rift. They'd drifted apart—but professionally and geographically more than emotionally. "It occurred to me while the play was in Cleveland and Jimmy in England that if we were finding it difficult to even arrange a wedding, what would it be like later on?" Audrey said at the time. "I decided it would be unfair for Jimmy to marry him when I was also in love with, and tied to, my work. He agreed."

Audrey also told columnist friend Radie Harris, "When I realized that I wouldn't even have time to select the furnishings for our home, I knew that I would make a pretty bad wife. I would forever have to be studying parts, fitting costumes, and giving interviews. What a humiliating spot to put my husband in—making him stand by, holding my coat while I signed autographs."

One can only wonder what Audrey Hepburn's life would have been like if she *had* married James Hanson, who today as Lord Hanson is one of England's wealthiest men, his Hanson PLC conglomerate reported to be worth £11.3 billion ($17 billion). He has been married only once, to the former Geraldine Kaelin. In 1993, the couple celebrated their thirty-fourth anniversary, having produced two sons and a daughter along the way.

When *Gigi* reached Los Angeles, Paramount's publicity department started the advance buildup for Audrey and *Roman Holiday*, which proved a real challenge because their new star hardly fitted the current Hollywood mold. She was neither blond nor busty, and her ladylike demeanor hardly suggested a sex kitten. Studio-arranged "dates" with Bing Crosby and then with the even older Groucho Marx generated more titters than press coverage.

But those who'd viewed the rough cut of *Roman Holiday* felt that Audrey would make it on her own talent and personality once the public saw her on-screen. "As I supervised the editing, I had that rare gut feeling that I was witnessing something very special indeed," William Wyler recalled. "Audrey *was* a princess—and she had so much poise, no doubt from her experience as a dancer and from her mother's aristocratic background. But she was also every eager young girl who has ever come to Rome for the first time, and she reacted with so natural and spontaneous an eagerness that I, crusty veteran that I was, felt tears in my eyes watching her.

"Audrey was the spirit of youth—and I knew that very soon the entire world would fall in love with her, as all of us on the picture did."

Paramount became even more eager to extend its hold on Audrey with a long-term contract. This time she accepted, provided that she received script approval and could reject what she didn't like. She also got the right to work in stage plays as long as they didn't conflict with her filming schedules. This was a freedom seldom granted in the Hollywood factory system of old, when contract stars usually made two or three films annually and were forbidden (even if they had time to spare) to do anything else but radio broadcasts to promote their work.

When *Gigi* ended its tour in San Francisco, Audrey grabbed a long-needed vacation and took off for London to visit her mother. With Audrey earning enough now to support them both, they'd moved up to a larger apartment in the same Mayfair building. England was still Audrey's official home, but with so much of her work focused in the United States now, it looked like she would have to settle in the U.S. and maybe even become an American citizen.

Gregory Peck, who'd remained in Europe after *Roman Holiday* to make *Night People* for 20th Century-Fox, also happened to be in London during Audrey's stay, so Paramount's PR department persuaded him to throw a Welcome Home cocktail party in her honor. The crowd of celebrities and journalists included one of Peck's closest friends, the American actor Mel Ferrer, who was in England getting ready to portray King Arthur to Robert Taylor's Sir Lancelot in MGM's *Knights of the Round Table*.

After Peck introduced Audrey to his chum, the two started chatting about the theater. Ferrer told her about the La Jolla Playhouse, a year-round summer theater in Southern California where he and Peck, together with others from Hollywood, produced plays and often acted and/or directed as well. "Audrey had been to a screening of my latest film, *Lili*, and very sweetly told me how wonderful she thought I was in it," Ferrer recalled. "We talked vaguely about doing a play together, and she asked me to send her a likely script if I found one."

Tall, slender, and off-beat handsome, thirty-six-year-old Mel Ferrer was then a contender for major Hollywood stardom, although he fancied himself more of a triple threat actor-director-writer in the mold of his idol Orson Welles, whom he strongly resembled in a slimmer version. It turned out to be a case of instant and mutual attraction as he talked with Audrey. "A sensitive man with a sensitive face. I could love him," she thought to herself.

"Is it any wonder that Mel Ferrer fell head over heels in love with such a provocative, desirable creature?" columnist Radie Harris would soon ask. "Mel has always been attracted to glamorous, successful women. But the chemistry works both ways. I can also understand why Audrey would fall for him. Mel has a quality rare in American men—he knows how to make a woman feel like a woman."

During Audrey's sojourn in London, Ferrer took her to the theater several times, but she was realistic enough to keep her emotions under control. Besides the twelve-year age difference, she would feel guilty about becoming involved with a man who had a wife and children back home in America. She was also caught up in the whirl of her career, which threatened to overwhelm her as *Roman Holiday* drew nearer to release.

chapter seven

HOLLYWOOD ROMANCE

When Audrey returned to Los Angeles from London in the late spring of 1953, she discovered that Paramount had snared the movie industry's most prestigious showcase, the 6,000-seat Radio City Music Hall in New York, for the world premiere engagement of *Roman Holiday*. Based on all the advance enthusiasm, the studio was in a fever to find another project for its new star. George Cukor, who'd missed out on directing Audrey in *Gigi* and yearned for another chance, suggested Edith Sitwell's *Fanfare for Elizabeth*, dealing with the romance between the queen's parents, King Henry VIII and Anne Boleyn, but Paramount gagged at the thought of a costly historical epic that would take a year or more to prepare and film.

One of the scouts in the story department who covered stage plays strongly recommended *Sabrina Fair*, a romantic comedy by Samuel Taylor due to open in November on Broadway with the luminous Margaret Sullavan in the title role. After reading the script, Audrey adored the Cinderella fable about a chauffeur's daughter pursued by two millionaire brothers, and needed no further persuading. Paramount then purchased the film rights for $150,000, much to the dismay of Margaret Sullavan, who'd hoped to star in the movie herself. Though a forty-four-year-old actress might be able to create the illusion of a twenty-three-year-old girl on the stage, it seemed a bit crazy to think that she could get by with it on the big screen.

Audrey had another piece of extraordinary luck when Paramount assigned Billy Wilder to direct *Sabrina Fair*, which immediately had its title shortened to *Sabrina* to stop the public from thinking it might be a sequel to the musty literary classic *Vanity Fair*. Like William Wyler, with whom he was often confused because of the similarity of names, Billy Wilder was also European-born but more broadly talented because he not only directed but also helped to write his productions. Prior to taking on *Sabrina*, Wilder had turned out such hits and award winners for Paramount as *Double Indemnity*, *The Lost Weekend*, *Sunset Boulevard*, and the just released *Stalag 17*.

While preparations went on for *Sabrina*, *Roman Holiday* finally entered release and more than fulfilled expectations. Publishing tycoon Henry Luce was so impressed by Audrey's performance that he instructed the editors of *Time* magazine to do a cover story about her for the issue of September 7, 1953, which was unusual for a Hollywood newcomer. From that time onwards, Audrey became a special pet of both *Time* and *Life*, turning up on their covers more frequently than any of her contemporaries, including Elizabeth Taylor and Marilyn Monroe.

That first *Time* embrace described Audrey as

"exquisitely blending queenly dignity and bubbling mischief . . . a stick-slim actress with huge, limpid eyes and a heart-shaped face . . . She sparkles and glows with the fire of a finely cut diamond." Reviews elsewhere were unanimously ecstatic about her vitality, beauty, and elfin charm.

Bosley Crowther, the film critic for *The New York Times*, said that Audrey was "alternately regal and childlike, with the qualities of someone who came from a better and purer world." In its 119 minutes running time, *Roman Holiday* made Audrey Hepburn the royal princess of the screen. Men found her irresistible and seemingly more attainable than glamour sirens like Monroe or Taylor. Women identified with Audrey and tried to emulate her pin-thin luster by going on diets and rushing out to buy full skirts and tailored blouses like those she wore in the film. What style maven Cecil Beaton described as Audrey's "rat-nibbled hair and moon-pale face" became known as the "gamine look" and was copied enthusiastically.

Roman Holiday made Audrey Hepburn an instant star all over the world, not only in England and Europe, where it might have been expected, but most astonishingly in Japan, where forty years later she's still a role model for young women and the favorite foreign actress of all generations of moviegoers. No doubt Audrey's delicate figure and slightly Asian-looking features made her easy to identify with. But her portrayal of a royal princess moving around freely in public and becoming involved with a commoner also provided a real cultural shock, since such behavior was impossible for Japan's own imperial family then. The fact that the princess finally chose her royal obligations over love also delighted the Japanese.

Audrey Hepburn also arrived at the right time for Japanese trendies, who'd had too much postwar exposure to American pop culture and saw her as the embodiment of European chic. Gregory Peck's agent would have thrown a fit if he'd known that Paramount-Japan gave Audrey top billing in its advertising for *Roman Holiday* in lettering twice the size of Peck's. In its initial Japanese release, Paramount estimated that the movie earned back a third of its production cost. (In a 1990 survey conducted by the NHK and JSB television companies, *Roman Holiday* turned out to be Japan's favorite foreign movie of all time, with *Gone With the Wind* ranking second.)

By the time Audrey started filming *Sabrina*, the Theatre Owners of America had dubbed her "Golden Girl of the Year" and rival gossip hens Louella Parsons and Hedda Hopper were unanimous for once in predicting that her work in *Roman Holiday* would be rewarded with an Oscar. Her new director, Billy Wilder, joined the rooters by noting that "After so many drive-in waitresses in movies—it has been a real drought—here is class, somebody who went to school, can spell and possibly play the piano—she's a wispy, thin little thing, but you're really in the presence of somebody when you see that girl. Not since Garbo has there been anything like her, with the possible exception of Ingrid Bergman."

Since Audrey had all but stolen *Roman Holiday* from Gregory Peck, it came as no surprise that Peck's close friend Cary Grant rejected Billy Wilder's bid to star opposite her in *Sabrina*. Instead the role went to Humphrey Bogart, who'd recently signed a three-picture contract with Paramount after spending most of his career at Warner Brothers.

Because Bogart was Grant's senior by five years and thus a full three decades older than Audrey Hepburn at twenty-four, Wilder tried to balance the difference by advancing the age of the third man in the romantic triangle. The role of Bogart's younger brother, originally intended for an up-and-coming star in Audrey's age bracket, was refashioned for thirty-five-year-old William Holden, then one of Wilder's preferred actors because of his terrific performances in the director's *Sunset Boulevard* and *Stalag 17*.

Audrey was less concerned about those changes than by Billy Wilder's decision to restrict her now trusted friend Edith Head to designing only her basic everyday clothes in *Sabrina*. The glamorous costumes that transform plain Sabrina Fairchild into a fashion plate would come from a twenty-six-year-old French wonder boy named Hubert de Givenchy, whom Wilder's wife had discovered during her last shopping expedition to Europe. With condolences to the outraged Edith Head, Audrey flew to Paris to confer with him, never dreaming that it would be the beginning of one of the most important and beneficial alliances of her life.

Givenchy was then competing with forty-eight-year-old Christian Dior for the leadership of French couture, dominated before World War II by two women, Coco Chanel and Jeanne Lanvin. His technique was heavily influenced by his great friend and mentor Cristobal Balenciaga. After apprenticing in the houses of Lucien Lelong and Elsa Schiaparelli, Givenchy opened his own salon on the Avenue Georges V, with financial backing from his family, which was one of the richest in France through ownership of the Gobelin and Beauvais tapestry factories.

Though his publicity tended to paint him as a devilishly handsome playboy and daring sports-car driver, Givenchy had not become a designer just to pass the time. His clothes were revolutionary for the era, austerely simple, yet feminine and beautifully tailored. They were the equivalent of picture frames, intended to make the women inside more beautiful without becoming the center of attention themselves.

Audrey's relationship with Givenchy did not begin auspiciously. As the designer recalled: "I was in the office of my salon when someone announced, 'Miss Hepburn's here to see you.' The film *Roman Holiday* had not yet been released in France and I'd never heard of Audrey Hepburn, so I was expecting to see walk in Katharine Hepburn, whom I'd long admired and had always wanted to meet. But in place of her I discovered in the doorway a thread of a girl with a very fragile look and the eyes of a doe. She was wearing a little pullover, checked cotton pants with ballerina shoes, and a gondolier's hat with 'Venezia' marked on it. She told me at once that she needed some clothes for a film and explained a bit of the story about a girl who comes to outfit herself in Paris.

"I told her the truth," Givenchy continued. "I was in the midst of putting together my next collection and didn't have the time to spend with her. She insisted. For the sake of peace and quietude, I said she could choose anything she liked from my current collection. That satisfied her and she selected several models. She knew exactly what she wanted. She knew perfectly her *visage* and her body, their fine points and their faults. I tried to adapt my designs to her desires. She wanted a bare-shouldered evening dress modified to hide the hollows behind her collar bone. What I invented for her eventually became a style, so popular that I named it *décolleté Sabrina*."

The enduring friendship started that same evening when Givenchy took Audrey to dinner in Saint Germain des Prés. "It was then that she truly won my heart," he recalled. "She told me of her life, her passion for the dance, her discovery by Colette. I saw that she was a woman very different from others, and I felt an extraordinary sympathy with her. Audrey, who was of admirable fidelity and loyalty, never forgot that first meeting. She had been very touched that I had consented to help her even though I didn't know her. For each of the films that she made afterwards, she wanted me to dress her or to help in the fittings of costumes that were not in my usual sphere."

Back in Hollywood again for the start of

Sabrina, Audrey got her first real taste of working in an American film factory, and it turned out a disillusioning experience. Making *Roman Holiday* on location in Italy had been an adventure, with everybody banding together like a family on vacation, but now she had to confront studio politics and egocentric co-workers who could turn into monsters when provoked. She was flabbergasted when Edith Head begrudgingly approved Givenchy's clothes and then went on to take credit for them herself, which Head was entitled to do in her contract as chief of Paramount's design department.

And for the three months needed to film *Sabrina*, Audrey had to endure shock waves created by Humphrey Bogart, who'd just finished portraying a psychopath in *The Caine Mutiny* and seemed to have permanently assumed Captain Queeg's snarling suspiciousness and foul temper. Perhaps Bogart was also suffering the first pain of the cancer that killed him four years later, but at the time his main irritation appeared to be Billy Wilder, with whom Bogart had never worked before and to whom he took an immediate dislike because of his autocratic ways of directing. Though Wilder was an Austrian Jew who'd fled Europe in 1933 because of the Hitler regime, Bogart kept calling him a Nazi to his face, which didn't help the atmosphere on the set.

In the plot of *Sabrina*, Audrey, portraying the daughter of a chauffeur to a rich family, becomes romantically involved with the two sons, first with rascal playboy William Holden, and then with solid businessman Bogart, who disapproves of his younger brother and tries to break up the lovers by pursuing the girl himself. The fun builds up considerable suspense over which brother will finally win Sabrina. In Samuel Taylor's original play, the older brother did, but to immerse the cast in their roles, Wilder made it a guessing game for them as well, handing out only a few pages of the script at a time and strongly hinting of pressure from Paramount's management to throw the ending to William Holden, who ranked well ahead of Bogart in the latest popularity polls. Needless to say, those tactics drove Bogart wild, which was probably Wilder's intention. The climax remained true to the play.

Because Wilder and Holden had become great friends during their two previous collaborations, Bogart started to believe that they were conspiring against him. He also became paranoid about Audrey, convinced that she would steal *Sabrina* just as she did *Roman Holiday*. He started making blunt statements to the press that Holden was a "dumb prick" and Audrey such an incompetent actress that she couldn't do a scene in less than a dozen takes. He also described *Sabrina* as "a crock of you know what," which didn't win him any allies in Paramount's executive suite.

Between Bogart's foul temper and his habit of isolating himself in his dressing room with a few flunkies and plenty of Scotch whisky, Audrey found no basis for even a casual friendship with her co-star, but something much more intense developed with William Holden, who had his hair bleached for a Jay Gatsby look in *Sabrina* and was probably one of the choicest hunks of beefcake in Hollywood at the time. It began innocently enough when Holden started watching over Audrey like a guardian angel to shield her from Bogart's unpleasantnesses.

"Before I even met Audrey," Holden recalled, "I had a crush on her, and after I met her, just a day later, I felt as if we were old friends, and I was rather fiercely protective of her, though not in a possessive way. Most men who worked with her felt both fatherly or brotherly about her, while harboring romantic feelings about her."

Ernest Lehman, Wilder's scriptwriting partner, was the first to discover a romance brewing between Audrey and Holden. Late one afternoon after shooting had just finished for the day, he stopped by Holden's dressing room to drop off some dialogue changes and walked in without knocking. To his surprise, he found Audrey and Holden standing face-to-face, staring into each other's eyes with their hands locked together. The embarrassed Lehman apologized for intruding and left, telling Billy Wilder afterwards that "something profound" seemed to be happening between the two stars.

William Holden differed from other Hollywood actors who had affairs with their leading ladies. He insisted on taking Audrey home to dinner one evening to meet his wife, Ardis, who'd been the promising movie star Brenda Marshall before retiring to raise their two sons. Mrs. Holden had too much invested in her husband's success to want to give him a divorce. They continued living together to preserve his public image as a solid family man and because she relished the prestige that went with being Mrs. William Holden. She tolerated his infidelities as long as they didn't become too serious or threatening.

Audrey, whose only serious romances had been with James Hanson and Marcel Le Bon, fell hard for Holden, and the feeling was reciprocated. After working at the studio, the lovers would head across the street to a secluded booth in Lucey's Restaurant for cocktails and dinner, then retreat to Audrey's temporary two-room apartment in Beverly Hills. Presumably they did more than just listen to Audrey's ever-burgeoning collection of classical and jazz records, which had become her favorite form of relaxation since she started living on her own.

Audrey was entranced by Holden's gentlemanly charm and keen sense of humor, but as she got to know him better she discovered him to be a hypochondriac, vain about his looks (as most actors are), and a heavy drinker who didn't know when to stop. But for Holden, Audrey had no flaws. She embodied everything he admired in a woman; her youth—eleven years his junior—was an additional attraction.

Swept away by her feelings for Holden, Audrey started daydreaming about marrying him and having babies that would grow up to be as bright and shining as Peter and Scott, the two that Ardis had given him. Holden was thrilled when Audrey confessed her fantasies, but felt honor-bound to tell her that one of them was impossible. After his wife had had a difficult birth with their last child, the couple decided that three were enough (she had a daughter from a previous marriage), and he'd undergone a vasectomy to make sure. In those days, the operation was irreversible. If Audrey wanted to have children with Holden, it would have to be as stepmother to those he already had or by adopting some.

But the unlikelihood of Ardis Holden agreeing to a divorce, combined with two demanding careers that could never mesh, made it plain that marriage was an impossible goal. The lovers decided to make the best of it while they could, realizing that when they finished working in *Sabrina* they had no excuse for being together that wouldn't cause scandal and unhappiness.

Meanwhile, Mel Ferrer made sure he wasn't forgotten by sending Audrey a play script that he believed would be perfect for them to act in together on Broadway. Written by Jean Giraudoux, the great modern French playwright, *Ondine* was a romantic fable about a medieval knight-errant and a fifteen-year-old water nymph. The play had been a huge hit with Louis Jouvet and Madeleine Ozeray in Paris in 1939, but the outbreak of World War II and Giraudoux's death in 1944 delayed its availability for a Broadway production.

Maurice Valency did the English adaptation of *Ondine*, which Giraudoux had based on a German fairy tale written in 1811 by Friedrich Heinrich Karl de la Motte Fouqué and subsequently produced as an opera in Berlin in 1816. Briefly, the story has the wandering knight, Hans, falling in love with a water nymph, who unfortunately carries a curse of death for any man who proves unfaithful to her. When Hans moves on to an affair with a mortal woman, he tries to save himself by having Ondine burned as a witch, but it's too late. He goes to a watery grave as Ondine returns safely to her undersea kingdom.

Audrey thought *Ondine* was one of the loveliest things she'd ever read. Instantly she phoned Mel Ferrer in New York and told him that she would do it. Ferrer then went to the production entity known as the Playwrights Company and obtained financial backing, with the understanding that the distinguished actor-director Alfred Lunt would do the staging. Lunt and his actress wife, Lynn Fontanne, scored one of their greatest triumphs in Giraudoux's *Amphitryon 38*, and the author had entrusted *Ondine* to them before he died. Too old to act in it themselves, they had once tried to persuade their close friends Laurence Olivier and Vivien Leigh to do it, but to no avail.

Since Paramount had no immediate plans for Audrey after *Sabrina*, the studio permitted her to do the play but made some strict demands, limiting her engagement to six months and extracting the right to produce a movie version of *Ondine* if the play became a hit. Happily for Audrey, MCA agent Kay Brown also did some fancy dealing with the Playwrights Company, landing her a minimum guarantee of $2,500 per week against a percentage of the box-office receipts. That proves what one solid movie success can do. For *Gigi*, Audrey had received a flat $500 per week.

Mel Ferrer, of course, would be Audrey's co-star in *Ondine*. In appreciation of his packaging efforts in behalf of the play, she also insisted that he receive equal-size billing. That didn't please the Playwrights Company very much, because Mel Ferrer had been on the scene for over a decade without becoming a major drawing card in either plays or movies. One of the reasons may have been that the public kept confusing him with non-relative Jose Ferrer, who *had* attained all the acting and directing success that Mel aspired to himself. Small wonder that gossip soon started— fair or not—that Mel Ferrer intended using Audrey Hepburn as his passport to the celebrity and wealth that had eluded him all those years.

Since Audrey had been instantly attracted to Mel when Gregory Peck introduced them in London the previous year, it seemed inevitable that a romance would develop when and if their paths converged for any length of time. In Audrey's case, it happened while she was recovering from her infatuation with William Holden and particularly vulnerable to the advances of any man, especially one as handsome, debonair, and smart as Mel Ferrer.

Born August 25, 1917, in the resort town of Elberon, New Jersey, Melchior Gaston Ferrer had a privileged background and some Hispanic and Irish ancestry. His father, a Cuban-born doctor, was a noted heart specialist. His mother, Irene O'Donohue, came from Newport, Rhode Island, society. Mel was educated in private schools and attended Princeton University, where he excelled in both acting and playwriting but quit after his sophomore year to pursue a theatrical career. In 1937, he married Frances Pilchard, an artist and sculptor whom he met at Princeton.

Mel performed in the chorus of Cole Porter's *You'll Never Know* on Broadway, acted in a couple of flop plays, and then had a mild bout with polio, which left him partially paralyzed in one arm for several years and kept him from serving in World War II. For a while he tried writing and had a modest success with a children's book entitled *Tito's Hat*, based on an idea that came to him during a vacation in Mexico. For adult readers, he compiled and edited *Granite Laughter and Marble Tears*, a collection of graveyard epitaphs.

Mel finally found a niche for himself in radio with NBC in New York as an announcer and actor, eventually producing and directing programs as well. In 1944 (the worst year of Audrey Hepburn's wartime suffering), his versatility induced Columbia Pictures to bring him to Hollywood to learn the ropes, starting as a dialogue coach. By the following year, he got his first chance to direct a movie, a *very* low budget remake of Gene Stratton Porter's *Girl of the Limberlost*, but Mel committed the unforgivable sin of going three days over the ten-day shooting schedule. Columbia, a studio that still prided itself on its penny-pinching beginnings on Poverty Row, promptly fired him.

Now with two children (Pepa and Mark) to support, Mel got help from his friend Jose Ferrer, who was getting ready to produce and direct a new play and who cast him in one of the leading roles. Lillian Smith's *Strange Fruit* had become a number one best-seller in 1944 after being banned in Boston and other cities for its bold depiction of miscegenation in the Deep South. The novel was considered too controversial for a movie version and possibly even for Broadway, so the play opened on the road and gradually worked its way toward the Main Stem. It finally arrived there in November 1945, lasting only sixty performances. Critics savaged it, but Mel received acclaim for his portrayal of a white man who has an affair with a beautiful black girl (played by Jane White) and then turns viciously against her when she becomes pregnant.

Mel's performance in *Strange Fruit* brought another offer from Hollywood, this time from independent producer David O. Selznick, who signed him to a three-way contract as an actor, director, and writer, but never actually used him for any of his projects. Instead, Selznick loaned him out at a considerable profit to RKO, where Mel worked as an assistant director to John Ford on *The Fugitive* and then attempted a salvage job as director on Howard Hughes's long delayed production of *Vendetta*, which, in the tradition of *The Outlaw* and Jane Russell, was intended to turn Hughes's latest discovery, Faith Domergue, into a goddess of the silver screen.

While waiting for a call that never came from Selznick himself, Mel became friendly with most of the producer's stable of stars, especially Gregory Peck, Joseph Cotten, and Dorothy McGuire, all stage-trained actors who rarely got a chance to work in the theater anymore because of their film commitments. With Mel as the catalyst and the principal producer-director, they formed the La Jolla Playhouse near San Diego, which had a resident company that the stars could join for a week or two in plays of their choice. The Playhouse also served as a training ground for young talent and a recruiting place for the scouts of the Hollywood studios.

Mel's first breakthrough in movies came in 1949, when he finished his Selznick contract with a loan-out to independent producer Louis de Rochemont for *Lost Boundaries*, which was deemed too controversial by the major studios and ended up being distributed by the second-grade Eagle Lion Films. Racist though it might seem now, Mel got the job because of his swarthy handsomeness. He portrayed a light-skinned Negro doctor, head of a family all trying to pass for white in a New England town. The white Beatrice Pearson portrayed Mel's wife, and their children were also acted by whites. Darker-skinned black characters, however, were cast accurately, with actors including Canada Lee, star of Orson Welles's Broadway production of *Native Son*.

Today, *Lost Boundaries* might seem like an embarrassment, but in 1949 it made a great impact in a wave of racially conscious movies that were also released that year, including *Intruder in the Dust*, *Pinky*, and *Home of the Brave*. Winning raves for his performance, Mel suddenly found himself in demand in Hollywood and accepted an offer from Howard Hughes to return to RKO as an actor-director. He started off the contract by

156

directing his first film since *Girl of the Limberlost*, a romantic melodrama with Claudette Colbert and Robert Ryan entitled *The Secret Fury* (remembered mainly for the film debut of Mel's stage actress friend, Vivian Vance, the future Ethel Mertz of TV's *I Love Lucy*).

Mel's first acting role for RKO was in *Born to Be Bad* with Joan Fontaine and Robert Ryan. On loan-out to Columbia, he got probably the best role of his entire career, as a Mexican peasant who rises to idolized matador in *The Brave Bulls*. Mel gave such a riveting performance that he seemed destined for an Oscar nomination, but both he and the movie became victims of director Robert Rossen's persecution by the House Un-American Activities Committee for his onetime membership in the Communist party.

Back at RKO again, Mel played Marlene Dietrich's outlaw lover in Fritz Lang's Technicolored *Rancho Notorious*, a most unusual western. He was fast becoming known for offbeat roles rather than typical romantic leads. MGM borrowed him for two pictures, first to menace Stewart Granger in the sword-swinging *Scaramouche*, then as the crippled puppet master bashfully in love with Leslie Caron in *Lili*.

By the time he met Audrey, Ferrer had been married three times, but twice to the same woman. He and Frances Pilchard had divorced when he fell in love with Barbara Tripp, a New York designer. Marriage to Tripp proved a quick mistake, and they divorced amicably so Mel could remarry Pilchard. Their two children couldn't have been happier. But when Frances

Ferrer discovered the growing rapport between her husband and Audrey, she wasted no time in consulting divorce lawyers again.

During the New York rehearsals for *Ondine*, Audrey and Mel started living together in her sublet apartment in Greenwich Village. The couple seemed a natural blending of opposite types: a delicately feminine woman and a macho man, a shy introvert and a domineering extrovert. But Mel's twelve-year seniority, his worldly experience as a husband and father, and his long involvement with the stage and movies dazzled the comparatively immature Audrey and made her worship the ground he walked on.

The seeds had been planted for a sort of Svengali-Trilby relationship, which may have been Mel's intention from the beginning. Many insiders who'd been following his career over the years believed that he had visions of them becoming the next Laurence Olivier and Vivien Leigh.

It certainly seemed that way as the *Ondine* rehearsals progressed. Mel started behaving as though he, and not Alfred Lunt, was directing Audrey in the play. There were frequent battles backstage and on, with the dignified and mild-mannered Lunt soon deciding to concentrate on the overall staging and to leave the star actress to the counseling of her lover.

"Mel was coaching Audrey at home every night and completely undoing whatever Lunt taught her during the day," the play's publicist recalled. "Poor Audrey was caught in the middle and going bananas. Since Mel was also the show's leading man, it wasn't helping his performance either. Lynn Fontanne, who sat out front during most rehearsals as her husband's eyes-and-ears, finally told him to let love have its way. Hopefully everything would all come together by opening night."

Actually, Mel was doing Audrey and *Ondine* a real service, because she needed all the help she could get in what was only her second major stage appearance. This one would dwarf *Gigi* and be housed at the 46th Street Theatre, which had three hundred seats more than the Fulton and would make greater demands on her vocal projection. Though hardly a musical, *Ondine* had an incidental score by Virgil Thomson and a cast of twenty-four actors, including dancers and singers. There were three acts instead of *Gigi*'s two, and panoramic scenic effects of castles and medieval landscape. Surprisingly, the production cost was only $113,000.

World War III nearly erupted over Audrey's hairstyling. Alfred Lunt wanted an ash blond Ondine, as suited a nymph of the salty deep, and as Madeleine Ozeray had played it in the original Paris production. But Audrey had such a pale complexion that she knew she'd look washed out as a blonde; she resisted Lunt's order to bleach her hair, and Mel backed her up. For the opening night of the try-out engagement in Boston, she relented, but after one look in the mirror she realized she'd made a mistake. Going back to her natural shade the next day, she experimented with a blond wig to appease Lunt. When that proved unsatisfactory, she settled on dusting her dark hair with a goldlike powder before each performance. That created an ethereal glow from the stage lights and could be easily shampooed out afterwards.

To the singularly named fashion designer Valentina fell the task of creating Audrey's minimal wardrobe, with a daring—for 1954—nude look. The costumes, all in pale aquatic colors, were no more than fish netting draped over a flesh-colored body stocking. Because Audrey required more than a bit of padding around the bust and buttocks, Valentina pasted synthetic seaweed in those strategic areas, as well as in the crotch.

When *Ondine* had its Broadway premiere on February 18, 1954, Audrey enjoyed another personal triumph, while also surprising those who had started to identify her with the virginal heroines of *Gigi* and *Roman Holiday*. Ondine was pure erotic fantasy—a teenage sexpot with supernatural powers.

Brooks Atkinson of *The New York Times* wrote: "Everyone knows that Audrey Hepburn is an exquisite young lady, and no one has ever doubted her talent for acting. But the part of Ondine is a complicated one. It is compounded of intangibles—of moods and impressions, mischief and tragedy. See how Miss Hepburn is able to translate them into the language of the theater without artfulness or precociousness. She gives a pulsing performance that is all grace and enchantment, disciplined by an instinct for the realities of the stage."

Atkinson described the production as "ideal from every point of view. Ideal literature, ideal acting, ideal theater—it hardly matters how you approach it." He said that Mel Ferrer "makes the perfect counterpart to Miss Hepburn's tremulously lovely performance. We are lucky. There's a magical play in town."

An unforgettable moment at every performance was the scene in which Audrey took advantage of her ballet training and leaped from a standing-still position into the lap of the seated Mel Ferrer.

From opening night onwards, the audiences always gave Audrey a roaring reception at the end of *Ondine*, applauding and cheering for curtain call after curtain call. But what they got was Audrey and Mel Ferrer, not Audrey alone. Gossip started that Mel insisted on the tandem bows because he was madly jealous of Audrey's triumph and craved being treated as her equal. Audrey laughed it off, telling columnist Leonard Lyons, "Why shouldn't Mel share my curtain calls? After all, it's his play, too, isn't it?"

Concurrent with the opening of *Ondine*, Audrey had yet another stroke of extraordinary luck when she received an Academy Award nomination for Best Actress of 1953 for her performance in *Roman Holiday*. Another Hollywood newcomer named Maggie McNamara was nominated for *The Moon Is Blue*, but insiders were betting that the Oscar would go to one of the three more established candidates: Deborah Kerr for *From Here to Eternity*, Ava Gardner for *Mogambo*, or Leslie Caron for *Lili*.

Audrey was shattered by Gregory Peck not being nominated for Best Actor, it seemed like recognizing Vivien Leigh without Clark Gable, but she kept her fingers crossed for William Holden, a candidate for *Stalag 17*. *Roman Holiday* got a total of ten nominations, including the very top Best Picture, as well as Best Director, Best Supporting Actor (Eddie Albert as Peck's photographer-sidekick), and Best Original Screenplay.

In those days, Broadway and Hollywood were so mutually dependent on talent that the annual Academy Awards ceremonies were a bi-coastal affair, telecast simultaneously from theaters in Los Angeles and New York. For the one held on March 25, 1954, Donald O'Connor emceed the proceedings at the Pantages in Hollywood, with Fredric March serving as host at the NBC-Century, an ex-legitimate house a block below Central Park South.

Because of the three-hour time difference between east and west coasts, Audrey was able to give a performance of *Ondine* before being whisked by limousine to the Century Theatre in time for the Best Actress presentation. While rushing to the backstage dressing rooms to change into a new Givenchy gown that she brought with her, she collided with rival nominee Deborah Kerr, who'd raced there from *her* play, *Tea and Sympathy*. They wished each other luck, though both expressed a belief that Leslie Caron would win for *Lili*.

Out in the packed auditorium, Audrey sat between Mel Ferrer and her mother, who'd been visiting from London since the opening of *Ondine*. According to Oscar etiquette, the Best

Actress award was supposed to be presented by the previous year's Best Actor winner, in this case Gary (*High Noon*) Cooper. But since Cooper happened to be making a movie on location in Mexico at the time, he prerecorded his participation, reading off the nominees and then asking Donald O'Connor, the live host in Hollywood, to help out by tearing open the envelope and announcing the winner.

When O'Connor whooped "Audrey Hepburn," emcee Fredric March stepped out onto the Century stage in New York and beckoned to her to join him. Amid thunderous applause, Audrey all but raced down the aisle and up the steps, in her blind excitement making a wrong turn and landing in the wings. There was a burst of affectionate laughter as she reappeared, made a charming frown of displeasure with herself, and then dashed over to the podium to accept the award from Academy trustee Jean Hersholt.

"It's too much," she sighed as she clasped the Oscar to her bosom. "I want to say thank you to *everybody* who these past months and years has helped, guided, and given me so much. I'm truly, truly grateful, and terribly happy." She then fled into the wings again, where she was ambushed by a gang of reporters and photographers. In the pandemonium that followed, she lost her gold-plated Oscar, but someone found it later in the ladies' room.

In those few minutes, Audrey missed the presentation of the Best Actor award, which went to William Holden for *Stalag 17*. Whether they would have wanted to or not, the lapsed lovers had no chance of celebrating together, because Holden's acceptance took place in Hollywood. But phone calls must have been exchanged before the next dawning.

Roman Holiday lost to *From Here to Eternity* as 1953's Best Picture, but it did win in the categories of original screenplay and costume design (Edith Head). With Dalton Trumbo among blacklisted script writers, the Academy of Motion Picture Arts and Sciences honored only his "front," Ian McLellan Hunter. The slight was corrected forty years later when an Oscar was presented posthumously to Trumbo's widow and three children.

When Audrey rejoined her mother at the conclusion of the telecast, the usual reserve between them lifted and they collapsed in each other's arms. Ten years ago, while they were starving in the war, who would have believed that life would ever get *this* much better?

Yet their incredible good fortune had not quite reached its peak. Three nights later, Audrey took Broadway's highest honor, an Antoinette Perry Tony Award, as Best Dramatic Actress of the 1953–54 season. No one except the judges knew who the other finalists were, but they almost certainly included the highly praised Deborah Kerr in *Tea and Sympathy*, Josephine Hull in *The Solid Gold Cadillac*, Geraldine Page in *The Immoralist*, and, ironically, Margaret Sullavan in *Sabrina Fair*.

Because of its original production in Paris, *Ondine* did not qualify for the Best Play Tony (won by *The Teahouse of the August Moon*), but Alfred Lunt received the Best Director award. Mel Ferrer, who was probably in the running for Best Actor, lost out to David Wayne of *Teahouse of the August Moon*. Friends said Mel seemed more than a bit rankled by those choices, having contributed more to Audrey's direction than Lunt did.

In the entire histories of the Oscars and Tonys, only one other actress had matched Audrey's coup of winning both honors in the same year, and none has done it since. Shirley Booth won a Best Actress of 1952 Oscar for *Come Back Little Sheba* (based on the William Inge play that had earned her a 1950 Tony) and a Tony for Arthur Laurents's *The Time of the Cuckoo*.

In Audrey Hepburn's case, the dual feat seemed even more remarkable than Shirley Booth's, which came when she was nearly fifty-six years old and had been acting since her youth. Audrey did it with her very first starring movie and second play. And unlike Booth, at not quite twenty-five she still had a long future ahead of her in romantic leading roles.

chapter eight

A SWISS WEDDING

Audrey Hepburn suddenly became the Crown Princess, if not the Queen, of Hollywood and Broadway. In recognition of her dual triumphs, the producers of *Ondine* insisted that she start taking solo curtain calls rather than sharing them with Mel Ferrer. Mel was furious but had to go along with it because everybody realized that without Audrey Hepburn the 46th Street Theatre wouldn't be playing to sellout business night after night.

In all other respects, Audrey and Mel had become inseparable, but friends said there were signs that Mel was exerting too much control over her.

Whether Mel posed a danger to Audrey or not, she seemed to blossom into full womanhood in his company. Her romance with James Hanson had suffered prolonged interruptions, while the affair with William Holden lasted only weeks. Audrey had reached the age of twenty-five without ever having a steady beau on the scene or experiencing the social activity that went with it. While working on Broadway in *Gigi*, she had usually ended her evenings in bed alone reading a book, but there was slight chance of that happening while involved with Mel Ferrer.

"Lanky Bones," as friends called him, was a night owl who loved New York, its swank supper clubs and its lowdown jazz joints. After a night on stage in *Ondine*, Mel insisted on taking Audrey to celebrity hangouts like El Morocco or the Stork Club to dine and dance, followed by a visit to Birdland or the Metropole. On their days off, they went sightseeing, visited museums, and rode the Staten Island ferry.

"Audrey tended to be very shy and serious, seeming much older than she really was, but Mel brought her out of that shell and made her young again. But at the same time he was the one who set the pace and called the shots. He was a man who really knew how to take command," a friend recalled.

Baroness Ella disapproved of the relationship. Mel was not only too old for her daughter, but he'd also been married before and had two children. "What difference does that make?" Audrey once asked her. "Need I remind you, Mother dear, that you were married and divorced twice, *and* that you had two sons by your first husband?" End of argument.

In the late spring of 1954, Audrey and Mel became engaged, announcing plans for a combined wedding-honeymoon in Europe as soon as their commitments to *Ondine* ended. No one could have taken the news harder than William Holden, who still carried a torch for Audrey and probably always would. Years later, he confessed that her engagement to Mel Ferrer left him so shattered that he persuaded

Paramount to send him on a worldwide promotional tour to forget her.

"I was determined to wipe Audrey out of my mind by screwing a woman in every country I visited," Holden recalled. "My plan succeeded, though sometimes with difficulty. When I was in Bangkok, I was with a Thai girl in a boat floating in one of the klongs. I guess we got too animated, because the boat tipped over and I fell into the filthy water. Back at the hotel I poured alcohol in my ears because I was afraid I'd become infected with the plague."

When Holden and Audrey eventually ran into each other socially in Hollywood, he told her what he'd done. As Holden remembered the encounter: "You know what she said? 'Oh, Bill!' That's all: 'Oh, Bill!' Just as though I were some naughty boy. What a waste!"

Impending matrimony raised questions over Audrey's and Mel's careers. When *Ondine* closed, the professional togetherness would end unless they decided to emulate the Lunts by becoming a regular team. But while Mel might have desired that, he must have been shrewd enough to realize that producers—especially those in Hollywood— would fiercely resist teaming Audrey Hepburn with a box-office lightweight after she'd been paired with the likes of Gregory Peck, Humphrey Bogart, and William Holden.

Surprisingly, Paramount wasn't pressuring Audrey to start another film. In that era before pay TV and VCRs, movies had a much longer theatrical life; to protect exhibitors, releases had to be at least five years old before they could be shown on television. Audrey's Oscar had proved such a box-office boost to *Roman Holiday* that Paramount wanted to squeeze whatever it could before opening *Sabrina*. The latter, pushed back to an October release to better position it for consideration for the year-end frenzy of award presentations, promised to be an even bigger hit because all three of its stars were now Oscar winners (Humphrey Bogart having received his for 1951's *The African Queen*).

Paramount had no immediate project in mind for Audrey anyway. Though it held an option on *Ondine*, the studio could not come to terms with Jean Giraudoux's literary executors, who were demanding what amounted to a literal filmed copy of the stage play. No opening-up into a big-screen epic would be permitted, and there could be no cuts in the text, much of which would never get by Hollywood's ultrastrict Production Code.

Paramount also wasn't sure if Audrey's next movie would even be for them. Now that she'd become an Oscar-winning star, Associated British Pictures was challenging the legality of the contract she'd signed with Paramount while still in ABC's employ. To settle the dispute, Paramount was willing to work out a rotating deal where the two companies took turns on her services. Right now it looked like ABC would have to be next, but the financially strapped company was having problems finding a big property that suited Audrey's new international stature.

The complexity of those matters caused Audrey to start looking for a new agent who could give her more personalized attention than she'd been receiving from the octopus known as MCA. She finally settled on fiftyish Kurt Frings, who'd been recommended to her by his poker-playing cronies William Wyler and Billy Wilder.

A onetime lightweight boxing champion of Europe and a nephew of a Roman Catholic cardinal persecuted by Hitler, the German-born Frings fled to Paris in 1937, where he met a vacationing American journalist Katharine (Ketti) Hartley, whom he eventually married. Several years later, she wrote a novel, *Hold Back the Dawn*, based loosely on her experiences helping him to become an American citizen. Paramount bought the screen rights and turned the writing over to the team of Billy Wilder and Charles Brackett, who took some liberties and changed the noble boxer hero into a conniving gigolo and the savvy reporter into a naive schoolteacher. Kurt Frings threatened to sue for libel, but changed his mind when Paramount claimed he'd gotten access to the script illegally and vowed to have him deported.

Hollywood legend has it that Kurt Frings became an agent to get even for his feelings of humiliation. His anger at Paramount widened to all the studios as he derived satisfaction from gouging them for all he could get and then some. In the early 1950s, when TV nearly killed the movie business and the studios abandoned the long-established contract roster system, he led in the development of independent freelance stars who got hefty guaranteed fees againt a percentage of the gross.

Frings was a jocular, shrewd, and volcanic character. Audrey took to him immediately, no doubt also attracted by his European heritage. As their relationship grew, he became the nearest thing to a father she ever had.

Meanwhile, *Ondine* continued to pack them in at the 46th Street Theatre. With her percentage deal, Audrey was earning about $3,500 a week. By June, however, after giving eight performances per week for almost four months, her health started to fail. Suffering from anemia and physical exhaustion, she lost fifteen pounds but kept on working. On their Sunday-into-Monday weekend breaks, Mel took her to Grossinger's Hotel in the Catskill Mountains, hoping that the combination of fresh country air and high-caloric Jewish cooking would build her up.

Through sheer will power, Audrey continued in *Ondine* without missing a single performance, but when the strain proved too much, her doctors finally persuaded the Playwrights Company to release her from her contract. An *Ondine* without Audrey Hepburn seemed unlikely to prosper without a star of equal charisma. Since there were none available that might have qualified (did one even exist?), the Playwrights Company decided to close *Ondine* at the end of its nineteenth week on June 26, 1954. In its 156 sold-out performances, the play earned a profit of $38,000, so none of the investors could really complain.

The main losers were the actors and the offstage personnel. The sudden termination of *Ondine* left 137 people unemployed, including, of course, Mel Ferrer. The first real test of his relationship with Audrey came when he accepted the offer of a leading role in *La Madre (The Mother)*, an Italian-French-Spanish co-production to be filmed in Rome that summer.

Audrey became very unhappy. In her rundown condition she could hardly risk traveling with Mel. She'd had more than she could take of Rome's heat and humidity while working there herself. But she also had no reason to stay on alone in New York. Finally, her doctor resolved the dilemma by recommending a rest cure in Switzerland. Mel could easily visit her by plane from Rome on the weekends.

The underlying cause of Audrey's frail health was the asthma and anemia that had plagued her since the war, combined with her addiction to cigarettes. As long as she continued to puff a pack or more of her favorite English-cut Gold Flakes per day, the wheezing and the coughing weren't going to disappear, but a month or two of supervised medical care in the rarefied mountain air might restore some of the bloom to her cheeks.

After an emotional parting from Mel Ferrer, who left New York for Rome the same day, Audrey took a Swissair flight to Geneva, where a chauffeured limousine picked her up for delivery to the Palace Hotel in Gstaad, the winter ski resort and summertime watering hole beloved by the international set. The town was 3,500 feet up in the Alps, with breathtaking views of mountains and lakes, but Audrey didn't expect to see much of it. Supervised by a local doctor and tended by a nurse-companion, she was supposed to spend her time resting, if not in bed then lazing beside the swimming pool or in the hotel's luxurious gardens.

While confined to her suite, Audrey enjoyed the peaceful solitude that had been denied her in a year of solid work. But whenever she ventured outside she was constantly pestered by autograph seekers or by reporters and photographers who'd learned of her residency. When she discovered that Gstaad's only cinema had booked a return engagement of *Roman Holiday* and expected her to attend the opening night, she decided to move to more protected surroundings.

On the advice of her part-time chauffeur, she had him drive her up into central Switzerland to Burgenstock, a resort complex south of Lake Lucerne. His description of an isolated and heavily guarded compound of hotels and fully serviced chalet-bungalows and villas sounded like a better place to get away from it all.

Owner Fritz Frey took Audrey on a grand tour of his Shangri-la, which stood 3,000 feet above Lake Lucerne and was surrounded by snow-capped mountains in every direction. There were 500 acres of gardens and parks, rolling green fields and dense forest. Indoor and outdoor swimming pools, tennis courts, a nine-hole golf course, and a health spa. The kitchens and wine cellars were five-star; the year-round staff of six hundred included medical professionals, electricians, mechanics, plumbers, all on twenty-four-hour call. Burgenstock, of course, had its own security police and fire brigade.

"If you haven't been able to find peace in Gstaad, Miss Hepburn, I can assure you that you will find it here in the Burgenstock," Frey said. Audrey didn't need any further convincing. She placed a few phone calls to Gstaad and made all the necessary arrangements for a transfer that same day.

Burgenstock's Grand, Park, and Palace hotels were the ultimate in luxury, with priceless antiques and paintings adorning many of the suites. But Frey guessed rightly that Audrey would be happier in one of the small chalets, which were two-bedroom duplexes with quaint Swiss exteriors and comfortably modern interiors. She chose one named "Villa Bethiana," which had enormous picture windows looking out on the Alps and an exquisite garden that evoked memories of her childhood in Linkebeek.

Audrey thrived in her new surroundings. Each day Frey filled the chalet with fresh flowers and delivered meals to die for—using farm-fresh ingredients and prepared by cordon bleu chefs. She couldn't get enough of the homemade chocolates—truly Swiss for a change—or the cream-rich cakes and pastries. Though she wanted to stop smoking, she couldn't. But she was trying to restrict herself to six cigarettes per day, using a filtered holder that her mother sent her from Dunhill in London.

As she began to feel better, Audrey missed Mel Ferrer more and more. Since he had a birthday coming up at the end of August (his thirty-seventh), she took a speedboat across the lake to Lucerne one day and bought him a platinum Rolex watch. On the back, she asked the jeweler to engrave "Mad About the Man" (the lovers were avid fans of Noel Coward's music). Needless to say, Mel was ecstatic when a courier delivered the package to him in Rome. That weekend, he flew to Switzerland and proposed marriage as soon as arrangements could be made.

Audrey needed no persuading. They set a date for late September, when Mel was due to finish his movie. After that they would spend their honeymoon in Italy. Mel adored the ancient wine-growing region in the Alban Hills, and Audrey had never been there. The climate was healthier than Rome's and shouldn't bother her.

The wedding took place in Burgenstock on September 25, 1954, in a small Protestant chapel built in the thirteenth century. Audrey intended keeping it a secret until after it was over, but when someone tipped off the press she reluctantly agreed to admit one reporter and one photographer selected at random from the rival international news agencies.

Heading the wedding party, of course, was Baroness Ella, escorted by Sir Neville Bland (ex-British Ambassador to the Netherlands and a longtime friend of the van Heemstra family), who would give the bride away in lieu of her father (still unheard from after all these years). Mel's two children, Pepa and Mark, came from New York with their aunt, Terry Ferrer. Gregory Peck, who had introduced Audrey and Mel, was supposed to be best man, but a last-minute change in his filming schedule caused him to cancel. The Burgenstock's Fritz Frey replaced him.

Dressed in a navy blue suit, with a white shirt

and white tie, Mel dared superstition (and may have jinxed the marriage) by delivering Audrey to the church himself. The bride wore an ankle-length Givenchy gown of white organdy, with puff sleeves and a billowy skirt. A crown of white roses adorned her short-cropped hair.

The fiftyish pastor, Maurice Eindiguer, performed the ceremony. Audrey liked him so much that he became a friend, confidant, and spiritual adviser for the rest of her life.

Following a private reception in the Grand Hotel, the newlyweds left for a honeymoon in Italy, or so they pretended. But after driving several miles, they returned to Burgenstock via a back road and stayed secluded in Audrey's chalet for four days. Then, instead of flying to Rome, they took the train from Lucerne. That way they succeeded in eluding the paparazzi who were always camped out at Rome airport to ambush arriving celebrities.

Unfortunately, the honeymooners were unable to sneak through Rome's Stazione Termini. By the time all their luggage was loaded into a waiting Mercedes Benz limousine, five cars of reporters and photographers were ready to pursue them to their rented villa near Anzio. At the end of the chase, they raced into the house and bolted the door behind them. When the horde kept rapping on the windows and throwing pebbles, Audrey and Mel finally agreed to come out and pose for a few pictures in exchange for solitude.

The rowdy pack left but kept returning in smaller numbers, hiding in the trees and bushes to snap off-guard pictures of the honeymooners. Audrey turned sullen and angry whenever she caught them, but soon realized there wasn't much she could do to stop them. If she wanted a career and the celebrity that inevitably went with it, she had to get accustomed to being examined through telescopic lenses.

Disturbances apart, it was a blissful honeymoon. Mel had found a perfect nest in the twenty-room former farmhouse, which overlooked a valley rich in ancient history, pungent flowers, and ripening vineyards. A resident staff of six looked after them like family. A collection of animals, including a donkey named Benito, a cow for milking, three dogs, and more cats than Audrey could keep track of, revived her childhood love for pets. Mel promised to buy her some as soon as they had a home of their own.

But for the moment it would be a vagabond existence. After a month in Italy, the Ferrers returned briefly to Burgenstock. At the end of October, Audrey traveled back to Holland for the first time since her movie fame, at the invitation of the BNMO (League of Dutch Military War Invalids). Accompanied by her husband, she made a five-day tour of Holland to help raise funds for the organization's welfare efforts. In Oosterbeek, near Arnhem, she participated in ceremonies commemorating the tenth anniversary of the tragic battle, laying a wreath at the inspiring Airborne Monument that had been erected there after the war. In Doorn, site of the splendid "castle" once owned by some of her relations, she attended the renaming of one of its avenues to Audrey Hepburnlaan.

She was also awarded the BNMO's Resistance Cross (*Kruis van Verdienste*) for her wartime contributions, though she said while accepting it that there were thousands who deserved it more than she did. It was all pretty heady stuff, Audrey's first lesson in how she could use her celebrity to help others. Huge crowds turned out to greet her and to donate money. The BNMO raised over 40,000 guilders during her brief visit.

The Ferrers also made a quick trip to New York and Los Angeles at Paramount's expense to attend the premieres of *Sabrina*. Audrey was shocked to find that by this time Billy Wilder had quit Paramount and was refusing to help in promoting the movie. The director went berserk when the studio wanted him to soften the anti-Nazi content of *Stalag 17* for the German release because the former enemy was now the top European market for Hollywood movies.

But with or without Billy Wilder's blessing, *Sabrina* became a hit and another personal triumph for Audrey Hepburn. Bosley Crowther, the often difficult to please film critic for *The New York Times*, wrote a virtual hymn to her "bewitching charm and grace." During the rest of his tenure at the *Times*, Crowther continued so rhapsodic about Audrey's performances that some readers suspected he was in love with her.

The rave reviews made it plain that *Sabrina* would earn Audrey another Academy Award nomination and perhaps her second Oscar in a row. Paramount was ecstatic but also in a state of panic. Exhibitors were asking about her next movie, which hadn't even been selected yet. The studio proposed teaming her with Cary Grant in *To Catch a Thief*, but director Alfred Hitchcock preferred blondes and instead demanded another Paramount contractee, Grace Kelly.

Meanwhile, Audrey became pregnant, which suddenly brought everything else to a screeching halt. Because of her delicate health, she couldn't possibly risk anything that might jeopardize the birth, so Paramount would just have to wait. For the time being, Mel Ferrer would be the only actor in the family. When he was offered a movie job in London, Audrey encouraged him to accept. She couldn't imagine getting through the coming months without her mother on the scene.

Baroness Ella found a furnished six-room apartment for the couple in Portman Square, ten minutes from her own flat in Mayfair. The proverbial mother-in-law problems started immediately. Ella not only disliked Mel (as she probably would any man who threatened the tight bond she had with her daughter), but also possessed the same sort of strong-willed, dominating character. All three people, Audrey included, were also impeccably polite, so they would never risk offending or saying what was really on their minds. There was always a strained atmosphere when the trio were together.

While her husband toiled at Elstree Studios in *Oh! Rosalinda!* (director Michael Powell's non-singing version of *Die Fledermaus*), Audrey stayed home and fretted about other women chasing him. She found him so irresistible that she thought everybody else did too. But apparently Mel's lean sensitivity, his morose eyes, and his receding hairline did not appeal to a majority of women or men, for he was not a major star by then.

Mel stood in danger of being swallowed up in his wife's skyrocketing celebrity. There were already signs of that while he was working in *Oh! Rosalinda!* The movie's publicist couldn't get any press coverage for Mel unless it involved Audrey. When she agreed to visit the set one day for a photo opportunity, the couple landed on the front pages of London tabloids.

While Audrey was infanticipating, she found herself caught up in an international race between American producer Mike Todd and the Italian combo of Carlo Ponti and Dino De Laurentiis to make a film of Leo Tolstoy's public-domain classic *War and Peace.* Both opponents wanted Audrey Hepburn to portray the pivotal role of Natasha Rostova. Todd's project promised to be the more prestigious, with playwright Robert E. Sherwood scripting and Fred Zinnemann directing.

Ponti-De Laurentiis had not gotten that far in their own planning, but to keep Audrey from possibly signing with Mike Todd, they shrewdly hired Mel Ferrer for the part of Prince Andrei. The opportunity for marital togetherness was too good to resist. Audrey promised Ponti-De Laurentiis that she'd do the movie, subject to Paramount's approval.

Although it might seem that Audrey had let her heart rule, *War and Peace* was something she would have wanted to do whether Mel was involved or not. She loved the novel, the reading of which had been one of her few pleasures during World War II. Ponti and De Laurentiis were intent on making an epic surpassing *Gone With the Wind*. If they only half succeeded, *War and Peace* could be one of the biggest hits of all time.

Once Audrey gave the nod to *War and Peace*, Paramount moved in and carved out a big chunk for itself. After some heated bargaining on both sides, Paramount became an equal partner in the project, loaning Audrey's services and also putting up $3 million of the expected $6 million budget. In return, Paramount received world distribution rights, then signed over the United Kingdom rights to Associated British Pictures to finally settle their long-simmering dispute over Audrey's contract. As part of the deal, Ponti-De Laurentiis also agreed to photograph *War and Peace* in Paramount's giant-screen VistaVision process, which had yet to win the industry-wide acceptance of 20th Century-Fox's Cinema-Scope.

Production of *War and Peace* would, of course, have to wait until Audrey had her baby, but that didn't matter, because Ponti and De Laurentiis were months away from starting anyway. Six scriptwriters were struggling to reduce Tolstoy's 650,000-word novel into about three and a half hours of screen time. While the Soviet Union had vetoed any location filming, negotiations were under way with Marshal Tito of Yugoslavia to photograph the battle sequences there, using Yugoslav Army extras. Dozens of indoor and outdoor sets also had to be built at Rome's Cinecitta studios, where most of the filming would take place.

War and Peace was one of the first truly international co-productions, so no one expected it to be made with clockwork precision. Though the behind-the-cameras personnel would be predominantly Italian, the acting would be in English and subsequently dubbed for countries like Italy, France, Germany, and Spain, where moviegoers preferred hearing their own language to reading subtitles. That enabled the producers to select their main actors from all over the world.

Audrey and Mel suggested their friend Gregory Peck for the role of Pierre. But Peck had other commitments, and the considerably older Henry Fonda was illogically chosen instead. Also signed were Italy's Vittorio Gassman, Hollywood Austrians Oscar Homolka and Helmut Dantine, Sweden's Anita Ekberg, the Czech Herbert Lom, and numerous British actors, including John Mills, Barry Jones, and Jeremy Brett.

In the footsteps of William Wyler and Billy Wilder, Paramount wanted another A-list director for Audrey Hepburn's third starring film. None being available for one reason or another, they settled for the somewhat faded King Vidor, who had epics like *Duel in the Sun* and the silent *The Big Parade* to his credit, but not recently. However, the sixty-year-old Vidor ranked high in the Hollywood pantheon and had also done vital salvage work on such trouble-laden productions as *Gone With the Wind* and *The Wizard of Oz*, so he got the job.

Since *War and Peace* would be Audrey's first movie to be photographed in color, a medium that could be crueler to beauty than the more easily controlled black and white, she took more interest in the choice of the cinematographer than of the director. After going through a list of candidates, she selected one in England—Jack Cardiff. If he could work the same kind of rainbow magic that he did for her dancing idol Moira Shearer in *The Red Shoes*, Audrey would die happy. The fact that Cardiff had also won an Oscar for the Technicolored *Black Narcissus* was an added inducement.

On February 12, 1955, Audrey received the not totally unexpected news that she had received her second Oscar nomination in as many years, this time for *Sabrina*. Since up to that time only the soulful Austrian beauty Luise Rainer had ever won Best Actress twice in succession, Audrey guessed that she had slight chance of repeating that feat. Especially since her competition consisted of Judy Garland for A *Star Is Born*, Grace Kelly for *The Country Girl*, Dorothy Dandridge for *Carmen Jones*, and Jane Wyman for *Magnificent Obsession*.

Gossip columnists were betting on Judy Garland to win because her performance marked a dazzling comeback after years of psychiatric problems. The dark horse, literally and figuratively, was Dorothy Dandridge, the first black actor or actress in Oscar history ever to be nominated in the topmost performance category.

Because of Audrey's pregnancy, doctors ordered her to skip the ceremonies and the grueling plane trip to Los Angeles, which took a minimum of twenty-two hours in that pre-jet era. Though her conscience nagged her a bit—as last year's Best Actress she was expected to present the Best Actor award—she cabled regrets. A replacement was quickly found for her in Bette Davis, another double Oscar winner, though not in succession.

Sabrina did not get nominated for Best Picture of 1954, but Billy Wilder was a candidate for Best Director, and the movie also qualified in the category of the best script based on adapted material (as opposed to one written originally for the screen). In those days, there were still enough black-and-white movies for the Academy to recognize the fact that visually, at least, they were an art unto themselves and had to be judged separately from those filmed in color. Thus, *Sabrina* received three black-and-white nominations for cinematography, art decoration/ set decoration, and costume design.

With a ten-hour time difference between London and Los Angeles, Audrey went to bed on March 30 not knowing whether she'd won another Oscar or not, though the suspense wasn't enough to keep her awake all night. She felt certain that the award would go to Judy Garland, so she was as shocked as most people were when she discovered that Grace Kelly had won for *The Country Girl.*

Perhaps it was just as well that Audrey missed the ceremony. Presenting the Oscar to Grace Kelly was William Holden, who'd had an affair with her while they were working together in *The*

Country Girl, right after his involvement with Audrey during the filming of *Sabrina.*

Sabrina ended up winning only one Oscar, the second in a row for designer Edith Head, following *Roman Holiday.* Such was Head's clout as chief of Paramount's wardrobe department that Hubert de Givenchy had no share in the award, even though his glamorous clothes were what made the Sabrina Look the sensation of the fashion world that year. Head's habit of taking credit for other people's work explained not only why she'd won more Oscars than any other designer but also why she was so despised by her peers.

Audrey felt so sorry for Givenchy that she phoned him immediately in Paris to apologize.

"I was very touched, but told her not to worry, because *Sabrina* had brought me more new clients than I could handle," Givenchy recalled. "But Audrey was still upset, and she made a promise to me that in the future she would make sure that it never happened again. And she kept her promise. This was one of the most marvelous things about her. She thought constantly of others."

As soon as Mel Ferrer finished filming *Oh! Rosalinda!* the couple returned to Burgenstock to await the birth of their first child. Audrey had fallen in love with Switzerland and wanted to settle there permanently. She felt welcome and protected; people treated her as if she'd lived there all her life, and not like a visiting Hollywood star.

No doubt the current tense relations between

the U.S.S.R. and the NATO nations affected Audrey's feelings. She'd lived through one war too many, and Switzerland was the last place to expect any. For a woman soon to be raising children, it boasted probably the best public education system in the world, with training in English, French, and German required. Last but not least, Switzerland's banking and tax laws were far more liberal than in the United States or England, which seemed the only other likely countries of residence for a family of film stars.

By this time, Dino De Laurentiis had started production of *War and Peace* in Yugoslavia with battle scenes and other exteriors that didn't require the main actors. The beginning of principal photography depended on the birth of Audrey's baby—as soon as she seemed strong enough to work, certainly by early summer if there were no complications.

While Audrey rested, the expectant parents read and reread *War and Peace*, trying to become more deeply involved with the roles of Natasha and Prince Andrei in the absence of a completed script. They also consulted whatever books they could find about Leo Tolstoy and the Russian aristocracy of the period.

Audrey became more tense and nervous as time passed. The usual morning sickness turned to steady nausea and stomach cramps. When she seemed to be going into premature labor, Mel rushed her to a hospital in Lucerne, but it proved too late. Audrey miscarried, though the exact cause was never made public.

Audrey, of course, was devastated. She wanted

a baby more than anything, but, as she kept telling herself, there's always a next time. Luckily, the increasingly hectic preparations for *War and Peace* kept her from falling into what might have been a long and debilitating depression. Between moving to Italy for the length of the production, costume fittings, and rehearsals, she had little time to fret or feel sorry for herself.

Audrey dreaded the prospect of working in Rome's sweltering summer weather, but Mel eased the problem by again renting their honeymoon villa near Anzio. About thirteen miles southeast of Rome, it seemed well worth combating the heavy traffic around Cinecitta Studios twice a day because of the fresh sea breezes and beautiful countryside.

Dino De Laurentiis made no secret of intending *War and Peace* to be another *Gone With the Wind*, which up to that time was the highest-grossing movie ever made. Of course, Tolstoy's novel had much in common with Margaret Mitchell's and probably even inspired her to write it. Tolstoy's Russo-French war of 1812 became Mitchell's American Civil War, the romantic triangle between Natasha Rostova, the intellectual Pierre, and the dashing Prince Andrei anticipated the one between Scarlett O'Hara, Ashley Wilkes, and Rhett Butler. For sheer spectacle, *War and Peace* had the burning of Moscow, *GWTW* the burning of Atlanta.

One important ingredient that *War and Peace* and *Gone With the Wind* didn't share was a huge readership salivating for the movie version. While *GWTW* had been a phenomenal best-seller before its filming, the daunting length of *War and Peace*, coupled with clumsy translations, had given it the reputation of a musty literary classic read mainly by high school and college students under coercion. De Laurentiis would have to overcome that if *War and Peace* was to be another box-office blockbuster.

As with *GWTW*, reducing *War and Peace* to a screenplay proved a nightmare task, compounded by the fact that De Laurentiis divided the job up between Italian, British, and American writers. Six finally got authorship credit, including director King Vidor, whose main contribution was cutting and pasting bits and pieces from the other five (Bridget Boland, Robert Westerby, Mario Camerini, Ennio DeConcini, and Ivo Perelli) into a cohesive shooting script.

De Laurentiis and his administrative partner, Carlo Ponti, had taken over all forty-eight acres and nine sound stages of Cinecitta, which, ironically, had served as barracks for German soldiers in World War II and a sanctuary for thousands of displaced persons immediately afterwards. *War and Peace* had over a hundred sets, including full-scale replicas of Moscow buildings and monuments. Snow machines would simulate Russian blizzard conditions while Rome sizzled outside.

As *War and Peace* was Audrey's Technicolor debut as well as her first historical movie, she made sure she looked her best by going to friends for help. Though early nineteenth-century Russia was hardly Hubert de Givenchy's métier, she arranged for him to fly in from Paris to supervise the fittings of the clothes that had been designed for her by period specialist Maria de Matteis.

"At fittings," Givenchy recalled, "Audrey liked to try out the motions of walking, sitting, dancing. This meant not only the clothes themselves but the underthings, the shoes, the hats, the gloves, or whatever else she wore with them. Once she worked out the mechanics, she was happy. Sometimes this took ten minutes, sometimes ten hours. She knew exactly what she wanted, and there were no limits to the time or work that she would put into it."

The Italian cosmetician Alberto di Rossi and his hairstylist wife, Gracia, who'd worked for Audrey on *Roman Holiday*, returned for *War and Peace* and ended up as regulars, eventually traveling all over the world with her. Di Rossi carried all his makeup and implements in a Louis Vuitton case that Audrey called his "magic box." From it came the legendary Audrey Hepburn Eyes, which was simply a matter of enhancing their mink-brown luminosity with just enough dark liner and mascara on the lashes to make them seem even more enormous and luxuriant.

"Audrey was born *photogénique*," di Rossi recalled. "She had such beautiful bone structure that her features did not need a lot of work. She had a very strong jawline, which in a sense I reversed by emphasizing her temples. She had thick eyebrows that always needed to be thinned out. Every picture we made together, I tried to reduce them a bit more than the time before, but without going to extremes. She had the kind of face that needed eyebrows."

With the character of Natasha Rostova being the deepest and most serious of her career so far, Audrey became determined to prove that she was more than just a lighthearted pixie. Unfortunately, the scriptwriters gave her little to work with. Most of Tolstoy's rich detail had to be sacrificed in condensing *War and Peace* to under four hours of screen time. Audrey lugged the novel to the set every day, looking for guidance from it. In key scenes where it might help her performance, King Vidor often permitted her to change some of her lines so they used some of the novel's dialogue.

War and Peace was also Audrey's first experience at working in a colossal epic, which by necessity had to be filmed in bits and pieces and rarely in the same order as the scenes would eventually appear on the screen. She had no chance to grow with the role as she did on stage in *Gigi* and *Ondine*, or in *Roman Holiday* and *Sabrina* either, which the directors filmed chronologically to make it easier for her. One day she had to portray Natasha as a naive teenager, the next day as a grieving widow. Enacting that emotional seesaw for months on end left her on the verge of cracking up.

"Nobody realizes what I've been going through," she said at the time. "I constantly have to tell myself, 'I must remember this line. I must summon the tears.' Acting doesn't come easily to me. I put a tremendous effort into every morsel that comes out. I don't yet have enough experience or store of knowledge to fall back on. Many of my reactions stem from instinct rather than knowing. So I must work very hard to achieve what I'm after."

Not surprisingly, the startling veracity of the grisly war scenes revived Audrey's memories of her own experiences. While that might have been just what she needed to get into the mood of the role, it also kept her awake nights, and she vowed to never do a war-related film again.

Since Mel Ferrer had fewer scenes in *War and Peace* than Audrey, he finished his work a month before she did and left for France to start another movie. It hadn't been planned that way, but the sudden offer to work with Ingrid Bergman and master director Jean Renoir in *Elena and Her Men* was too good to resist. It was the Ferrers' first separation since they married over a year before.

Audrey took it badly, Mel less so because it gave him a chance to get out from under his wife's professional shadow. While Ingrid Bergman was still on Hollywood's blacklist because of her illicit affair with director Roberto Rossellini (by now her husband), she retained a divine luster that couldn't help raising Mel Ferrer's leading man status several notches. Completing the romantic triangle in the boudoir comedy was France's dashing Jean Marais, in private life the lover and muse of avant-gardist Jean Cocteau. Though *Elena* had no Hollywood financing, Jean Renoir was making separate French and English versions, with provision for dubbing or subtitles in other languages.

To make the work separation easier for Audrey,

Mel flew from Paris to Rome on the weekends. When she finally finished *War and Peace*, she joined him in Paris for the duration of his assignment. Where their determination to be together would lead was anybody's guess. But their agents were dropping unsubtle hints that projects involving both Ferrers had a better chance of getting a go signal. That didn't necessarily mean as co-actors. With Mel's credentials as a director, he could easily work with his wife from behind the cameras rather than in front of them.

Meanwhile, Audrey had her contract with Paramount to contend with. While she was still filming *War and Peace*, the studio sent Tennessee Williams and producer Hal Wallis to Rome to persuade her to take the leading role in the film of the playwright's *Summer and Smoke*, which had been a flop on Broadway in 1948 and not purchased by Paramount until 1952, following its smash off-Broadway revival. Wallis must have drugged Tennessee Williams into making the trip to Rome, since Audrey Hepburn seemed an unlikely choice for the part of Alma Winemiller, a Southern minister's daughter who ends up as the town prostitute.

Surprisingly, Audrey expressed interest in the spinsterish role, provided that Wallis gave serious consideration to casting Mel Ferrer as the lustful doctor who drives her down the primrose path. But sanity prevailed, and the movie did not get produced until 1961, when Wallis finally decided to take a chance on Geraldine Page (star of the off-Broadway revival) in tandem with Laurence Harvey.

Paramount next proposed a top-secret project that involved loaning Audrey to rival Metro-Goldwyn-Mayer. When she heard the details, Audrey thought they must be joking. Happily, they weren't.

chapter nine

PARIS IN THE SPRING

Several nights after the liberation of Arnhem, the sixteen-year-old Audrey Hepburn saw her first Hollywood movie since before the war when the Canadian troops ran an outdoor screening in the town square, using a projector plugged into one of their electric generators. The film was *Top Hat*, with Fred Astaire and Ginger Rogers. Eleven years later, Audrey found herself not only partnered with Astaire, probably the greatest song-and-dance star of all time, but getting top billing. How's that for a fairy tale come true?

The $4 million Technicolor musical *Funny Face* would have more gloss than any of the black-and-white Astaire-Rogers classics made for comparative peanuts during the Depression years, but the premise was basically the same. Had it been played by Ginger Rogers, the character Jo Stockton might have been a sassy soda jerk in Walgreen's, but in Audrey Hepburn's case she was a shy bibliophile clerking in a rare and secondhand bookshop in Greenwich Village. When a topflight photographer happens in and notices her loveliness, the plot follows predictable lines as he talks her into modeling for a cover story that he's shooting for a major fashion magazine.

Funny Face grew out of a collaboration that

started between lyricist and music arranger Roger Edens and the younger writer Leonard Gershe when they were matched up to collaborate on special material for Judy Garland in *A Star Is Born*. Edens asked to see some of Gershe's previous work and became intrigued with an unproduced play entitled *Wedding Day*, in which Gershe based the leading character, Dick Avery, on photographer Richard Avedon, a longtime friend. Edens, a main component of Arthur Freed's eminent production unit at MGM, saw the basis of a musical for Fred Astaire and persuaded Freed to buy it.

Edens earned his stripes on Broadway and had an encyclopedic knowledge of show music that told him *Wedding Day* would adapt perfectly to a score that George and Ira Gershwin had written for the 1927 *Funny Face*, one of Fred Astaire's biggest stage hits when he was still partnered with his older and perhaps even more talented sister, Adele. For the sake of just the songs and the title, MGM bought the movie rights to *Funny Face*, but found nothing worth salvaging in the libretto about a jewel heist in an Atlantic City boardwalk hotel.

By that point, no one had envisioned Audrey Hepburn as Fred Astaire's co-star, but when Edens and Gershe went through the list of MGM contractees, they came up empty. Leslie Caron had already been teamed with Fred Astaire with dismal results in *Daddy Long Legs*. Debbie Reynolds and Cyd Charisse didn't suit either. Grace Kelly would have been perfect, but she was quitting MGM and moviemaking for a royal marriage.

Looking outside MGM, it didn't take Edens and Gershe long to fix on Audrey Hepburn, who not only possessed cover girl qualities but was also a trained dancer. Paramount wasn't exactly eager to loan Audrey to MGM, but since the studio had nothing of its own ready for her, it at least agreed to talk.

While negotiations were going on, MGM assigned Stanley Donen, director of such hits as *Singin' in the Rain* and *Seven Brides for Seven Brothers*, to direct *Funny Face*. Roger Edens persuaded Kay Thompson, a chichi cabaret entertainer who'd long been a fixture of the Freed unit as a vocal coach and arranger, to make her acting debut in the chief supporting role. The character of Maggie Prescott was based on one of Richard Avedon's editors, Diana Vreeland, the *monstre sacré* of *Vogue* magazine (called *Quality* in the film).

As the various pieces of *Funny Face* fell together, Paramount became covetous of the project and offered to buy it outright from MGM, complete with the whole creative team assembled by Arthur Freed. Since MGM had several other expensive musicals on Freed's agenda at the time, it finally agreed, provided that Paramount sweetened the pot with a loan of Audrey Hepburn. Her next movie after *Funny Face* would have to be for MGM.

At Audrey's insistence, Paramount hired Hubert de Givenchy to design her clothes in *Funny Face*, which made perfect sense given that her role as the model for "The Quality Woman" required wearing the ultimate in Paris chic. That infuriated studio designer Edith Head, who in order to stay on the project had to settle for outfitting Kay Thompson and the other actresses and models in the cast. Head also had to agree to Givenchy receiving equal credit to hers in the opening titles, which meant she couldn't pull another fast one on him when Oscar time rolled around.

Audrey's Givenchy wardrobe took months to execute, including suits, dresses, evening gowns, and even a bridal costume. Ironically, the outfit that had the greatest impact on fashion when *Funny Face* came out was the simplest: a black turtle-neck sweater and tight black pants worn with white anklet socks.

At the close of 1955, Audrey and Mel spent a very white Christmas in Burgenstock, their last rest break before she started *Funny Face*. Since she was apprehensive about her first musical role, and especially about working opposite Fred Astaire, Mel canceled or postponed all commitments of his own so that he could be with her throughout the production. Expected to take three to four months, the filming would start at Paramount's studio in Hollywood and eventually move to France in the spring when the weather would hopefully be appropriate for the many outdoor locations that were required.

Although married now for over a year, the Ferrers still had no permanent home of their own. They traded their rented Swiss chalet for an oceanside house in Malibu leased from director

Anatole Litvak, who was another of Kurt Frings's clients and busy filming in Europe at the time. After the grueling schedule of *War and Peace* in Rome, where everybody worked a six-day week, Audrey looked forward to Hollywood's less stringent Monday-to-Friday standard, which would enable her to spend the weekends on the beach.

By this time, the Ferrers were accustomed to living in temporary dwellings and had standard household items that always accompanied them. Since Audrey's contracts required her employers to pay her transportation expenses, the couple never worried about airline overweight charges, generally traveling with fifty or sixty pieces of luggage between them. Besides the expected clothing and personal effects, the contents included tableware, bed linens, and prized knicknacks, as well as their favorite paintings, photographs, books, and phonograph records.

Audrey had never met Fred Astaire. Before she did, she insisted on practicing with a coach to get back into dancing condition. Eugene Loring, one of the choreographers assigned to *Funny Face,* took on the job, which proved more spasmodic than Audrey anticipated. Going on twenty-seven, she was no longer as limber as she'd been at twenty in London revues. When she tried her first plié, she could almost hear the bones creak. For the first week, her calf and thigh muscles were so sore that she required Swedish massage and hot towel treatments at the end of each session.

When the introduction to Fred Astaire finally came, he turned out to be less formidable than

Audrey expected. "I remember he was wearing a yellow shirt, gray flannels, a red scarf knotted around his waist instead of a belt, and the famous feet were clad in soft moccasins and pink socks. He was also wearing that irresistible smile," she said later. "One look at this most debonair, elegant, and distinguished of legends and I could feel myself turn to solid lead, while my heart sank into my two left feet. Then suddenly I felt a hand around my waist and, with his inimitable grace and lightness, Fred literally swept me off my feet.

"He said, 'Come on, let's have a little go together,' and we just danced around together. He just took me and turned me around, or whatever. It was such fun, it was so divine. We were laughing and having fun. It was great. I didn't feel too self-conscious, in the sense that I was meeting the great Fred Astaire. I mean, I knew I wasn't a very good dancer, so I never expected to be a great dancer. I just hoped he would deal with my lack of whatever it was, and he really did sweep it away. He gave me such confidence. We practiced a lot, which is an understatement. For hours, and hours, and hours, and hours, and hours. But Fred was so easy. With that wonderful nonchalance of his, you didn't want it to end."

Astaire was nearly fifty-seven and making his first movie since his wife, Phyllis, had died from lung cancer two years before. Like many stars who'd been on the scene for decades (in his case, since age five), he'd become extremely sensitive about his age, especially since the blasting he received for romancing the then-twenty-two-year-old Leslie Caron in *Daddy Long Legs*, which offended some critics into labeling it musicalized pedophilia. Though Audrey Hepburn was two years older than Leslie Caron, that still made her young enough to be Fred Astaire's daughter, which meant treating the age difference with more finesse in *Funny Face* to escape similar attacks.

Director Stanley Donen and the scriptwriters wisely arranged things so that there were virtually no kisses or passionate clinches between the two stars. The romance was expressed through the musical numbers, which included such Gershwin heartstoppers as "How Long Has This Been Going On?" "He Loves and She Loves," and "S'Wonderful." Not all of the original songs from *Funny Face* suited the totally different plot about the world of high fashion, so Roger Edens and Leonard Gershe wrote three new ones, "Think Pink!" "Bonjour, Paris!" and "On How to Be Lovely."

To overcome Audrey's limitations as a singer and dancer, she had only two solo numbers, one a vocal of "How Long Has This Been Going On?" and the other some jazzy high kicking in a beatnik nightclub. Both scenes were filmed in Hollywood before production shifted to France. Kay Thompson, who'd coached Judy Garland and many other MGM luminaries, taught Audrey to pay close attention to the lyrics of the songs and to use a parlando style closer to reciting poetry than true singing.

Fred Astaire also tried to help. "We were getting ready to record the vocal track for their duet of 'S'Wonderful,'" director Stanley Donen recalled. "It was also Audrey's first time with Fred in front of a full orchestra, so she was very ill at ease and nervous, as anybody would be. I was in a mixing booth, and they were out on the stage, and she made a mistake, so I said, 'Hold it.' She said she was terribly sorry, and we started again. She made a mistake again, and this time she stopped and asked to start again. The third time we went through it, she made a mistake, and Fred jumped in and did something wrong on purpose. He said, 'Oh, I'm sorry. I've ruined it. Can we do it again?' It was so wonderful, and I'm not sure that she ever realized. He was so fabulous."

In the spring of 1956, the filming of *Funny Face* shifted to Paris, where Audrey and Mel took up residence in the sumptuous Hotel Raphaël (at Paramount's expense, of course). Following them was everything they'd taken with them to California, plus several more crates of purchases made there. Most of the furnishings provided by the hotel were removed from their suite and sent to the basement storeroom. Audrey spent several days unpacking and making sure that the couple's new surroundings were as close to "home" as living out of suitcases permitted.

Audrey learned the practice from her mother, but it dated back centuries among Europe's wealthy aristocrats. Audrey kept it up most of her life, cataloging every item in a loose-leaf book. Each one was marked with a number so that she knew exactly what she had with her at any particular time and where the rest was stored.

After everything was unpacked, Audrey liked

to rearrange the furniture, summoning the hotel staff to move the heavier pieces. At the Raphaël, she remembered a table that had been in one of her rooms on a previous visit. When she asked the concierge to get it for her, he said he couldn't because it was being used in another suite. "I'm afraid the other suite will just have to do without it," she politely insisted. Needless to say, the table arrived within minutes.

April in Paris turned out a soggy version of the classic song. Exceptionally cold and rainy weather caused long delays in the filming because *Funny Face* called for a magical city bathed in golden daylight. Tourists were also a constant nuisance, so shooting had to start at dawn to avoid the crowds attracted to landmarks like the Arch of Triumph, Notre Dame Cathedral, Montmartre, and, of course, the Eiffel Tower.

Richard Avedon served as visual consultant on the movie and also shot all the still photographs that were supposedly the work of Fred Astaire. Avedon also became Audrey's photographer of choice for many years, although he always claimed he found her impossible to photograph.

"However you defined the encounter of photographer and subject, Audrey won," he once said. "I couldn't lift her to greater heights. She was already there. I could only record. I could not interpret her. There was no going further than who she was. She paralyzed me. She had achieved in herself the ultimate portrait."

In an extended scene in *Funny Face* where Astaire takes Audrey around Paris snapping pictures of her in different Givenchy getups,

Avedon and director Stanley Donen alternated live action with freeze-frame enlargements of the shots that would eventually appear in the fictitious *Quality* magazine.

The sequence, filmed like the rest of the movie by Hollywood ace Ray June, included what is perhaps Audrey Hepburn's supreme pictorial moment. Dressed in a strapless red evening gown and long white gloves, she emerges from hiding behind the legendary Winged Victory statue in the Louvre, unfurls a filmy red shawl behind her, and turns into the goddess Nike with arms as she runs down a white marble staircase toward photographer Astaire at the bottom.

"I thought I would slip and break my neck because I was wearing high heels and there were about thirty marble steps to maneuver without looking down at them," Audrey remembered. "I made up my mind I was going to do it in one take and I did, but I think it was just good luck, actually."

The final production number, a fantasy danced to "He Loves and She Loves" with Audrey wearing a Givenchy wedding dress and Fred Astaire his usual tweeds, had to be filmed outdoors in the lush countryside near Chantilly. "It had been raining for weeks and weeks, but finally we went out to shoot on this little island, which was not much more than a strip of grass between two streams," director Stanley Donen recalled.

"The grass was ankle deep in bog. Audrey had on white satin dancing shoes made in Paris, very expensive. She had about nine pairs standing by because they kept getting black in the mud. Fred got very crotchety and said to me, 'I can't dance in that. Fix it.' I told him we'd do what we could, but how could we fix it? He said, 'I don't care! Put down a wood floor and paint it green.' Everyone was tense until Audrey suddenly quipped, 'Here I've been waiting twenty years to dance with Fred Astaire, and what do I get? Mud in my eye!'"

Early in the filming of *Funny Face* in Hollywood, Audrey had been approached by Billy Wilder about taking the title role in *Ariane*, a sophisticated bedroom comedy intended as the director's homage to his great friend and inspiration Ernst Lubitsch, the acknowledged master of boudoir farce. Audrey owed so much to Wilder for the success of *Sabrina* that she agreed to do the movie even before Wilder had a finished script. But she left agent Kurt Frings to work out a deal that would be acceptable to Paramount and MGM, the latter due to be her next employer in the *Funny Face* swap arrangement.

Since MGM had not yet selected a property for Audrey, it agreed to become second in line for her services. Paramount raised no objections. Between *Funny Face* and the still unreleased *War and Peace*, the studio had enough of an Audrey Hepburn inventory to satisfy its needs for the foreseeable future. Paramount considered her too special a personality to risk overexposure in more than one release a year.

Ariane would be produced by Allied Artists, which sprang from the corporate shell of the defunct Monogram Pictures and was trying to become a major force in Hollywood by signing deals with top directors like Wilder and William Wyler. The latter had just made *Friendly Persuasion* for the company, with Gary Cooper as star. Cooper had another commitment to Allied, so he became a part of the *Ariane* package. Billy Wilder had first tried to sign Cary Grant, but the latter, having already passed up starring opposite Audrey in *Sabrina*, still considered himself too old for the romantic shenanigans involved.

Though Gary Cooper was three years older than Cary Grant, he seemed less bothered by his twenty-eight-year age difference with Audrey. Unintentionally she seemed to be becoming the mature gent's dream girl. With the exception of Gregory Peck and William Holden (neither of whom won her at the end of the films), all of Audrey's starring roles hurled her into the arms of men old enough to be her father—Humphrey Bogart, Henry Fonda, Fred Astaire, and now Gary Cooper.

Once Audrey and Cooper were set as the stars, Billy Wilder and his new writing partner, I. A. L. Diamond, rushed through the script so production could start as soon as she had a chance to rest up from *Funny Face.* When one of the world's most romantic personalities, Maurice Chevalier, signed on for another major role, *Ariane* screamed out for a title change and got one with *Love in the Afternoon.* (Based on a novel by Claude Anet, *Ariane* had been filmed twice before, first as a French silent and then in England in 1931 with the legendary Elisabeth

Bergner, who had a waiflike quality similar to Audrey's.)

Eighteen-year-old Ariane Charasse, an aspiring cellist studying at the Paris Conservatory of Music, is the only child of a private detective specializing in marital infidelities. When Ariane overhears one of her father's clients threatening to murder his wife and her lover, she rushes to their trysting place in the Ritz Hotel to prevent it, only to fall in love herself with the man in the case, a dashing American millionaire playboy named Frank Flannagan.

Amusingly, before any of the present stars entered the project, Wilder and Diamond intended patterning the playboy after Prince Aly Khan, with Yul Brynner in the role. But after doing some research they considered Khan too unsavory a character, so they switched the model to Howard Hughes, who had yet to start the tragic and reclusive decline he's best remembered for today.

Love in the Afternoon provided another opportunity for Givenchy to design Audrey's clothes, this time without Edith Head to contend with. Working in black and white instead of Technicolor film, Givenchy stressed soft tones and flowery prints. The high-waisted so-called Ariane Look became a favorite of women who wanted to appear eighteen again.

Though the four months of filming *Funny Face* had left Audrey exhausted, *Love in the Afternoon* would also be filmed in Paris, so the Ferrers were spared moving from their suite in the Raphaël Hotel. They just locked the door behind them and took off for a month's vacation in Burgenstock. A vacation, that is, for Mrs. Ferrer, since her husband continued professionally idle. During *Funny Face*, he'd hung around the set holding her hand and occasionally an umbrella to shield her from the frequent rain showers.

That ill-balanced situation improved a bit when they returned to Paris from Switzerland and Mel's agent secured him a co-starring role with Pier Angeli and John Kerr in *The Vintage*, a less than topgrade melodrama being produced by MGM in the winemaking South of France. It meant a separation, but at least the Ferrers would be close enough geographically for weekend visits.

To compensate for his absence, Mel gifted Audrey with an adorable companion—a Yorkshire toy terrier that she gleefully named "Mr. Famous," or "Famous" to skip the formality. With his trusting eyes and long, silky coat of steel blue and tan, Famous became a surrogate child for the one she had been unable to have so far. Audrey gave her precious the full star treatment, with red ribbons in his hair and jeweled collars from Cartier's and Van Cleef and Arpels. His weekly shampoos and pedicures were done by the same doggie salon that took care of the Duchess of Windsor's dogs.

Though Audrey had become intimately involved with one of her co-actors during the making of her previous Billy Wilder film, there seemed slight chance of that happening during *Love in the Afternoon*. First of all, she was now a married woman and devoted to her husband.

Second, while Gary Cooper and Maurice Chevalier had once been two of the busiest skirt chasers in showbiz, both were well past their prime. Audrey had never been attracted to older men who were *that* much older. Also, it's doubtful that either Cooper or Chevalier had any designs on Audrey. Both had reportedly sworn off sex and booze for the duration of the filming to protect their deteriorating looks.

Since the sixty-eight-year-old Chevalier was portraying Audrey's father in the movie, his age caused worry mainly to his own ego. But in Cooper's case, the fifty-five-year-old actor had to try to shave at least ten years off his appearance to avoid looking like a pervert courting an eighteen-year-old heroine. Because heavy makeup would have made Cooper look even more ridiculous, Billy Wilder had to resort to the gauzy filters usually reserved for withering movie queens. Cooper's face was often photographed in shadow. Many scenes were shot with the camera behind his shoulder. Since most of the action of the black-and-white movie took place indoors, it would be hard to detect the manipulated shots in the finished film.

Needless to say, Audrey also benefited from the lighting and camera tricks, even though they were meant primarily for Cooper. She was never more exquisitely photographed than she was in *Love in the Afternoon* by William Mellor, whose Oscar-winning work on the 1951 *A Place in the Sun* had served Elizabeth Taylor equally well.

The age disparity between Ariane and her American millionaire caused problems during the making of *Love in the Afternoon* and later during its release. Many critics, as well as film censors and other guardians of morality like the Catholic Legion of Decency, would be outraged by its cradle-snatching escapades. Yet it was usually Billy Wilder's style to provoke controversy.

The relationship that worked best in the film was between Audrey and Maurice Chevalier. "The way she talked to him, the way they embraced, the way they looked at each other, they made you believe they were father and daughter," Billy Wilder recalled. "Audrey understood the character, and she knew how to make it true. You always knew what was going on in her mind. She made it so clear that her acting partners had to react the proper way. She drew them into reality."

In the midst of the filming, Audrey and Chevalier received a visit from playwright-lyricist Alan Jay Lerner, who'd flown over from California to offer them starring roles in the musicalized version of *Gigi* that he and composer Frederick Loewe were preparing for MGM as their first endeavor since that year's phenomenal Broadway hit, *My Fair Lady*. Chevalier needed no coaxing, since Lerner had written the part of Gaston's bon-vivant uncle (who didn't appear in the Anita Loos play) especially for him.

Audrey, however, wasn't interested. Though *Gigi* had been the making of her on Broadway, five years had elapsed. She thought she'd grown too old for the role and didn't want to risk unkind comparisons to the dewy innocence of her original interpretation. Lerner, of course, moved on to MGM contractee Leslie Caron, who'd also won critical acclaim for *Gigi*, in her case on the London stage after Audrey declined that opportunity.

Meanwhile, Paramount was about to launch *War and Peace*. In a classic case of bad timing, most of the theaters that specialized in reserved-seat road shows were tied up with *Around the World in 80 Days* or Paramount's *The Ten Commandments*, which meant that *War and Peace* had to skip the red carpet treatment and go directly into standard continuous-performance release. That's hardly the best way to showcase an epic running nearly three and a half hours.

War and Peace had the additional bad luck of being released at the same time as another biggie of similar length, Warner Brothers' *Giant*. Moviegoers soon made it plain that if they had only one afternoon or evening to spare, they preferred spending it in Edna Ferber's Texas with Elizabeth Taylor, Rock Hudson, and the late James Dean (his final performance), rather than in Leo Tolstoy's Russia with Audrey Hepburn, Henry Fonda, and Mel Ferrer.

While not a box-office disaster, *War and Peace* never came close to equaling the hoped for success or acclaim of *Gone With the Wind*. Critics were quick to compare the two, but always to the detriment of *War and Peace*. The general consensus was that the heart and soul of the novel had been sacrificed in the oversimplification of the story and characters, but there was considerable praise for the pageantry and the luminous camera work of Jack Cardiff and his Italian associate, Aldo Tonti.

Many reviewers, including Audrey's number-one fan, Bosley Crowther, considered her Natasha to be her best screen performance so far. Despite predictions, she failed to win even an Oscar nomination. But her acting was undoubtedly one of the reasons why King Vidor was nominated for Best Director, thought the winner turned out to be George Stevens for *Giant.*

Unfortunately, Mel Ferrer was roundly panned for a stiff and uncharismatic performance as Prince Andrei. The failure of the Ferrers to ignite sparks as an acting team raised serious doubts about their landing in the elite company of the Lunts and the Oliviers.

But they made another attempt—this time on American television—in a new version of *Mayerling* for their friend Anatole Litvak on *Producers' Showcase,* an anthology series of plays and musicals that aired usually once a month on NBC. Litvak had also directed the memorable 1936 French film of *Mayerling,* with Charles Boyer and Danielle Darrieux in the leads. Ironically, the source material was a novel by Claude Anet, the author of *Ariane,* who drew his speculative story from the tragic love affair between Austria's Crown Prince Rudolph and a commoner, Marie Vetsera. To this day, no one knows the whole truth behind the apparent double suicide in the hunting lodge known as "Mayerling."

Audrey loved the script, as well as the opportunity to earn $150,000 for only three weeks of work—a week of rehearsals and two more for the taping in New York City. Most of TV's "quality" programs were still being produced in New York, which, as culture capital of the nation if not the world, had a more diverse talent pool to draw from than Hollywood.

Mel Ferrer may have seemed an unlikely replacement for Charles Boyer, one of the screen's most adored (and imitated) great lovers. But in order to obtain Audrey Hepburn for what amounted to her television debut and would almost certainly hype the Nielsen ratings of *Producers' Showcase*, NBC had to hire him as well, though for a comparatively paltry $25,000. Hopefully, Anatole Litvak would be able to work the same wonders with Mel as he did with Boyer, whose spotty career took off like a rocket after *Mayerling*.

When Audrey finally finished working in *Love in the Afternoon* in December 1956, the Ferrers flew to California for a vacation and spent the Christmas holidays at the desert resort of La Quinta, near Palm Springs. Mel's two children, Pepa, aged fifteen, and Mark, twelve, joined them, so it made for a happy family of five, counting Mr. Famous.

Produced by the highly regarded Fred Coe, *Mayerling* was one of the most expensive and elaborate productions since the start of the so-called television revolution in 1948. Audrey alone had twelve costume changes (her outfits copied from nineteenth-century originals), almost as many as she had had in *War and Peace*.

There were thirty indoor sets, spread around studios on lower Sixth Avenue that had once been some of Manhattan's original department stores.

The cast of 107 actors included such notables as Raymond Massey, Diana Wynyard, Basil Sydney, Judith Evelyn, and Lorne Greene. Although 99.9 percent of American homes still had only black-and-white receivers, the program was shot and broadcast in color. Most of NBC's specials were, in order to create a demand for the color sets manufactured by its parent company, RCA.

To defray some of the expense of *Mayerling*, NBC made a deal with Paramount to release the program as a theatrical movie overseas. The production values were far in excess of what TV viewers were accustomed to seeing in most foreign countries. Outside the United States, television had developed along non-commercial lines: government controlled, inexpensive programming, and a restricted broadcasting day that usually started at evening and ended by midnight.

Anatole Litvak encountered problems directing the married couple. "When Audrey played Marie in a love scene with the prince, she was also Audrey being held in the arms of her husband. I had a lot of trouble getting them to turn on the heat. Audrey seemed to have a better rapport with that Yorkshire terrier of hers," Litvak said later.

Audrey had grown so accustomed to the long gap between a movie's completion and its release that she could hardly believe it when *Mayerling* hit the airwaves only two weeks after the New York production ended. According to the A. C. Neilsen ratings, the broadcast on February 4,

1957, reached the largest audience of any *Producers' Showcase* program since Mary Martin's phenomenal *Peter Pan* in March 1955. *Mayerling* also topped the ratings of *The Petrified Forest*, with Humphrey Bogart, Henry Fonda, and Lauren Bacall, and the musicalized *Our Town* with Frank Sinatra, Paul Newman, and Eva Marie Saint.

Press reviews, however, were less than raves. While Audrey received praise for her heart-stopping beauty, vulnerability, and poise, Mel got clobbered for being too stiff and lacking in charisma. As columnist Sheilah Graham put it, "The lovers seemed more fated to bore each other to death than to end their illicit alliance in a murder-suicide pact."

After *Mayerling*, Audrey took a break while Mel accepted a prestigious offer to enact one of the leading roles in Darryl F. Zanuck's adaptation of Ernest Hemingway's Lost Generation classic *The Sun Also Rises*, for 20th Century– Fox. With *Funny Face* and *Love in the Afternoon* still to be released, Audrey was really more intent on starting a family than on rushing into more film commitments. Mel's assignment would give the couple what amounted to an all-expenses-paid vacation in Spain and Mexico during the location filming. Hopefully, the sun and relaxation would be conducive to Audrey conceiving again.

Meanwhile, offers poured in for Audrey's consideration, but she kept rejecting them. Several carried reminders of her personal sufferings in World War II, an additional reason for turning them down. Director George Stevens pursued her for the film of *The Diary of Anne*

Frank, though how Stevens expected a twenty-eight-year-old woman to pass for a girl barely into her teens is anybody's guess (nineteen-year-old Millie Perkins finally played the part and even she couldn't get away with it).

Paramount had optioned convent dropout Maria von Trapp's best-seller about her adopted family's escape from Nazi-occupied Austria for a dramatic epic and wanted Audrey to play the lead. When she passed, Paramount dropped its option on the book, which two years later was transformed by Rodgers and Hammerstein into the Broadway smash *The Sound of Music*, starring Mary Martin.

Ironically, there was another postulant in Audrey's future in a project being peddled around Hollywood by director Fred Zinnemann, but without any takers so far. No one saw any possibilities beyond a TV documentary in *The Nun's Story*, Kathryn Hulme's nonfiction best-seller about a Catholic missionary in the Belgian Congo. Zinnemann went ahead anyway and commissioned a script from Robert Anderson, the prize-winning playwright of *Tea and Sympathy*. A copy landed with Audrey's agent, Kurt Frings, who loved it and urged her to do it.

The story of a young woman training to be a nun and medical missionary, her inner struggle between blind obedience to God and sensual feelings for a doctor she meets in Africa, and her eventual decision to leave the convent to aid the displaced victims of World War II, covered a period of nearly twenty years and offered Audrey

215

the most dramatically challenging role of her career so far. It also had eerie parallels to her own life. The nun known as Sister Luke is Belgian-born. When war breaks out, she shelters a downed British flier from the Nazis. One of the nun's brothers is in the underground Resistance, another a prisoner of the Germans.

Audrey read both the script and the book, and agreed to make the movie. With Audrey Hepburn's name attached to it, *The Nun's Story* suddenly became a hot property. Paramount, which had first call on Audrey's services, dropped out when it saw Zinnemann's projected budget of $4 million. Rival mogul Jack Warner, however, had been covetous of the star for a long time and offered a deal at Warner Brothers.

Before scheduling could be arranged, every-body had to contend with Audrey's commitment to MGM in the swap arrangement with Paramount on *Funny Face*, a deal that stipulated mel Ferrer would direct whatever project was chosen. The Ferrers had been pushing for their long-cherished *Ondine*, with the more box-office-worthy Charlton Heston replacing Mel as the knight errant, but the Giraudoux estate still wouldn't approve the epic approach that MGM wanted.

But while sifting through properties that MGM had acquired over the years, Mel found some-thing similar in W. H. Hudson's classic fantasy novel *Green Mansions*, which, instead of a water nymph, had an elfin jungle goddess named Rima as its central character. Envisioning an adult and more romantic version of *Tarzan of the Apes*,

Audrey at age ten. There would be fewer smiles during the war-torn years soon to begin.

Geared up for a ride in the open cockpit of an airplane, Audrey gets moral support from half-brothers, Ian, left, and Alexander Quarles van Ufford. Photographed by their mother during a family vacation, circa 1937–38.

1

2

3

A rare photo of Audrey's parents, Ella and Joseph Ruston, here enjoying a swim around the time of their marriage in the Dutch East Indies in 1926.

Dutch artist Max Nauta did this wash drawing of Audrey in 1948, not long before she and her mother moved to England.

A rare view of Audrey as a blond, from one of her ballet scenes in the British film, *The Secret People*.

Audrey visited her "discoverer,"
Colette, in Paris in 1951.
The novelist died three years later,
at age eighty-one.

Audrey became an
overnight sensation as Gigi.
She was twenty-one when she
portrayed the sixteen-year-old
schoolgirl on Broadway.

Audrey and fiancé
James Hanson share a
zebra-striped
banquette at New
York's legendary
nightspot El Morocco,
in 1952.

9

Shooting this scene with Gregory Peck on Rome's Spanish Steps attracted thousands of spectators who constantly heckled and second-guessed William Wyler's direction.

10

Audrey accepts her *Roman Holiday* Oscar from Jean Hersholt. Thirty-one years later, for her work for UNICEF, she was awarded posthumously the humanitarian Academy Award given in the actor's memory.

11

Hubert de Givenchy dressed Audrey for the first time in 1953 in *Sabrina*. This bare-shouldered ball gown of white organdy embroidered in black started a vogue for the "décolleté Sabrina."

12

A real romance developed between Audrey and William Holden during the filming of *Sabrina*.

13

Humphrey Bogart won the girl in *Sabrina*, but he and Audrey were cordial at best while working together.

Audrey and future husband Mel Ferrer teamed on Broadway in 1954 in *Ondine*, with Alfred Lunt as director and Peter Larkin as scenic designer.

14

Henry Fonda as Pierre and Audrey as Natasha in *War and Peace*, a failed attempt at turning Tolstoy's classic into another *Gone With the Wind*.

Two faces of Audrey in a scene from *Funny Face* with Fred Astaire. His character was loosely modeled on photographer Richard Avedon, who really snapped the picture Astaire is holding.

15

16

Gowned in red by Givenchy, Audrey became a Winged Victory with arms in *Funny Face*. The scene was actually filmed in the Louvre during non-visiting hours.

There was no getting away from Gary Cooper as he made his pitch in *Love in the Afternoon* in his suite at the Ritz Hotel.

Prior to starting *The Nun's Story,* Audrey consulted with author Kathryn Hulme and director Fred Zinnemann.

19

20

21

Seventeen years separate these hallowed images of Audrey as Sister Luke in *The Nun's Story,* made in 1958, and as the Abbess in *Robin and Marian,* filmed in 1975.

Audrey's beloved Yorkshire terrier Mr. Famous traveled with her to Africa during the filming of *The Nun's Story.*

Audrey and Mel Ferrer trained the fawn in *Green Mansions* by raising it at home and acting as its parents.

While recuperating from a serious horseback riding accident, Audrey had to rest on a folding cot between takes for *The Unforgiven* in Durango, Mexico. Co-star Burt Lancaster commiserates.

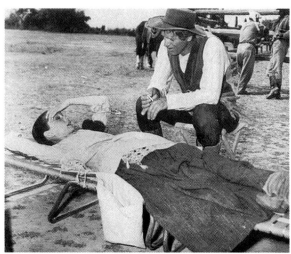

The proud parents show off their first child, Sean Ferrer, born on July 17, 1960, in Lucerne, Switzerland.

Truman Capote wanted Marilyn Monroe for Holly Golightly but had to settle for Audrey, who received another Oscar nomination for her performance.

Mel Ferrer and Eddie Fisher swap wives at a Hollywood party. Even in stockinged feet, Audrey was taller than the spike-heeled Elizabeth Taylor.

Audrey and Shirley MacLaine played teachers being persecuted for an alleged lesbian relationship in *The Children's Hour,* one of the first movies produced under Hollywood's liberalized censorship code of the 1960s.

Though she had the day off, Audrey came to watch William Wyler, left, shoot an exterior for *The Children's Hour* in the countryside near Los Angeles.

Audrey and Hubert de Givenchy were the greatest of friends for more than forty years. She frequently visited him in Paris to replenish her personal wardrobe.

Filming a scene for *Charade* with Cary Grant alongside the Seine in 1963. The City of Light was the principal setting for five of Audrey's movies.

Director George Cukor huddles with Audrey and Rex Harrison during a break from *My Fair Lady*, which was filmed in its entirety at Warner Brothers' studio in Burbank, California.

Audrey and her mother, Baroness Ella van Heemstra, were escorted to the 1964 Oscar presentations by George Cukor, who ended up a winner for his direction of *My Fair Lady*. Audrey, who wasn't even nominated for her performance in the film, handed out the Best Actor Oscar, which went to co-star Rex Harrison.

33

Audrey and Albert Finney became very close during the filming of *Two for the Road*. He later said that their relationship, while short-lived, was "one of the closest I've ever had."

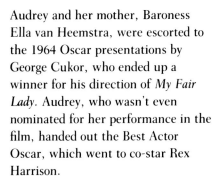

The blind heroine of *Wait Until Dark* checks the time on her kitchen clock. Audrey's performance earned her her fifth and last Oscar nomination.

34

35

The bride wore pink at her 1969 wedding to Italian psychiatrist Andrea Dotti, nine years her junior. The civil ceremony took place in Morges, Switzerland, near Audrey's home in Tolochenaz.

Audrey escorting youngest son Luca Dotti to school during their residence in Rome. Fears and threats of kidnapping eventually made that impossible.

After a nine-year gap, Audrey restarted her film career as Maid Marian to Sean Connery's Robin Hood in *Robin and Marian*.

Eldest son Sean
Ferrer, left,
joined Audrey
and her longtime
companion,
Robert Wolders,
at a Hollywood
gala in 1981.

Audrey had a
featured part as a
heavenly angel in
what turned out
to be her last
movie, Steven
Spielberg's
Always, released
in 1989.

With her ancestral Huis Doorn in the background, Audrey and Robert Wolders posed for a family photo with her aunt, Baroness Jacqueline van Heemstra, onetime lady-in-waiting to Crown Princess Juliana. The occasion was the introduction of the Audrey Hepburn Tulip in Holland in April 1990.

41

Audrey in the role for which she will perhaps be best remembered, as a traveling goodwill ambassador for UNICEF, here surrounded by children she met in a tour of refugee camps in famine-wracked southern Sudan.

MGM turned it over to staff producer Edmund Grainger for immediate activation.

While Kurt Frings dickered with Warner Brothers and MGM over the order in which *The Nun's Story* and *Green Mansions* would be made, the Ferrers traveled to Spain and Mexico for Mel's assignment in *The Sun Also Rises*. Presumably, with two major movies on the horizon, Audrey wasn't trying too hard to get pregnant again.

Mel had the role of Robert Cohn, a Jewish-American writer and former college boxer, in the film, which starred Tyrone Power as Jake Barnes, Ava Gardner as Lady Brett Ashley, and Errol Flynn as Mike Campbell. Eddie Albert, who had worked with Audrey in *Roman Holiday*, was also in the cast, as well as her Paris friend Juliette Greco, the beatnik chanteuse and mistress of Darryl Zanuck, the film's producer. It was a highly congenial group, and Audrey enjoyed being an outsider for a change. During the day she went shopping, sightseeing, or to the beach. In the evenings, everybody got together and made the rounds of the local restaurants and night-clubs.

"It was the first time that I felt like a real wife," Audrey recalled. "My husband went to work in the morning and I had the whole day to myself to do as I pleased."

When Mel completed his scenes, the Ferrers returned briefly to Switzerland, then flew to Los Angeles because Audrey had promised Paramount and Allied Artists to help in the publicity hoopla for *Funny Face* and *Love in the*

Afternoon, which were scheduled for release only two months apart. *Funny Face,* in fact, had already opened in an advance engagement, heading the Easter holiday show at New York's Radio City Music Hall. *Love in the Afternoon* would debut nationwide in June.

Surprisingly, neither movie became a box-office hit, though *Funny Face* started out breaking records at the Music Hall (as any movie would, given the circumstances). The musical received generally enthusiastic reviews for advancing the art of that particular genre of film making, but it was apparently too sophisticated for the mass audience, and it failed to recoup its $4 million cost. The pairing of Audrey with the aging Fred Astaire may have offended people as well, which also seemed the case with Gary Cooper in *Love in the Afternoon.* Audiences stayed away from that one in droves, perhaps nauseated by misleading advertising that suggested a ménage à trois between Audrey, Cooper, and the even older Maurice Chevalier.

Both movies, however, and especially *Funny Face,* solidified Audrey's reputation as one of the world's most beautiful and best-dressed women. She was becoming more than that—an icon, an inspiration for women and for the fashion world, not only for that time but for later generations that would see her films and repeatedly recreate her special look.

During their trip to Los Angeles, the Ferrers finalized plans for *The Nun's Story* and *Green Mansions,* which would be produced in that order. Since Mel was involved only with the

218

second of those movies, it would save a lot of time if he took care of the preparation while Audrey was busy elsewhere. It would also give him something to do during the six months or so that *The Nun's Story* would take. To simply travel with Audrey all that time, playing the star's husband, wasn't something he relished, though neither was happy about being separated.

Before that happened, however, Mel accepted another offer of an acting job from 20th Century–Fox, this time co-starring with Dana Wynter (protégé of Darryl Zanuck's attorney, Greg Bautzer) in a Cold War thriller entitled *Fräulein*. Because all the filming would be in Munich and West Berlin, Audrey decided to not accompany her husband in his travels. After her war experience, she vowed never to set foot in Germany.

Instead, she lingered on in Los Angeles and started learning what it takes to be a nun and medical missionary.

chapter ten

A NUN IN AFRICA

The character Sister Luke, or Gabrielle van der Mal in her previous worldly existence, was based on the real life Marie-Louise Habets, who, after seventeen years as a missionary nun, renounced her vows at the outbreak of World War II and joined the Belgian Resistance against the Nazis. At the end of the war, Habets became a nurse at a United Nations Relief and Rehabilitation Agency camp for displaced persons in Germany, where she became close friends with her superior, Kathryn Hulme. In time, Habets confessed to a "shameful" past as a failed nun. Hulme helped Habets to gradually come to terms with her guilty conscience, and the end result was *The Nun's Story*, which Hulme wrote as a follow-up to *The Wild Place*, a book about her own experiences helping war refugees.

Oddly enough, the idea for a film of *The Nun's Story* originated with Gary Cooper, who loved the book and strongly urged it on close friend Fred Zinnemann, the director of his Oscar-winning performance in *High Noon*. That happened before Cooper got to know Audrey during *Love in the Afternoon*, so she was not part of his recommendation. But Zinnemann wanted her.

"With the exception of Ingrid Bergman, there was at that time no star as incandescent as Audrey," he recalled. "She was shy, coltish, and intelligent; she looked delicate, but there was a hint of iron in the jawline that signified a stubborn will. I thought she would be ideal."

When Audrey discovered that Habets and Hulme were now living in Los Angeles, she arranged to meet them for coaching in the role of Sister Luke. She knew very little about the nursing profession and even less about the Roman Catholic nunnery. Though she had not been raised in any particular faith, she considered herself a Protestant, a product of her father's Church of England and her mother's Dutch Reformed.

Though out of the convent now for eighteen years, the fiftyish Habets was still very shy around strangers, but Hulme coaxed her out of her shell, and she warmed to Audrey immediately. For several weeks, Audrey visited the two women every afternoon and learned the basics of being a postulant. By the time she finished, she knew all the prayers and services, the garb and the sacred articles, and how to walk and talk (or not talk), even how to prostrate herself and to kiss the feet of her superiors.

Still working part-time as a private nurse, Habets took Audrey to a hospital to study operating room procedures and to learn how to handle surgical instruments. They also spent an afternoon in a research laboratory, familiarizing Audrey with microscopes, Bunsen burners, and sterilizing test tubes.

When Audrey finished her crash course with Habets and Hulme, she decided that she must spend some time in an actual convent. Hopefully it would be the Sisters of Charity in Ghent, Belgium, where Habets herself had trained. Fred Zinnemann and his producer, Henry Blanke, were negotiating to shoot some of the scenes there.

Meanwhile, the casting of the other key roles in *The Nun's Story* continued. Though Audrey had dropped several hints that Mel Ferrer would be an ideal choice for the cynical European tempter, Dr. Fortunati, Fred Zinnemann pretended not to hear. He got turned down by two Frenchmen, Gerard Philipe and then Yves Montand, before settling on Peter Finch, who happened to be British but adept at foreign accents.

In the supporting cast, Zinnemann selected some fine actresses for his principal nuns, including England's Edith Evans and Peggy Ashcroft, and Mildred Dunnock, Patricia Collinge, Beatrice Straight, and Ruth White from the United States. While Audrey had the contractual right to reject any of them, she didn't, unlike some stars who might have considered them potential scene stealers. Audrey knew that acting in such distinguished company could only enhance her own performance.

Audrey once again had the good luck of linking up with a master director. Fred Zinnemann had three recent award-winning hits to his credit: the diversely different *High Noon*, *From Here to Eternity*, and *Oklahoma*! Like William Wyler and

Billy Wilder before him, he had a European (Austrian) sensibility that meshed well with Audrey's. She couldn't believe it when he told her the story of being fired from his first major Hollywood film, *The Clock*, because its star, Judy Garland, claimed she couldn't relate to a foreigner (actually a lame excuse for her lover and future husband, Vincente Minnelli, to replace him).

When first published, *The Nun's Story* infuriated many officials in the Catholic Church because of its harsh depiction of convent life, the implied sexual attraction between Sister Luke and Dr. Fortunati, and the fact that an ex-nun had made best-selling capital of her experiences. As a consequence, the convent in Belgium where Marie-Louise Habets took her vows refused to cooperate in the filming, forcing Zinnemann to look elsewhere for a location site. French Catholics were less concerned about retaliation from the Vatican than their Belgian neighbors, and the Order of the Sisters of the Assumption at Froyennes, near Paris, agreed to cooperate, in return for a substantial cash contribution from Warner Brothers. The Mother Superior also permitted Audrey to visit for a short residence in one of the guest rooms. Accompanied by a chaperone, she could observe some of the nuns' activities but not socialize with them.

Zinnemann also arranged for Peggy Ashcroft and Edith Evans to stay in other convents in the vicinity of Paris at the same time. Each morning he visited them by taxi to see how they were doing. "The January weather was freezing and the convents were hardly heated," he recalled. "My 'nuns' would come out of the cloisters absolutely purple with cold but fascinated by what they were involved with and very excited by the way they were getting prepared for their characters."

Audrey emerged from her retreat a changed woman, or so the publicity for *The Nun's Story* claimed. She ate and dressed spartanly, never looked at herself in a mirror, because it was forbidden for a nun of Sister Luke's order to do so. She could not play radios, phonographs, or television sets, because these activities were considered frivolities that were banned from convent life.

Needless to say, Hubert de Givenchy did not design Audrey's wardrobe for *The Nun's Story*. That job went to Marjorie Best of the Warner Brothers costume department in California, working with guidance from Marie-Louise Habets herself. But before Audrey would approve anything, she had the sketches airmailed to Givenchy in Paris for his opinion. Later he also supervised her fittings.

After five major films, Audrey had started to build a list of cinematographers and other personnel whose work pleased her and whom she would request whenever she thought their expertise suited her latest project. For *The Nun's Story*, she obtained Franz Planer, who had won an Oscar nomination for photographing *Roman Holiday*, and scenic designer Alexander Trauner from *Love in the Afternoon*, who had to recreate the convent interiors on studio sound stages.

Audrey also brought along her usual team of cosmetician Alberto di Rossi and his hairstylist wife, Gracia, who ended up portraying the role of the nun who shears off Sister Luke's long locks when she starts her novitiate. Audrey wore a wig for the scene. Gracia's expertise avoided the nervousness and fumbling that an actress might have shown in applying scissors to Audrey Hepburn's head.

The di Rossis had it easy through most of *The Nun's Story* because only Audrey's face, from mid-forehead down, showed through the wimples that she wore. In the final scenes where Sister Luke becomes Gabrielle van der Mal again, Audrey had a disagreement with Fred Zinnemann, who wanted her hair streaked with gray to denote the passage of seventeen years. Guess who won?

In that era of so-called runaway production, none of *The Nun's Story* was filmed in Hollywood, even though the Warner Brothers studio in Burbank could easily have accommodated it. But the Hollywood labor unions had such high pay scales that nearly a million dollars could be shaved off the budget by shooting the interiors at Cinecitta in Rome, which also had the advantage of being near artisans and technical advisers trained in church traditions. Besides exteriors at the French convent in Froyennes, there was filming in Belgium in Ghent and the surrounding countryside, but the longest—and most distant—location was at Stanleyville in the Belgian Congo (now known as Kisangani, Zaire).

Thoughts of the African trip terrified Audrey

because of her delicate health. She was well aware of actress Edwina Booth's near death from tropical fever during the 1930 filming of *Trader Horn*, as well as the more recent sufferings of Katharine Hepburn and Deborah Kerr while making *The African Queen* and *King Solomon's Mines*. She therefore insisted that there be a top doctor available who could handle any type of emergency and would have all the latest drugs and medications that might be needed.

While Audrey filmed *The Nun's Story*, Mel would be in Hollywood preparing *Green Mansions*. To keep his hand in, he also accepted an acting role at MGM co-starring with Harry Belafonte and Inger Stevens in *The World, the Flesh and the Devil*, a bizarre three-character melodrama about the only survivors of a world-wide nuclear disaster.

For companionship while she was traveling, Audrey insisted on bringing Mr. Famous with her. Not an unreasonable demand, except that Italy and the Belgian Congo had strict quarantines against domestic pets. Warner Brothers spent weeks contacting government officials and greasing palms before finally getting permission. But Famous had to take enough inoculations to immunize the entire terrier race.

In mid-January 1958, after a few days in Rome for rehearsals, Audrey and Famous flew to Stanleyville on a chartered Sabena airliner also carrying Fred Zinnemann, Peter Finch, Peggy Ashcroft, some other supporting actors, and the production crew. Since forty-one-year-old Finch had a reputation for getting romantically involved with his leading ladies (most notably Vivien Leigh), those expecting sparks to ignite with Audrey would be disappointed. During the fourteen-hour flight, he fell for a Sabena stewardess who made the run twice a week and became his steady bedmate for the duration of the filming.

It's doubtful that Finch would have found Audrey in a receptive mood anyway, given her devotion to her husband as well as the nunlike regimen she'd adopted for herself during the filming. Before going to bed each night, she always scribbled a two- or three-page letter to Mel to go in the next day's airmail pouch to Warner Brothers' California studio, where it would be immediately delivered by motorcycle messenger to Mel at MGM. Such were the perks of a star on location.

The Congo was then nearing the end of more than eighty years of Belgian colonialism, with racial tensions escalating wildly. There was a curfew for blacks, who were banned from the European sectors after dark. Little did anyone know that a clerk in the Stanleyville post office named Patrice Lumumba would be appointed premier in 1960. Many of the local people who worked on *The Nun's Story*—both blacks and whites—were killed during the pre-independence fighting.

Like all of the visiting movie group, Audrey lived in Stanleyville's only hotel, a glorified guest house operated by Sabena Airlines. Her suite was modestly furnished in bamboo and had only a noisy circulating fan until Fred Zinnemann phoned Jack Warner in California to fly over an air conditioner. Someone got their orders wrong and a dehumidifier arrived instead. With the outdoor temperature hovering around 100 degrees even at night, and water strictly rationed because of drought, Audrey had to suffer along with the rest, though the long-haired Famous felt it even more.

Audrey's scrawniness offered some protection, since thin people can generally tolerate torrid weather better than more corpulent ones. Audrey's spartan diet, adopted years before she discovered its similarity to that of a nun in a convent, usually consisted of two boiled eggs, unbuttered toast and black coffee for breakfast; cottage cheese and fruit salad for lunch; and a dinner of fish or lean meat and two vegetables. Presumably she had the cottage cheese flown in from California, since it was unavailable in Africa in those days.

One secular pleasure that Audrey didn't give up was smoking cigarettes, which she did even in her nun's habit while relaxing on the set between takes. One day when Audrey and some of the other "nuns" were sitting smoking and gabbing, some local bystanders educated by ascetic Belgian missionaries mistook them for the real thing and got very upset. To calm them down, a member of the production crew explained, "They're American nuns." One African thought a moment and said, "Ah, yes, now I understand."

To get a head start on the heat, everybody got up at five in the morning and began working at six. The main locations in Stanleyville included a mission run by the Assumptionist order, an

228

orphanage, and the separate European and black hospitals. During the two-month location, there were also frequent jaunts into the jungle and to villages. The production unit always lugged along wind and rain machines in case nature failed to deliver when required.

For four days the unit worked in a real leper colony situated on an island in the midst of the Congo River, fifteen miles downstream from Stanleyville. In advance, Fred Zinnemann took Audrey and some of the others to meet Stanley Browne, the English Baptist missionary doctor who ran the colony like a military outpost.

Audrey never forgot the voyage aboard a coal-burning river steamer with a crew of black sailors and a white captain. Production manager Julien Derode had organized a champagne lunch. As the boat chugged along, she saw long stretches of lush jungle, interspersed with settlements where adults and children rushed to the riverbanks to wave at the passers-by. Dozens of hippopotamuses also raised their heads out of the water to give them the once-over.

When the group arrived at the leper colony, Dr. Browne and his wife took them to a service in the small wood-frame chapel. Never having met victims of leprosy, Audrey expected distressing sights, but she was amazed to discover that medical advances of recent years had made the disease more treatable than in the past. She saw slight evidence of hideous deformities or missing limbs or digits. The lepers sat through the church service like ordinary people, except that some had great difficulty kneeling during prayers.

Afterwards, the visitors were taken to an assembly hall, where twenty patients were awarded their discharge papers as being completely safe after treatment with new sulfone drugs. They could now return to the villages that had exiled them and also stop wearing the jingling bells that were a warning signal of a leper's presence. Audrey shed tears during the ceremony, which concluded with everyone singing a hymn to the tune of the "Ode to Joy" chorale from Beethoven's Ninth Symphony. The lyrics were handed around on printed cards, translated into English, French, Lingala, and Swahili. It made for a cacophonous but deeply felt performance.

Audrey and her group were still a bit nervous about possible danger to themselves, but Dr. Browne assured them that "You have less risk of getting leprosy here than catching a cold in the New York subway." But just to be on the safe side, during the four days of filming, everyone wore gloves and covered themselves whenever possible. When it was all over and they were ready to return to Stanleyville, Dr. Browne thought it only fair to announce that the incubation period for leprosy was seventeen years.

The Congo location shots were finally completed in early March 1958. Although Audrey left with many vivid memories, the strongest were of the missionary nuns she met and the serenity with which they went about their duties and devotions. One elderly Dutch nun had been there for thirty-five years, nursing terminal leprosy cases. Little did Audrey know that she herself would be returning to Africa three decades later to do similar missionary work.

At the same time that Audrey returned to Rome for the remaining scenes in *The Nun's Story*, Mel Ferrer took off for the jungles of South America with a camera crew to survey locations for *Green Mansions*. They visited Venezuela, the novel's actual locale, as well as Colombia and British and Dutch Guiana, the latter, ironically, once governed by Audrey's grandfather. When the sites were decided on, she had another long stretch of living in the rough to look forward to.

Although she escaped serious illness in Africa, Audrey had an attack of kidney stones soon after returning to Rome. The condition had probably started developing in the Congo; people living in hot climates tend to sweat more and urinate less, which can cause a buildup of stone-forming calcium in the kidneys. Hoping to spare Audrey an operation, doctors prescribed drugs and a couple of weeks of bed rest, during which filming of *The Nun's Story* continued around its star. Mel interrupted his South American trip to be with her. The Baroness van Heemstra, who had little occasion to visit her daughter these days, flew in from London to supervise the nursing.

Audrey recovered quickly and with no need for surgery, but Mel realized that by the time she finished *The Nun's Story*, it would be inadvisable to subject her delicate health to another endurance test in the wilds of South America. When he returned to Los Angeles, he persuaded MGM to shoot *Green Mansions* at its Culver City studio.

231

Since many of the scenes took place in dense rain forest where light barely penetrated, he thought he could fake most of them and rely on scenic footage photographed during his South American survey trip for the rest.

Just after Audrey resumed working in *The Nun's Story*, she had a surprise visit from her younger half brother, Ian Quarles van Ufford, who ended up appearing in the movie, though not in the expected way. Fred Zinnemann persuaded him to model for a photograph that was needed for a key scene and supposed to represent Sister Luke's brother, a member of the Belgian Resistance. Not quite type-casting, given Ian's forced labor service in Nazi Germany during the war.

Now an executive with Unilever in Holland, Ian brought with him wife Yvonne and their four-year-old daughter, born while the couple were residing in Indonesia. Not surprisingly, they named the child Audrey. Her aunt—who was also her godmother—absolutely adored her. The trip to Rome marked their first meeting in a year. Aunt Audrey was in heaven.

No doubt the end of the visit left Audrey with empty feelings as well as doubts about her ability to have a child of her own. Co-workers spotted signs of neurosis in her treatment of Famous, whom she brought to the studio every day and kissed and cuddled like a baby instead of a pet.

One morning, Audrey happened to compliment British actress Rosalie Crutchley on her two young children, who'd visited the set the previous day. "How fortunate you are to have such a lovely son and daughter," Audrey said a bit glumly. "I do terribly want to have a child—more than anything else in the world. How have you managed to have children *and* maintain a career?"

"Unlike you, Audrey, I am not a globe-trotting film star," said Crutchley, who made few movies and worked mainly in the London theater and on television

"Yes, that might be the stumbling block," Audrey sighed.

The filming at Cinecitta was nearly over. "I have never seen anyone more disciplined, more gracious, or more dedicated to her work than Audrey. There was no ego, no asking for extra favors," Fred Zinnemann recalled. "To spare her injury, I wanted to use a stunt woman in the scene in the lunatic asylum where she's attacked by one of the inmates, but she refused. Audrey could have broken her back, but her dancer's agility helped her and we were able to shoot the scene in one take."

Looking at the movie many years later, the director was still impressed by what Audrey brought to the role of Sister Luke. "The subconscious quality of independence is present in all her actions," Zinnemann said. "When she comes running in late for the Service her haste betrays the inner calm she should be developing. In the scene when the girls are admitted as postulants and prostrate themselves on the floor in front of the Mother General, Audrey peeks out of one eye, curiosity getting the better of her. Her performance is put together of dozens of moments of independence, such as the medical exam she is asked to fail in order to prove her humility."

From Rome, Audrey and company (eighty-two people in total) moved to Belgium for the remaining exterior scenes. To avoid the touristic hordes attending the World's Fair in Brussels, the group stayed in Ostend, a resort town on the North Sea. But on a day off between filming in Bruges, Antwerp, and Ghent, Audrey sneaked into Brussels for a visit to the old house on the winding Rue Keyenveld where she was born. As luck would have it, she missed the twenty-ninth anniversary of that moment by a matter of only a few days.

Toward the end of June, after six months of arduous filming under the European system of six-day workweeks, Audrey removed her nun's gear for the last time and took off for Los Angeles for a reunion with her husband. The couple had again arranged to rent director Anatole Litvak's Malibu beach house during the production of *Green Mansions*, now expected to take no more than three months because of the cancellation of South American locations. Hopefully the more relaxed working conditions would be conducive to Audrey becoming pregnant again. Just in case, she instructed Kurt Frings to go slow in negotiating future projects.

Like *War and Peace*, *Green Mansions*, originally published in 1904, had a built-in readership of millions, as well as the same taint of a literary classic. To make it seem more exciting to current moviegoers, MGM tried to market the heroine as a female Tarzan of the Apes by labeling her

"Rima the Bird Girl," though she's never called more than "Rima" in W. H. Hudson's novel. Unlike Tarzan, she seemed more myth than muscle.

Certain masterworks of literature are better left to the printed page, and *Green Mansions* may have been one of them. Its mystical qualities seemed to defy screen treatment and might have been better served by a Disney animated feature. Amusingly, to capitalize on its huge success with *King Kong* in 1933, RKO Radio came near to filming it as a follow-up, with the exotic Dolores del Rio ruling a jungle filled with mechanized creatures and birds.

Since *Green Mansions* had already defeated the diversely talented Vincente Minnelli in a previous MGM attempt to film it with Pier Angeli in the lead, one can only guess what Mel Ferrer expected to bring to it as director. Up to then, he'd directed only three movies, *Girl of the Limberlost*, *The Secret Fury*, and *Vendetta*, all insignificant black-and-white potboilers.

By the time Audrey arrived from Europe, Mel had almost finished preparing for the filming. Twenty-five acres of backlot at MGM had been converted into jungle terrain to match the exteriors already photographed in South America. Art director Preston Ames, who had accompanied Mel on that trip, had shipped back 300 tons of cargo for his replica of a native village, including turf, boulders, canoes, grass huts, blowguns, trees, plants, as well as live birds and reptiles.

Audrey was delighted by Mel's choice of Anthony Perkins for the co-starring role of Abel

Guevez de Argensola, poet, naturalist, and gold prospector. After a long run of Bogarts, Astaires, and Coopers, it seemed about time that she should be paired with someone nearer her own age (Perkins, in fact, happened to be three years younger). Though not yet a major star, Perkins seemed well on his way after winning acclaim for his recent work in *Friendly Persuasion* and *Fear Strikes Out*. Fan magazines had him pegged as the next big Hollywood dreamboat if he continued to get worthy roles.

For the main supporting cast, Mel selected two great character actors more for their prestige value than for their suitability to the roles. Lee J. Cobb, the original Willy Loman in *Death of a Salesman* on Broadway, played Old Nulfo, Rima's grandfather. Sessue Hayakawa, the onetime silent movie idol who made a comeback with his Oscar-nominated portrayal of the Japanese prison-camp commandant in *The Bridge on the River Kwai*, enacted Runi, a native chief.

Before starting *Green Mansions*, Audrey had to establish a relationship with another of her co-actors, a fawn that trails Rima round like Mary's proverbial little lamb. Experts told Mel that young deer are so excitable and ornery that the only sure method of training one for the film was for Audrey to take in a newborn animal and care for it just like her own baby. After a few weeks of such nurturing, the fawn would supposedly follow Audrey everywhere.

The Fawn came from Jungleland theme park. With his huge eyes, he did look a bit like Audrey, and she soon named him "Ip," the sound he made when sucking on his bottles of goat's milk. Of course, Mama's other baby, Famous, became jealous and Audrey had to make sure they were kept apart. At night, while Ip bunked in the tub in the guest bathroom, she made it up to Famous by permitting him to sleep with her and Mel in the master bedroom.

That summer, Audrey decided that it was high time that she learned how to drive. She may have been suffering from freeway fever, that peculiar disease that often strikes visitors to Los Angeles when they discover it's impossible to get around that sprawling metropolis without a car. She'd also grown tired of having to depend on her husband or a hired chauffeur. Her friends had a snazzy sports car or two to zip around in whenever they wanted to go shopping or visiting.

So Audrey took lessons with a private instructor, passed the road test on her second try, and rented a convertible from Hertz for the duration of her stay. One day while she was driving through the business section of Beverly Hills, she swerved to avoid an oncoming car and crashed into another one parked at the curb. Though frightened out of her wits, she escaped injury. But a woman sitting in the parked car wasn't as lucky and had to be rushed to the hospital by ambulance.

The injured Joan Lora was a twenty-two-year-old actress and dancer. Claiming to have suffered severe neck and back injuries, she later filed suit against Audrey to collect her medical expenses plus $45,000 in lost earnings. The court eventually ordered Audrey to pay her $4,500.

Audrey took the matter so hard that she told friends she'd never get behind the steering wheel again. Because of newspaper suggestions that Audrey was drunk or driving on the wrong side of the road, there was a lot of negative publicity. This was Audrey's first taste of such publicity and it left bitter memories for years.

Another crisis developed during the camera tests for *Green Mansions*, which MGM intended filming in the CinemaScope process. Up to then, all of Audrey's movies had been shot in VistaVision or equivalent, with a frame of about 1:66 to 1. No one had given much consideration to how she would photograph in CinemaScope's much wider 2:33 to 1. With her rather square features, it wasn't an attractive sight, at least to Audrey. She thought she looked like a balloon in the close-ups.

Horrified by the test footage, Audrey refused to start work until MGM rectified the problem. Luckily, it was one already being worked on by a small company called Panavision, which had come up with an anamorphic lens superior to the one made by Bausch & Lomb for CinemaScope. The inventor, Robert E. Gottschalk, brought one to MGM for a demonstration.

"We made some test shots of Audrey, dollying-in for some big closeups as she peeked out from behind some jungle foliage," Gottschalk recalled. "As soon as the film was processed, we rushed into a projection room and ran it. Audrey looked perfectly normal—beautiful, as always—and her face didn't expand. Everybody in the room, Audrey and Mel included, broke out in spontaneous applause." Gottschalk later credited Audrey's square face for Panavision's eventual triumph over CinemaScope as the industry standard.

Green Mansions was another missed opportunity for Hubert de Givenchy. Rima's dresses needed to look like they were woven by spiders and also had to serve as camouflage from animal predators and hostile Indians. Mel gave the job to Dorothy Jeakins, a specialist in ethnic assignments much admired for her contributions to the original Broadway production of *South Pacific*.

Given Audrey's modest dimensions, Jeakins had to give her an alluring appearance without tarting her up like another Sheena, Queen of the Jungle. The result was a filmy knee-length shift that Jeakins made up in a variety of jungle pastels to set off Audrey's bare shoulders and long, graceful arms.

Jeakins's keen eye for color delighted Audrey. "You give Dorothy a piece of cloth and she will strip it, redye it and overdye it until she gets just the color she has in mind," she said at the time.

To complete Rima's mystical look, Audrey had to rely on MGM's legendary hairstylist Sidney Guilaroff, who'd worked on every crowned head from Greta Garbo and Joan Crawford to Elizabeth Taylor and Grace Kelly. After numerous experiments, they decided that her hair should be long and flowing down her back, with bangs across the forehead. How much of it was Audrey's own hair is anybody's guess, but in some scenes she seemed to be wearing a full wig.

Though William Henry Hudson probably

would have disapproved, scriptwriter Dorothy Kingsley heated up the romance in *Green Mansions* to present a sexier Audrey Hepburn than usual. MGM's advertising campaign declared, "Young lovers in a jungle Eden where menace lurks amid the orchids . . . Rima, the untouched, the girl of the virgin forest, meets her first man!"

Easier claimed than accomplished. Mel Ferrer was probably not the best person to direct his own wife in love scenes with another man. Also, Tony Perkins happened to be bisexual and couldn't work up much steam whenever he took Audrey in his arms.

When *Green Mansions* wrapped, the Ferrers lingered on in Hollywood while Mel supervised the editing. With two unreleased films under her belt, Audrey was in a mood to take a long rest, but she couldn't resist a $250,000 offer from United Artists for one of the leads in *The Unforgiven*. Bizarre though it might seem, she was keen on doing a western. This one promised to be more prestigious than most, with another great master, John Huston, directing a script by Ben Maddow, his associate on *The Asphalt Jungle*.

The Unforgiven had come up suddenly, so Huston could fill time while Arthur Miller did some polishing on the screenplay for a collaborative effort entitled *The Misfits*, which would team Miller's wife, Marilyn Monroe, with Clark Gable and Montgomery Clift. Huston intended putting his *Unforgiven* salary toward the restoration work on his newly purchased home, a 150-year-old Georgian manor near Galway, Ireland.

Huston called *The Unforgiven* his first western, forgetting perhaps that his 1948 *Treasure of the Sierra Madre* had been marketed in that category. Based on a novel by Alan LeMay, *The Unforgiven* was being made by Hecht-Hill-Lancaster Productions, actor Burt Lancaster's independent company, managed by producer Harold Hecht and writer James Hill. They had hit paydirt with *Marty* (a multi-Oscar winner in which Lancaster didn't appear) and were one of the top independent units affiliated with United Artists.

UA had built a reputation for fearless and controversial movies like Otto Preminger's *The Man With a Golden Arm*, which dealt with drug addiction, and Stanley Kramer's *The Defiant Ones*, a plea for interracial brotherhood. John Huston's *The Unforgiven* would also deal with racial prejudice, pitting whites against North American Indians in frontier Texas.

While Huston prepared the movie, the Ferrers flew to Switzerland for their first Burgenstock vacation in more than a year. The vacation seemingly did the trick. Audrey turned out to be pregnant again. She cursed herself for taking on *The Unforgiven*, but it was too late to cancel. She'd just have to be extra cautious and pray that everything went safely.

chapter eleven
MOTHERHOOD AT LAST

If Rima the nature goddess seemed an unlikely role for Audrey Hepburn, she stretched the limits of credibility with the part of Rachel Zachary, a full-blooded Kiowa Indian adopted in infancy by a Texas ranch family and raised as white. When the secret of the "red nigger" is revealed, all hell breaks loose, spreading across the Panhandle in a bloody war between cowboys and Indians.

Burt Lancaster, one of the producers of *The Unforgiven*, portrayed Ben Zachary, the eldest son and head of the clan since his father's death. Not surprisingly, Ben and the adopted Rachel become romantically involved when she grows up. In the end, she must choose between killing her Kiowa kin or seeing them slaughter the man she loves.

John Huston picked Audie Murphy, real-life World War II hero and star of the director's *The Red Badge of Courage*, to play Lancaster's hottempered brother. Lillian Gish, the symbolic hand that rocks the cradle of D. W. Griffith's *Intolerance*, portrayed the Zacharys' widowed mother. When she hears the Kiowas making war music in the surrounding hills, she has the family's piano carried out into the yard so she can answer back with Bach and Mozart.

Unlike the spaghetti westerns that Hollywood

studios were grinding out cheaply in Italy and Spain, *The Unforgiven* would be supergrade, budgeted at nearly $6 million. A quarter of a million went to a replica of a ranch home that in 1860 would have cost almost nothing. Built with a steel frame, the structure had invisible hinges to provide breakaway walls to admit the camera crew and allow filming from all angles. In the soddy style of the time, the grass-covered roof extended into the side of a hill and served as pasture for the family's cow.

Because Texas no longer looked as it did in the 1860s, John Huston opted to film *The Unforgiven* entirely on location in rugged terrain near Durango, Mexico, about 600 miles south of the U.S. border, another lengthy hot-weather expedition for Audrey, who at least this time could bring her husband along for companionship. The Ferrers' home away from home was the Casa Blanca Hotel, which turned out to be as bottom-line-basic as the Sabena guest house in Stanleyville.

Audrey struck up an instant rapport with John Huston, a crusty man's man who took his craft less seriously than Fred Zinnemann or William Wyler and treated everybody like family. By coincidence, Huston had directed the screen's more senior Hepburn in *The African Queen,* so he and Audrey often swapped stories about their jungle experiences.

With *The Unforgiven*, Huston hoped to make a serious statement about racial intolerance and the persecution of the American Indian, but United Artists was mainly interested in getting a blood-and-guts action film. The director had a rough time with Burt Lancaster, who, as co-producer, naturally wanted the movie to turn out a box-office hit.

As a result, *The Unforgiven* had less Hustonian allegory than usual and some of it became unintentionally funny when Audrey Hepburn became involved. In the scene where Huston made symbolic use of wild geese migrating north, no Kiowa woman, unless educated in a British boarding school, would have sounded like Audrey did spouting, "They're human, too, Maw; they jest fly a mite higher than us, that's all."

By giving the producers the near formula western that they wanted, Huston violated his own credo never to undertake a film he didn't believe in, and *The Unforgiven* turned sour as production progressed. "Everything went to hell," Huston said later. "It was as if some celestial vengeance had been loosed upon me for infidelity to my principles. Some of the things that happened are painful to remember."

Painful memory number one involved Audrey, who throughout the film had to ride bareback on a magnificent gray stallion named "Diablo," once owned by Cuban dictator Fulgencio Batista. Audrey was terrified about the riding, not only because of her pregnant condition but also because of a spill from a pony in childhood. But John Huston pledged every safeguard, plus the employment of a stunt double in shots where her face didn't come into view.

Audrey practiced with Diablo every lunch

break. One day, while technicians were testing some blank ammunition, the stallion got startled by the gunfire, bucked, and threw Audrey over his head onto the ground. She landed on her back with an audible shattering of something.

John Huston and Burt Lancaster, who happened to be nearby, zoomed over with the Mexican doctor assigned to emergency duty with the production unit. Mel Ferrer was absent, having stayed at the hotel in Durango that day. Audrey was semiconscious, in terrible pain, and pleading in a quavering voice, "Please don't tell Mel. . . . He worries so much."

While waiting for an ambulance to arrive, the doctor gave Audrey a sedative. Before passing out, she joked to Burt Lancaster, "I had to do something to get out of this hellhole."

By the time Audrey was delivered to the hospital in Durango, her husband was waiting for her. X rays revealed several broken vertebrae, but Mel had a low opinion of the Mexican medical profession and insisted on sending for Audrey's Los Angeles physician, Dr. Howard Mendelson. The latter flew down in a chartered plane, accompanied by ex-nun Marie-Louise Habets, who volunteered to be Audrey's nurse for as long as needed.

Mendelson's examination confirmed four broken bones, torn muscles in the lower back, and a sprained foot. To Audrey and Mel's enormous relief, the doctor found no evidence of fetal damage and predicted a safe delivery if she adhered to the usual prenatal precautions.

Mel didn't want to take any chances and

thought that Audrey should not return to *The Unforgiven* when she recovered. He begged John Huston and Burt Lancaster to cancel the movie, which should cause no financial loss because the production was heavily insured with Lloyd's of London. But United Artists wouldn't agree and said it could live with doctors' estimates that Audrey's convalescence should take no longer than six weeks. In the meantime, Huston was instructed to finish all the scenes in which she didn't appear, as well as any of Audrey's where he could get away with using a double.

A chartered plane took Audrey on a stretcher back to Los Angeles, where Mel had hastily rented a furnished house in the upper reaches of Beverly Hills for the duration of her treatment. With the devoted Marie-Louise Habets taking care of her between daily visits from medical specialists and physical therapists, she was able, by the fifth week, to stand unassisted and walk a few steps. Though still in great pain, she got fitted for a steel back brace that she would need to wear throughout the filming and probably for several months afterwards until her injuries were completely healed.

Unable to sit comfortably with the brace installed, Audrey had to be flown back to Durango the same way she left—prone on a stretcher. John Huston had a mariachi band and a fireworks display waiting to welcome her back. She spent a week rehearsing her remaining scenes, rethinking the movements so she'd be able to accomplish them wearing the brace under her costumes.

To spare Audrey some of the torture of being driven back and forth to the locations on the bumpy roads, the transport manager fitted out the back of a station wagon with two layers of foam rubber mattresses for her to stretch out on. On the set, her canvas chair was replaced by a folding cot, with her name similarly stenciled on it.

Unavoidably, in order to match the scenes with those filmed before the accident, Audrey had to ride Diablo one more time before finishing *The Unforgiven*. There was a moment that John Huston couldn't fake with a double, so he saved it until the very last day. Audrey simply had to canter straight toward the cameras from a distance of fifty yards. Huston personally lifted her onto the stallion and made sure that she was securely fastened. There were no mishaps this time. Diablo had been sedated as an extra precaution.

At the windup of *The Unforgiven*, the Ferrers returned to Burgenstock in Switzerland for the duration of Audrey's pregnancy. But again she suffered a miscarriage, which may or may not have been the result of her horse-riding accident. "I was fuming," she recalled. "I blamed God. I blamed myself. I blamed John Huston. I was a bundle of anger and recrimination. I couldn't understand why I couldn't have children. Mel and I were so much in love."

Audrey fell into what she later described as a "black decline," turning into a nervous wreck who smoked three packs of cigarettes a day. Her weight dropped to under a hundred pounds.

Then, in October 1959, she tested pregnant again. Having just celebrated their fifth wedding anniversary the previous month, the Ferrers considered it a belated gift from heaven.

Realizing that there might not be any more chances after this third one, Audrey swore to take life easy and to give up working until after the baby was born. *The Unforgiven* would not be released until the spring of 1960, so she would be well represented on theater screens.

By this time, *Green Mansions* had come and gone, but *The Nun's Story* was still current. Though *Green Mansions* was made after *The Nun's Story*, the editing went faster and it reached theaters first, premiering at New York's Radio City Music Hall in February and released broadly in March. Audrey received her usual love sonnets from Bosley Crowther and others, but the movie and especially Mel Ferrer's direction were blamed for making a stolid mess out of a literary classic. *Green Mansions* never recouped its $3 million investment, and it killed all likelihood of the Ferrers' teaming professionally again. It must have been a bitter blow to Mel's ego and to his own directing aspirations. Friends say he never got over it, to the detriment of the marriage as time went on.

In May, *The Nun's Story* also opened at Radio City Music Hall, but in this case receiving rave reviews and breaking box-office records. Bosley Crowther described Audrey's performance as "fluid and luminous. From her eyes and her eloquent expressions emerge a character that is warm and involved." Crowther and many other critics predicted that Audrey would win another Oscar. *The Nun's Story* became Warner Brothers' biggest hit of 1959, with rentals of about $7 million in U.S. and Canada (and probably an equal amount abroad, given Audrey's popularity in England, Europe, and Japan).

Studio head Jack Warner breathed a huge sigh of relief. The movie's cost of $3.5 million made it one of the most expensive he'd ever turned out. Fearing that the title of *The Nun's Story* might keep people away, he'd once suggested changing it to *I Kicked My Habit!* (one of many reasons why he was known as Hollywood's clown prince of bad jokes).

While Audrey was resting easy and knitting baby booties, director Alfred Hitchcock tried to tempt her into working for him in *No Bail for the Judge*, a suspense thriller to be produced in England for Paramount Pictures. Hitchcock had commissioned Samuel Taylor, author of *Sabrina Fair*, to write the screenplay, based on Henry Cecil's novel about a woman barrister who has to defend her own father, a court judge, against a charge of murdering a prostitute.

Audrey was flattered that Hitchcock, one of the most revered film directors at that time, thought her worthy, but she had reservations about the script, especially a scene where she would be attacked by a rapist. Mel, to whom she always turned for advice in such matters, guessed that Hitchcock intended it as a sick joke at the expense of Audrey's virtuous image. She told Kurt Frings that she couldn't possibly accept the role, and to use her pregnancy as an excuse so Hitchcock didn't get too upset.

But Hitchcock boiled over anyway. Using Audrey's name as bait, he'd already persuaded Laurence Olivier to play the father and Laurence Harvey the romantic lead. Now both weren't interested when Hitchcock proposed Lee Remick as a replacement for Audrey. In the end, *No Bail for the Judge* was never filmed. Instead, to prove that he could manage very nicely without Audrey Hepburn or other major stars, Hitchcock chose to make a low-budget chiller entitled *Psycho*, never dreaming that it would become the biggest box-office hit of his entire career.

Paramount, however, kept pressuring Audrey. If she didn't want to do the Hitchcock film, she must pick something, because since *Funny Face*, they'd been very understanding while she made four movies for other studios. Among a batch of scripts submitted to her, the only one that intrigued her was *Breakfast at Tiffany's*, a novella by Truman Capote that had been expanded into a full-blown screenplay by George Axelrod, author of *The Seven Year Itch*. At Capote's urging, Axelrod tailored the leading role of Holly Golightly for Marilyn Monroe, but producers Martin Jurow and Richard Shepherd were unable to borrow her from 20th Century–Fox.

"Within forty-eight hours, we were told by Monroe's dramatic adviser, Paula Strasberg, that she would not have her play a lady of the evening," Jurow recalled.

A native of the Texas boondocks, Holly Golightly has left a husband and stepchildren for the glitz and high life of Manhattan. Not exactly a role for her, Audrey thought at first reading. Besides being the antithesis of Marilyn Monroe, she doubted that she had the comic flair for a kooky extrovert who supports herself as a call girl while dreaming of a more permanent liaison with a multimillionaire. But Mel urged her to do it, reasoning that she needed to stretch her talent with something different from her usual ingenuous roles.

When Paramount sent Jurow and director Blake Edwards to Switzerland to persuade her, Audrey finally capitulated. Considerably younger than the directors she'd worked with in the past, the thirty-eight-year-old Edwards seemed more attuned to contemporary material than a Billy Wilder or a Fred Zinnemann would have been.

"She still had qualms about playing the role, until I said that it was not a lady of the evening that we sought but a lopsided romantic, a dreamer of dreams," Jurow remembered.

Breakfast at Tiffany's would have to wait until Audrey had her baby. She wanted three months off after that to get back into condition, so Jurow and Edwards flew back to Hollywood with a deal and a tentative staring date of October 1960.

In Burgenstock, Audrey suffered through a bitterly cold winter while awaiting the baby's arrival. At Christmas, Mel brought his two teenaged children from the United States to cheer her up. Her spirits were further buoyed by the news that the New York Film Critics Circle had voted her Best Actress of 1959 for *The Nun's*

Story, which virtually guaranteed a nomination in the approaching Academy Awards competition.

Audrey's determination to stay home and rest made it awkward for Mel, who had his own career to consider. She didn't want to risk traveling and he didn't fancy being inactive all those months. To keep busy and still be close to home, he accepted offers of starring roles in *The Hands of Orlac* and *Blood and Roses,* both being made in Europe with co-financing by French, British, Italian, American, and German interests. While the jobs paid well, they must have dented Mel's ego; his wife got all the plum assignments, while he was accepting unmemorable roles.

Mel also must have been a bit jealous when Audrey received another Oscar nomination—her third in the category of Best Actress—for *The Nun's Story.* Unwilling to jeopardize her health, she declined to fly to Los Angeles in April for the presentation ceremonies, which was just as well, because Simone Signoret turned out the winner for her performance in *Room at the Top.* Also in contention were Doris Day for *Pillow Talk* and Elizabeth Taylor and Katharine Hepburn for *Suddenly Last Summer,* the first time that the two Hepburns were rival nominees.

The Nun's Story received a total of eight nominations, including Best Picture of 1959, but won none. The winner of the top Oscar was William Wyler's *Ben-Hur,* in a field that also included *Anatomy of a Murder, The Diary of Anne Frank,* and *Room at the Top.*

In May, Audrey turned thirty-one and wished that she were twenty-one again for the sake of her childbearing powers. As the months ticked by, she ballooned in size. She waddled around the house as best she could, but spent most of her time in bed to avoid any strain that might cause another miscarriage.

Since her first pregnancy, Audrey had been praying for a son. Because her half brother Ian van Ufford had done her the honor of naming his first child after her, she had intended reciprocating until someone pointed out that the baby's monogram would be "IF." A happy compromise was "Sean," an Irish variant of "Ian" and said to mean "gift of God," which the baby surely would be to the long-suffering prospective mother.

As if on cue, Sean Ferrer arrived in the midst of a thunderstorm on July 17, 1960, at the cantonal hospital in Lucerne. The birth couldn't have been easy for the slenderly built Audrey. Sean weighed in at a hefty nine and a half pounds, or about a tenth of his mother's usual weight.

According to one of the delivery-room nurses, Audrey cried out, "Let me see my baby, let me see it at once. Is it all right? Is it really all right?" When told that *he* seemed perfect, she squealed with joy and then passed out from exhaustion.

Two days later, to pacify a mob of press photographers camped in the hospital lobby, Audrey and Mel selected one at random and permitted him to come to her room to shoot some pictures to be shared by all. Still too weak to get out of bed, Audrey clutched Sean to her bosom while Mel plopped down beside them for a family grouping. It was the last public view of Sean for a long time. Audrey worried that someone might try to kidnap him.

The new mother and child received flowers and gifts from all over the world, so many that the Ferrers had to hire a van to take them home. Audrey's first weeks with Sean at Burgenstock were her happiest ever. "Like all mothers I couldn't believe at first that Sean was really mine, and that I could keep him and take him home," she said at the time. "I'm still filled with the wonder of his being, to be able to go out and come back and find that he's still there!"

For Sean's baptism, Audrey asked Givenchy to design them matching outfits. Her half brother Ian and Mel's sister, Terry Ferrer, were chosen as godparents. The ceremony was held in the same little Protestant chapel in Burgenstock where the Ferrers were married six years before.

Pastor Maurice Eindiguer again officiated. "Audrey was radiant with joy," he recalled. "Mel read a passage from the Bible. I had to ask the godfather and godmother to repeat the name of Sean, which was not a familiar one in our country."

As the minister sprinkled holy water on his head, Sean bawled so robustly that his grandmother, the Baroness, couldn't resist quoting an old Dutch proverb for everybody to hear: "A good cry at the christening lets the Devil out!"

Also attending the service was Henry Taylor, Jr., the U.S. Ambassador to Switzerland, who afterwards presented the parents with Sean's American passport. Like Audrey, who was also born on foreign soil, Sean took the nationality of his father, though in his case he had the option of switching to Swiss citizenship when he turned twenty-one.

At an impromptu press conference for all the reporters and photographers who turned up uninvited, Audrey said, "I would like to mix Sean with all kinds of people in all countries, so that he will learn what the world is all about. If he's the right kind of person, he should take his own small part in making the world a better place."

Motherhood proved a real tonic for Audrey. Friends said they had never seen her happier or more radiant. Like most first-timers, she was afraid to leave her baby for even a minute, but she finally agreed to Mel's suggestion that they hire a full-time nanny, which would be essential when Audrey resumed working. They settled on a plump Italian woman named Gina, who spoke only her native language but gradually picked up smidgens of English, French, German, and Spanish from her multilingual employers.

Silly as it might seem, Audrey fretted over how Mr. Famous would accept the new baby. The terrier had become the equivalent of an oldest child, and Audrey expected a jealous reaction. "I knew that Famous would be upset," she recalled, "and he was, by Sean wailing in the nursery upstairs and obviously now the center of gravity in the family. Everybody was fussing over Sean, so I realized I would have to make a special effort to soften the blow to Famous's self-esteem." After several nights of rare privilege—being permitted to sleep at the foot of Audrey's bed instead of in his doghouse—Famous stopped growling and accepted Sean as his brother.

One night Audrey woke up in the midst of a tremendous mountain storm. "A huge thunderbolt crashed into the forest," she remembered. "I was seized by an irrational fear that Sean might be in danger and ran up to his room. There I saw a wonderful sight. He was sleeping peacefully in his crib, with Famous keeping vigil beside him."

Meanwhile, preparations for *Breakfast at Tiffany's* were continuing. At Audrey's insistence, Blake Edwards hired Franz Planer as cinematograper, marking their fourth collaboration after *Roman Holiday*, *The Nun's Story* and *The Unforgiven*. No other cameraman had worked with Audrey more than once. Both in black and white and color, and dealing with radically different subject matter, Planer always knew exactly what lighting, lenses, and camera angles were best for her.

After a three-year lapse, Audrey was able to choose Hubert de Givenchy to design her wardrobe. In fact, one of the main reasons she chose to do *Breakfast at Tiffany's* was the opportunity to wear his creations again, though no one knew at the time how enduring these would be. The so-called little black dress that Givenchy designed for Audrey's Holly Golightly is still fashion shorthand for all things glamorous. Equally influential was a black sleeveless evening gown accessorized with long gloves, a pearl choker, and a foot-long cigarette holder.

With Audrey's approval, Blake Edwards chose

blond and blue-eyed George Peppard, one year her senior and a rising star from the Broadway stage, to play Holly's upstairs neighbor, Paul Varjak, an aspiring novelist and kept man. Patricia Neal would portray his rich protector (wearing clothes designed for the film by Pauline Trigère), with Buddy Ebsen as Holly's ex-husband, Doc Golightly, and Martin Balsam as talent agent O. J. Berman. Mickey Rooney, a longtime buddy of Blake Edwards, was signed to play Holly's constantly complaining Japanese neighbor, complete with slanty eyes and buck teeth. Someone apparently forgot that World War II had been over for fifteen years.

With *Breakfast at Tiffany's* due to start production in October, Audrey was faced with the first real test of motherhood. Production was divided between New York City locations and Paramount's Hollywood studio, so it seemed advisable to leave her three-month-old son behind in Switzerland with Nanny Gina and his doting grandmother, Baroness Ella. Audrey's husband would, of course, accompany her to New York. Among other things, she depended on Mel to take Famous for his walks when she couldn't.

The New York location work for *Breakfast at Tiffany's* had to be done first, before cold weather set in. There were only two weeks' worth, several street scenes and filming inside and outside Tiffany & Company, the legendary jewelers founded in 1837 and situated since 1940 on the southeast corner of Fifth Avenue and Fifty-seventh Street. Because that intersection is one of

Manhattan's busiest, Blake Edwards scheduled those scenes for an early Sunday morning. But a crowd of several hundred people built up as strollers saw the protective squads of New York City cops and thought a jewel robbery was in progress.

"Breakfast" was the take-out variety, a danish pastry and a container of coffee, which Holly Golightly (wearing dark glasses, a black evening gown, long gloves, and a rhinestone tiara in her upswept hair) consumes while admiring one of Tiffany's window displays on her way home from an all-night party. Always nervous when she knew people were watching her work, Audrey became terrified by the swelling crowd of spectators. She spoiled take after take, finally so unnerving Franz Planer that he accidentally touched a high-voltage cable and received a jolt that sent him hurtling off the camera platform onto the side-walk. No serious harm was done, but when Audrey realized that she might have killed her favorite cinematographer, she pulled herself together and did the scene perfectly on the next take.

Blake Edwards also took advantage of Tiffany's Sunday closure to film the only scene set in the interior, filling the main floor with actors and dress extras posing as sales clerks and customers. The store hired twenty additional security guards to keep an eye on the $25 million worth of gems and jewelry that were within reach on the counters and in the display cases.

The scene called for Audrey and George Peppard to shock an uppity sales clerk by asking to see something in the ten-dollar range. As Holly puts it, "I think it's tacky to wear diamonds before I'm forty." The salesman (played by John McGiver) winds up showing the pair a sterling silver telephone dialer for $6.75, which they decline. Instead they settle for a five-dollar engraving on the inside of a ring that Holly is wearing, which came originally as a prize in a box of Cracker Jack.

Scenes were also photographed outside the Women's House of Detention in Greenwich Village, where Audrey has supposedly spent the night after being falsely arrested and is released into Peppard's waiting arms. A town house at 171 East Seventy-first Street was chosen to represent the exterior of Holly's apartment building. Interiors, however, would be shot at Paramount in Hollywood, with set designers taking the liberty of building an enormous pad for Holly that could never have fitted into that narrow Manhattan brownstone.

Audrey found it difficult working with George Peppard, her first leading man from the Lee Strasberg school of acting. His reliance on the Method was the opposite of her own technique, which was no method at all. "I never really became an actress—in the sense that when people ask me how I did it, my only answer is 'I wouldn't know.' I just walked on the set knowing my lines and took it from there," she once said.

When production of *Breakfast at Tiffany's* shifted to Hollywood, Audrey had her first meeting with Holly Golightly's coyly named "Cat," played by a tiger tom descended from the one who enacted Rhubarb in Paramount's 1951 comedy about a feline that inherits a baseball team. Since Audrey brought Famous to work with her every day, she feared that the two animals wouldn't get along, but much to her relief they did. Perhaps Famous felt sorry for Cat for having to be drenched to the skin for several days running for a scene with a simulated rainstorm.

Audrey started another longtime collaboration during *Breakfast at Tiffany's*, this time with Henry Mancini, then known mainly as a music arranger and composer of the themes for Blake Edwards's TV series *Peter Gunn* and *Mr. Lucky*. Edwards thought it was time that Mancini did a movie score and gave him the job.

Since Mancini didn't write lyrics, he recommended Johnny Mercer, master of homespun classics like "Lazybones" and "I'm an Old Cowhand," to contribute the words for the song that Holly Golightly croons while strumming the guitar on the fire escape outside her apartment window. The number was supposed to establish Holly as a homesick country girl at heart. The result was "Moon River." The unforgettable words "my huckleberry friend" became permanently attached to Audrey Hepburn.

"It's usual to write a song to fill a need in a script, but in this case we were really inspired by Audrey Hepburn herself," Henry Mancini recalled. "When we met Audrey for the first time, we knew the song had to be as special as she was and keyed to the exact quality of her voice. It was one of the hardest melodies I ever had to write because I couldn't figure out what this lady would sing. Would it be a pop tune, a folk song, a blues? It took me almost a month to get it. Though the song went on to be a big hit for Andy Williams and has had over a thousand recordings over the years, no one ever performed it with more honesty, feeling, or understanding than Audrey did in the movie."

Amusingly, Johnny Mercer told Audrey that he'd taken extra special care in writing the lyrics to "Moon River" to make up for the ones he wrote for the title song for *Love in the Afternoon*, set to music by Matty Malneck. The opening went "Love in the afternoon was as sly as a wink, and as gay as a pink balloon," which proved that even Johnny Mercer had his bad days.

For the duration of the Hollywood filming of *Breakfast at Tiffany's*, the Ferrers rented a house with a swimming pool in Coldwater Canyon. At Christmas, they sent for Sean and his nanny, which made for a very happy reunion. "At last I have my two men together," Audrey told Blake Edwards.

It made residing in California more bearable for Audrey. Although the perpetual sunshine had its advantages over Switzerland in winter, she disliked the casual lifestyle, which was the antithesis of her formal European upbringing. Her refusal to drive a car after her unfortunate accident added to her feelings of isolation. Her friends were mainly those she'd acquired through Mel, who'd known most of them many years. Gregory Peck and his French wife, Veronique, and producer Jerry Wald and wife, Connie, were the closest.

Agent Kurt Frings tried to encourage a friendship between Audrey and his other superstar client Elizabeth Taylor, who'd just arrived in Los Angeles to convalesce from a near-fatal bout with pneumonia in England while filming *Cleopatra*. The Ferrers began socializing with Taylor and her husband, Eddie Fisher, but the two women never grew close, probably because they were incompatible types. Audrey was refined and caring of others, Taylor ribald and totally self-centered.

Their husbands got along better, with the common bond (and mutual dilemma) of being married to two of the world's reigning beauties. Mel was unemployed, so he volunteered to lend Fisher a hand in preparing for his pending comeback at the Desert Inn in Las Vegas. The singer's career had been dormant since he married Taylor in 1959 and got submerged in her activities. Mel worked several weeks with Fisher, helping him to pick material for a new act and coaching him in stage technique.

In April, the Ferrers and Fishers attended the Academy Awards ceremonies at Santa Monica Civic Auditorium, Audrey gowned by Givenchy and Elizabeth by Dior. No nomination for Audrey Hepburn this year (*The Unforgiven* being her only 1960 release), but she was handing out the Best Picture award. Nominee Elizabeth Taylor, sporting a tracheotomy scar, was expected to win the sympathy vote and the Best Actress Oscar for *Butterfield 8*, which she did. The tumultuous standing ovation for Taylor was a hard act to follow, but Audrey at least had the pleasure of presenting the Best Picture Oscar to her beloved Billy Wilder for *The Apartment*.

While Audrey was in the midst of filming *Breakfast at Tiffany's*, William Wyler offered her one of the leading roles in a new version of Lillian Hellman's first Broadway play, *The Children's Hour*. The director had previously filmed it for producer Samuel Goldwyn in 1935 as *These Three*. At that time, the play's focus on an alleged lesbian relationship between two teachers had caused such a public outrage that Hollywood's ultrastrict moral guardian, the Hays Office, not only insisted on changing it into a heterosexual love triangle, but also ruled that no mention of the original title could be used in the credits or in the advertising and publicity.

Audrey couldn't very well say no to the director who helped her to win an Oscar for *Roman Holiday*, but she wondered if she needed the dubious honor of being in one of the first films to take advantage of the industry's recently liberalized Production Code. A quarter of a century after *These Three*, themes of unconventional sexuality were now permissible, provided they were treated with "care, discretion, and restraint."

Audrey was even more concerned about the cast of *The Children's Hour*, which would be the first movie where she wasn't the sole female star. Though she'd proved that she could stand up to the likes of Gregory Peck, Humphrey Bogart, and Gary Cooper, would she be able to hold her own opposite another woman, especially one with the scenestealing reputation of Shirley MacLaine, whom Wyler wanted as Audrey's co-star?

Signing for *The Children's Hour* also meant that the Ferrer family would have to extend their stay in Los Angeles, but in the end Audrey decided to risk it. William Wyler's last movie, *Ben-Hur*, had won a record twelve Oscars and grossed $100 million. Saying no to him would have been tantamount to rejecting God.

chapter twelve
SHIRLEY, BILL, AND CARY

After Holly Golightly, Karen Wright, Audrey's character in *The Children's Hour*, seemed downright drab. The co-owner of a private girl's school where she also teaches, Karen is getting ready to marry the town doctor when a disgruntled student starts rumors that Karen is involved in an "unnatural" relationship with Martha Dobie, the school's other owner-teacher.

Because of the recent death of her longtime companion, novelist Dashiell Hammett, Lillian Hellman resigned the job of rewriting her 1935 screenplay. John Michael Hayes, best known for his scripts for Alfred Hitchcock's *Rear Window* and *To Catch a Thief*, took over, restoring the lesbian content and contemporizing the action to the 1960s. Interestingly, Hellman got the idea for her original stage play from a famous scandal in Scotland in the early nineteenth century, although she transposed her fictional account to New England in the 1930s.

James Garner, a muscular actor who gained stardom portraying gambler cowboy Bret Maverick in a long-running TV series, got the role of Audrey's lover (acted in *These Three* by Joel McCrea). For the publicity value, William Wyler tried to persuade his original Karen and

Martha, Merle Oberon and Miriam Hopkins, to enact supporting roles in the movie. But only Hopkins seemed able to accept the fact that she'd reached an age for character work. She took on the role of Martha's selfish aunt, with Fay Bainter replacing Oberon as the imperious grandmother of the troublemaking student.

After agreeing to make *The Children's Hour*, Audrey became nervous about the lesbian content. To placate her, the "L" word was never actually spoken in the script by anyone. The burden of proof, so to speak, fell to Shirley MacLaine, whose Martha is a fairly obvious "butch." But it's never made clear whether Karen feels anything more than platonic friendship for Martha. In the end, Martha commits suicide from guilt over the chaos that her infatuation with Karen has caused.

Years later, Shirley MacLaine expressed regret at the bland way in which homosexuality was portrayed in the movie. "I should have fought more with Willie Wyler to investigate the lesbian relationship," she said. "John Michael Hayes had not pulled any punches in the script. In one scene, I baked a chocolate cake for Audrey, cut it like a work of art, placed the slices on doilies just so. Every nuance was the act of a lover. There were several scenes like that, but Wyler was afraid, so they were cut from the script the day before we started shooting. And I'd built the concept of my character on precisely those scenes."

Off-camera, Audrey and MacLaine became great friends, surprising those who thought the latter might be too far-out for the reserved princess. MacLaine's marriage to theatrical producer Steve Parker was one of the most unconventional in Hollywood; he lived and worked in Tokyo, where he also had charge of their five-year-old daughter, Stephanie Sachiko. Fancy that happening in the Ferrer family.

"I had plenty of qualms when I met Audrey for the first time during rehearsals," Shirley MacLaine recalled. "It took me quite a while to thaw her out—about three hours. From then on, it was one big kick. We had a running gag all through the making of the picture. She was supposed to teach me how to dress and I was supposed to teach her how to cuss. Neither of us succeeded."

For the black-and-white movie, Audrey's first since *Love in the Afternoon,* both women went along with William Wyler's dictum of conservative wardrobes appropriate to small-town school mistresses. Since it was hardly an assignment for Givenchy, Audrey picked Dorothy Jeakins, her designer for *Green Mansions* and *The Unforgiven.* MacLaine was in awe of Audrey's fashion sense and chose Jeakins as well.

During the filming at Samuel Goldwyn Studios, Audrey often made it her own children's hour, bringing her two babies, Sean and Mr. Famous, with her. Sean was just starting to walk and spent most of his time in a playpen in Audrey's dressing trailer, looked after by his nanny when Mama had to be on the set. Not so easily contained, Famous had a tendency to run off and get lost. One day, after he'd been missing for an hour, Audrey sent the entire studio police squad to find him. When finally located, Famous was sitting atop a high brick wall on the backlot and petrified of coming down.

Audrey rushed to the scene, but no amount of coaxing would bring the terrier down. Apparently he'd gotten there via some scaffolding attached to the wall, so Audrey finally climbed up and swept him into her arms.

Several weeks later, while the whole family was visiting some friends in Los Angeles, Mr. Famous slipped out of the house and was run over by a car on Wilshire Boulevard. Audrey mourned him like a mother who had just lost her first-born child. Fortunately, this one could be replaced. Mel soon surprised her with another Yorkie from the same breeding kennel in Paris. Named "Assam of Assam," he became known as "Sam." His new mother adored him. Her family was complete again.

After Audrey finished *The Children's Hour*, the Ferrers returned to Europe. Now it was Mel's turn to work, but the rest of the family would stay in Burgenstock while he traveled to France for *The Longest Day*, Darryl F. Zanuck's $15 million epic about the Allied invasion of Normandy. Portraying the American Major General Robert Haines, Mel was part of a huge international cast headed by John Wayne, Robert Mitchum, Henry Fonda, Richard Burton, and Sean Connery.

Audrey didn't accompany Mel on the trip because she thought that watching the re-creation of World War II combat would be too upsetting. She would never forget hearing about the D-Day invasion on Radio Orange in Holland, or the despair that she suffered when it took almost another year for the Allies to liberate her homeland.

When Mel got back from France, life settled down to as close to normal as it ever would be for the Ferrers. Audrey devoted herself to being a full-time wife and mother, the roles she'd dreamed of all her life. With help, of course, from nanny Gina and other servants, she tended Sean, supervised the meals, puttered in the garden, and so forth. Mel usually played tennis or golf every morning in the Burgenstock facilities. The couple made a weekly shopping trip to Lucerne but otherwise stuck close to home, taking hikes in the country, catching up on their reading, going to bed early. Neither did much skiing; they didn't want to risk any accidents that could ruin their filming schedules.

In October, *Breakfast at Tiffany's* broke box-office records in its premiere at Radio City Music Hall (as might be expected for a movie with Audrey Hepburn *and* New York City as its stars). Surprisingly, the movie did not become a huge blockbuster, doing well only in so-called urban sophisticated markets in the United States and ending up with about $4 million in domestic rentals (for comparison purposes, Paramount's most successful release of that year, *The World of Suzie Wong*, returned $7.5 million in the U.S.). Internationally, where Audrey always enjoyed her greatest popularity, the movie did better than in the U.S., earning another $6 million. Many countries changed the locally meaningless title. In France, it was released as *Diamants sur Canapé*.

Though Truman Capote described the movie as "a mawkish valentine to Audrey Hepburn," her performance was warmly received by most critics and made an enormous impact at the time. Holly Golightly became the free spirit of the Kennedy generation, with "Moon River" one of its theme songs. Young women made a craze of little black dresses, beehive hairdos, and enormous dark glasses. Animal adoption agencies couldn't keep up with the demand for orange-colored cats.

In December, United Artists rushed out *The Children's Hour* to qualify for the 1961 Oscar derby. Amusingly, UA had fears of the public confusing it with a Disney movie and had almost changed the title to *Infamous*, which Lillian Hellman vetoed. Later, when the movie bombed at the box office, she agreed to the title *The Loudest Whisper* for the overseas release.

United Artists tried to market the movie on its bold content, which apparently wasn't explicit enough to attract the prurient-minded. Critic Pauline Kael called it "a portentous, lugubrious dirge." The teaming of Hepburn and MacLaine didn't impress either. Archer Winsten wrote, "Instead of being wowed by an off-beat combination, we get a pair of off-hand performances in a sentimental slob of a film." *Time* magazine said that Audrey gave "her standard, frail, indomitable characterization, which is to say that her eyes watered constantly (frailty) and her chin is forever cantilevered forward (indomitability)."

UA's gifts to the press that Christmas must have been unusually generous. Columnists were predicting an Oscar race in which Audrey and Shirley would not only be competing against each other for Best Actress, but ending in a dead heat and sharing the award.

Chances of that happening ended in February 1962 with the announcement of the 1961 Oscar nominations. The only woman nominated for *The Children's Hour* was Fay Bainter, who played the role of the grandmother, as Best Supporting Actress.

Audrey Hepburn was nominated for Best Actress (the fourth time since the first in 1953), but for her performance as Holly Golightly in *Breakfast at Tiffany's*. Also nominated were Piper Laurie for *The Hustler*, Sophia Loren for *Two Women*, Geraldine Page for *Summer and Smoke* (a role first offered to Audrey), and Natalie Wood for *Splendor in the Grass*.

Surprisingly, though *Breakfast at Tiffany's* had been one of the most memorable movies of 1961, it failed to be nominated for Best Picture. (*Fanny*, *The Guns of Navarone*, *The Hustler*, *Judgment at Nuremberg*, and *West Side Story* were.) But George Axelrod did receive a screenplay nomination for his adaptation of Truman Capote's novella.

Leaving Sean behind with his nanny, Audrey and Mel flew to Los Angeles for the presentation telecast on April 9. Audrey purchased a new Givenchy gown for the occasion, but on Oscar night found herself sick in bed with the flu at the Beverly Hills Hotel. "I could kick myself," she told Louella Parsons by phone. "It was a long way to come just to watch a television show in a hotel room."

Audrey wasn't too surprised when Sophia Loren won for *Two Women*, making Oscar history with the first foreign-language performance to be so honored. Audrey received a consolation prize of sorts when Henry Mancini and Johnny Mercer paid tribute to her while accepting the Best Song Oscar for "Moon River." Mancini won an additional Oscar for his background score to *Breakfast at Tiffany's*.

Incredibly, "Moon River" almost ended up on the cutting room floor. "We previewed the movie in San Francisco and went to a nearby hotel to discuss what had obviously been a very good audience reaction," Henry Mancini remembered. "We all deferred to Paramount's new president, who paced the room puffing a cigar and whose first utterance was 'Well, I can tell you one thing, we can get rid of that song.' Audrey shot right up out of her chair and said, 'Over my dead body!' Mel Ferrer had to put his hand on her arm to restrain her. That's the closest I ever saw her come to losing control."

Although *Breakfast at Tiffany's* had a major influence on fashion that year, it failed to even get nominated for costume design. The Oscar winner was Irene Sharaff for *West Side Story*. The other nominated films were *Babes in Toyland*, *Back Street*, *Flower Drum Song* and *Pocketful of Miracles*. Ironically, in the separate category for black-and-white films, Dorothy Jeakins received a nomination for *The Children's Hour*, but Piero Gherardi ended up winning for *La Dolce Vita*.

While in Los Angeles, the Ferrers did some business dealing. Despite the fiasco of *Green Mansions*, Mel was determined to make another movie with Audrey. This time he came up with an idea that suited her perfectly—the title role in *Peter Pan*, the boy who never grew up (traditionally enacted by a woman, starting with Maude Adams on the stage in 1905 and most recently with Mary Martin on television in 1955). With himself as producer-director, Mel envisioned casting Peter Sellers as Captain Hook and Hayley Mills as Wendy, but the project eventually encountered opposition from the British charitable trust that owned the rights to James M. Barrie's play. Because of a protective clause in a deal made with Walt Disney for a 1953 cartoon version, no film could be made in competition for twenty-five years.

Instead, Audrey became a victim of circumstances when Paramount suddenly realized that her contract was due to expire at the end of 1962 and that she still owed the studio one picture. As luck would have it, Paramount found itself in a similar situation with William Holden, so production head Martin Rackin decided that the most expedient and economical solution would be a teaming of Audrey and Holden rather than separate films for each.

One can only imagine what a tizzy that caused the story department in trying to find a suitable property, but George Axelrod, the scriptwriter of *Breakfast at Tiffany's*, suggested an adaptation of one of his favorite foreign movies, Julien Duvivier's *La Fête à Henriette (Holiday for Henrietta)*, a French comedy that briefly played the American art circuits in 1955. Audrey and Holden seemed ideally suited for the story about a secretary who helps a famous screenwriter to come up with ideas for a romantic comedy to be filmed on location in Paris.

Paramount wanted George Axelrod to collaborate again with director Blake Edwards, but the latter had other commitments and recommended his friend and mentor Richard Quine. Paramount approved. Quine had previously directed Holden in the highly successful *The World of Suzie Wong* and also managed to control the actor's drinking problem during the filming.

Audrey panicked when Paramount confronted her with the project, which Axelrod had entitled *Paris When It Sizzles* (lifted from the lyrics to Cole Porter's "I Love Paris"). She doubted that she could cope with Bill Holden after the disastrous love affair that took place during the filming of *Sabrina*. Though eight years had passed, she still received birthday flowers and occasional phone calls that made it plain he still cared deeply for her.

Ironically, Holden also now resided in Switzerland, about 150 miles west of Burgenstock in St. Prex, near Lausanne. While still married to Ardis (the ex-Brenda Marshall), who lived there full-time with their two sons, he spent most of his time traveling for film assignments or checking on his extensive business holdings in the Far East and Africa. While making

The Lion in Kenya in 1961, Holden started what developed into a long but sporadic liaison with his French co-star, Capucine. (Born Germaine Lefebvre, she adopted the French word for nasturtium as a professional name in a prior career as a fashion model.)

Paramount sent Richard Quine to Burgenstock to talk Audrey into accepting *Paris When It Sizzles*. The director and ex-actor was experiencing romantic trauma of his own at the time, having just been jilted by Kim Novak, so he was sympathetic to Audrey's apprehension about working with Holden and managed to calm her fears. Quine believed that the only problem with Holden would be in trying to keep him away from booze.

The role of secretary Gabrielle Simpson found Audrey Hepburn pounding a typewriter for the first time, though the character wasn't the typical office drudge. With her vivid imagination, she helps blocked writer Richard Benson knock out a complete movie script in forty-eight hours. Before committing the major scenes to paper, they act them out in fantasy, so *Paris When It Sizzles* often turns into a movie within a movie.

The City of Light was fast becoming the dominant setting of Audrey's movies, with *Paris When It Sizzles* the third so far. Production became a problem in logistics for the Ferrer family because Mel had a conflicting commitment. He could only spend two weeks with Audrey and Sean in Paris before leaving for a role in *The Fall of the Roman Empire*, an all-star epic with Sophia Loren, Alec Guinness, Stephen Boyd, and James Mason being filmed at the Samuel Bronston Studios in Madrid.

Now with a rambunctious nearly two-year-old son to contend with, Audrey considered the Raphaël Hotel, her usual Paris home, too confining, so Paramount found a furnished house that suited her requirements. Built in the eighteenth century on what was then the only connecting road to Fontainebleu, the Château Crespierre was near the Studios de Boulogne and came equipped with twenty-four-hour-a-day security guards to scare off potential burglars and kidnappers.

Ironically, while the Ferrers were settling in, someone broke into their chalet in Burgenstock and stole many items, including Audrey's Oscar for *Roman Holiday*. Police eventually found everything in the possession of Jean-Claude Thouroude, a third-year university student and lovesick Audrey Hepburn fan who confessed to robbing the place in disappointment over not finding her at home! Amusingly, a tenderhearted magistrate ruled that "love is not a crime." Thouroude got off lightly with a fine of 250 francs (about fifty-five dollars) and a suspended sentence of six months in jail.

Filming of *Paris When It Sizzles* began in July 1962. William Holden later confessed to arriving in the city feeling like "a condemned man walking the last mile. I realized that I had to face Audrey and I had to deal with my drinking. And I didn't think I could handle either situation."

If Audrey was shocked by Holden's deterioration in the eight years since their affair, she kept it to herself. To Holden, she seemed as irresistible as ever, which only made him suffer more. No doubt he was also tormented whenever Audrey brought Sean to the studio. If Holden had been capable of siring, they might have married and had their own children by this time.

Partly for selfish reasons and partly out of concern for Holden's weathered looks, Audrey got very upset when she saw the first rushes taken by cinematographer Claude Renoir, a nephew of master director Jean Renoir and a grandson of the great Impressionist painter Pierre Auguste Renoir. Though Claude had created beautiful canvases of his own in classics like his uncle's *The River* and *The Golden Coach*, he preferred working under natural conditions and avoided the lighting tricks and lens filters that helped many Hollywood stars appear more beautiful or handsome than they really were.

"Audrey could be very, very critical of herself on-screen," Richard Quine recalled. "She just hated the way that she and Bill Holden looked, which wasn't necessarily Claude Renoir's fault but I had no option but to discharge him. Of course, firing a Renoir is tantamount to treason in France, so the unions raised hell and threatened to go on strike. But Claude proved a real sport, finally persuading them to permit Charles Lang to come over from Hollywood. Charlie won an Oscar nomination for photographing *Sabrina*, Audrey and Bill's previous picture together, so he knew exactly what was needed to keep both of them happy."

Among other things, Lang knew how to deal

with one of Audrey's major obsessions, a crooked front tooth. After she saw the scenes photographed by Claude Renoir, she was so horrified that she wanted to have it straightened.

"Holden and I threatened to absolutely maim her if she changed that tooth," Richard Quine said later. "It was one of the oddities that made her special. She was the charmer of the world and a delight to work with. She didn't have a false bone in her body, absolutely not a flaw, professional, kind, gentle, considerate, no temperament at all."

Though Audrey portrayed a low-paid secretary, the movie's fantasy scenes gave her plenty of opportunity to wear elegant ensembles designed by Hubert de Givenchy. Audiences watching *Paris When It Sizzles* would not be able to detect it, but she also spritzed herself with Givenchy's L'Interdit. His screen credit would read "Miss Hepburn's wardrobe and perfume by Hubert de Givenchy," the first time since the 1960 *Scent of Mystery* (produced in the Smell-O-Vision process) that a movie left itself wide open for critical branding as a stinker.

L'Interdit was a fragrance that Givenchy created for Audrey's personal use in 1957 as a surprise. Perhaps he thought he could also have no better guinea pig to test its appeal. In any case, so many of her friends loved it and wanted some for themselves that she kept urging Givenchy to put it on the market. He was now getting ready to launch it, and Audrey had offered to help by lending her face to the advertising campaign. Magazine readers all over the world would soon see a stunning full-page color ad of her veiled *visage*, photographed by Richard Avedon. The minimal pitch read: "Once she was the only woman in the world allowed to wear this perfume. L'Interdit. Created by Givenchy for Audrey Hepburn."

Besides perfume, Richard Quine and George Axelrod sprayed *Paris When It Sizzles* with some surprise guest appearances, including one by Mel Ferrer turning up at a costume ball disguised as Dr. Jekyll and Mr. Hyde in a two-sided rubber mask. The epicene Noel Coward portrayed a starlet-chasing producer named Alexander Meyerheim. Marlene Dietrich, now residing in Paris when not globe-trotting with her one-woman concert show, played herself, speaking not a word as she stepped out of a white Rolls-Royce dressed in a gorgeous white suit and hat designed by Christian Dior.

Production originally scheduled for three months took four because of William Holden's heavy drinking. He hit the bottle early and continued through the day. "Bill was like a punch-drunk fighter, walking on his heels, listing slightly, talking punchy. He didn't know he was drunk," Richard Quine recalled.

Some mornings Holden arrived with a pet African bush baby on his shoulder and a big grin on his face. "We knew we were in for trouble," Quine said. "Audrey tried to stay calm, cool, and collected, but working with Bill was a torment for her."

One evening at quitting time, Quine and George Axelrod walked a tipsy Holden to the studio parking lot, intending to send him home safely in a limousine. Holden suddenly glanced back in the direction of his co-star's dressing room and said, "Oh, I forgot to say good night to Audrey." Before Quine or Axelrod could stop him, he was climbing up the building wall to her suite, which was located on the second floor.

Hearing the commotion, Audrey stuck her head out the window and tried to shout him down. "You stop that, Bill!" she yelled. But he continued, finally getting close enough to give her a kiss on the cheek. Then he suddenly lost his grip and fell backwards, landing with a thud on the hood of a parked car. He seemed unhurt, but came to work limping the next day.

Paramount flew in Holden's wife from Switzerland to try to control him, but that only angered him, and he soon sent her packing. Richard Quine finally persuaded Holden to enter the Château de Garche, a hospital for alcoholics, for an eight-day drying-out treatment. George Axelrod hurriedly wrote some scenes for another guest star, Tony Curtis, who flew over from Hollywood so they could keep the cameras grinding during Holden's absence.

Upon his release, Holden returned to work exhilarated. He behaved as if nothing had happened, and no one dared remind him. Quine and Axelrod tried to make up for lost time by rewriting the script and removing any strenuous physical action that Holden might not be able to handle.

Meanwhile, Mel Ferrer had been working in Spain in *The Fall of the Roman Empire*. The gossip press was having a field day speculating on his activities—and Audrey's—while they were separated. In Madrid, Mel was often seen in the company of the young and beautiful Duchess of Quintanilla. In Paris, Audrey had been spotted dining with Holden at Tour d'Argent and Maxim's. Questions about infidelities, divorce, and remarriage were raised. None were answered.

Prior to starting *Paris When It Sizzles*, Audrey had been visited by Stanley Donen, director of *Funny Face*, who now had an independent company called Grandon in partnership with Cary Grant. The duo had already produced two films with Grant starring and Donen directing: *Indiscreet*, co-starring Ingrid Bergman, and *The Grass Is Greener*, with Deborah Kerr, Robert Mitchum, and Jean Simmons.

Donen brought Audrey something to read, a script by Peter Stone entitled *Charade*. The romantic thriller poked gentle fun at some of Cary Grant's collaborations with Alfred Hitchcock, especially *To Catch a Thief* and *North by Northwest*. Audrey loved it, as well as the chance it offered to finally work opposite Grant. They'd come close three times, first with *Roman Holiday*, and then with *Sabrina* and *Love in the Afternoon*. But Grant chickened out each time because of the quarter-century age gap between them.

Audrey agreed to make the movie, but only after agent Kurt Frings made sure that she got a percentage of the gross in addition to her $750,000 fee. Cary Grant stood to earn $5 million in percentages from his latest hit, *A Touch of Mink*. Why shouldn't Audrey get a slice of this one, even though it would be smaller than Grant's, since he was co-producer as well as star.

As luck would have it, Donen and Grant intended filming *Charade* on location in Paris. Audrey had insisted on taking a month's break in Switzerland after finishing *Paris When It Sizzles*, but that became impossible because of the delays on the Paramount movie. Her new employer, Universal Pictures, took over the lease of the Château Crespierre, which spared the upset of moving to another temporary home.

Mel rejoined his family there when he finished working in Spain. The Duchess of Quintanilla no longer seemed a threat to the marriage, if she ever was one. As for William Holden, he'd gone to Africa with Capucine to make another movie.

In *Charade*, Audrey portrayed Regina Lambert, a recent widow being stalked by a gang hunting for a stolen fortune that her husband may have hidden before his murder. A mysterious stranger who changes his name as often as his Savile Row suits comes to her rescue, but Reggie gradually comes to suspect him as her husband's killer.

Charade marked Cary Grant's seventieth movie, as well as the thirtieth anniversary of his film career (preceded by fourteen years in vaudeville and stage plays). At age fifty-eight, he was the oldest of Audrey's leading men so far, and extremely sensitive about it. By his decree, there would be only one passionate kiss between them in the entire movie.

Writer Peter Stone recalled that Grant

"thought he'd be called a dirty old man. He made me change the dynamic of the characters and make Audrey the aggressor. She chased him, and he tried to dissuade her. She pursued him and sat in his lap. She found him irresistible, and ultimately he was worn down by her. I gave him lines like 'I'm too old for you, get away from me, little girl.' And 'I'm old enough to be your father.' And in the elevator: 'I could be in trouble transporting you beyond the first floor. A minor!' This way Cary couldn't get in any trouble. What could he do? She was chasing him. He wasn't coming on. There's even a line where she kisses him—while they're dining on the *bateau-mouche*—and he says, 'When you come on, you come on.' And she says, 'Well, come on.'"

Throughout the film, Grant kept dropping lines like "At my age, who wants to hear the word 'serious'?" whenever Audrey started getting romantic notions about him. But Audrey's doelike eyes gazed on him with such longing that it was plain their ages didn't matter. When she asks Grant, "Do you know what's wrong with you?" she immediately supplies her own answer. "Nothing!"

Most of the loveplay was done humorously. Teasing Grant about his dimple, Audrey asks him, "How do you shave in there?" Grant's answer—"Very carefully!"—might have been even funnier if he'd been permitted to use Peter Stone's original line, "Like porcupines make love. Very carefully!" But Production Code censors considered it too risqué for the movie-going public of 1963.

Stanley Donen, who directed Audrey previously with Fred Astaire, had no problem with her playing the younger lady to the older man. "It was believable because Audrey had a maturity. She was vulnerable, but she had confidence. You might say that she had such self-confidence in what she was doing that she made those relationships work," he recalled.

Surprisingly, Audrey and Grant had never actually met before, so Donen eagerly looked forward to introducing those two magical personalities. The director remembered: "I arranged a dinner at a wonderful Italian restaurant in Paris. Audrey and I arrived first. Cary came in, and Audrey stood up and said, 'I'm so nervous.' He said, 'Why?' And she said, 'Meeting you, working with you—I'm so nervous.' And he said, 'Don't be nervous, for goodness' sake. I'm thrilled to know you. Here, sit down at the table. Put your hands on the table, palms up, put your head down and take a few deep breaths.' We all sat down, and Audrey put her hands on the table. I had ordered a bottle of red wine. When she put her head down, she hit the bottle, and the wine went all over Cary's cream-colored suit. Audrey was humiliated. People at other tables were looking, and everybody was buzzing. It was a horrendous moment. Cary was a half hour from his hotel, so he took off his coat and comfortably sat through the whole meal like that."

Audrey's own memory of that incident: "Cary took it so well, rather like he did in *Charade* itself when I dropped the ice cream on his suit. That scene came out of the experience in the restaurant. Can you imagine how I felt? I wanted to crawl into a hole. I felt terrible and kept apologizing, but Cary was so dear about it. The next day he sent me a box of caviar with a little note telling me not to feel bad."

Heading the supporting cast of *Charade* were two actors who later became stars in their own right, Walter Matthau and James Coburn. Because of the popularity of "Moon River," Stanley Donen re-teamed Henry Mancini and Johnny Mercer to write the title song for *Charade*, with Mancini also composing the film's background score. Givenchy again designed Audrey's wardrobe; her short-jacketed suits, pillbox hats, and head scarves worn with huge sunglasses started fashion fads.

As a result of the delays on *Paris When It Sizzles*, the filming of *Charade* had to take place in Paris when the city can be bone-chilling, starting at the end of October 1962. Since it turned out to be France's coldest fall and winter in more than a century, the Ferrer family shuttled back and forth between the Hotel Raphaël and their rented Château Crespierre, which lacked central heating and became uninhabitable during the frostier spells. It reminded Audrey all too painfully of her last winter in Arnhem before the war ended.

With large portions of *Charade* taking place outdoors, working conditions were often unbearable. At Audrey's insistence, Stanley Donen had retained Charles Lang from *Paris When It Sizzles* to be the cinematographer. This time Lang had not only Audrey to please but also Cary Grant, who was even more demanding. Nearing sixty,

285

Grant needed to be lighted very carefully and preferred three-quarter shots to close-ups because of his weathered looks.

Perhaps for lack of anything better to do, the Paris press hinted that Grant, recently divorced from actress Betsy Drake, had taken a romantic interest in Audrey, but nothing could have been further from the truth. Grant had fallen hard for a twenty-five-year-old starlet named Dyan Cannon, who was then getting ready to appear in a Broadway play and couldn't be with him.

Audrey and Grant were, at best, a mutual admiration society. "I think he understood me better than I did myself," she said years later. "He was observant and had a penetrating knowledge of people. He would talk often about relaxing and getting rid of one's fears, which I think he found a way to do. But he never preached. If he helped me, he did it without my knowing, and with a gentleness which made me lose my sense of being intimidated. I had this great affection for him because I knew he understood me. It was an unspoken friendship, which was wonderful. He would open up his arms wide when he saw you, and hug you, and smile, and let you know how he felt about you. We lived at other ends of the world, but it was always the same."

Audrey added, "While you might not think it, Cary was a vulnerable man, and he recognized my own vulnerability. We had that in common. He had more wisdom than I to help me with it. There was something mystic about Cary which I've never been able to put my finger on, but I think he had a deep perception of life. He said one thing very important to me one day when I was probably twitching and being nervous. We were sitting next to each other waiting for the next shot. And he laid his hand on my two hands and said, 'You've got to learn to like yourself a little more.' I've often thought about that.''

By Christmas, Dyan Cannon's Broadway play, *The Fun Couple*, had opened to nasty reviews and closed after only three performances, so Grant flew her to Paris to spend the holidays with him. On New Year's Eve, Audrey and Mel invited them to a small dinner party, together with a select group from the *Charade* unit.

Scriptwriter Peter Stone recalls: "Audrey had a marvelous château outside Paris and a staff that served with white gloves. It was very formal, very fancy living. For New Year's Eve there were eight of us, Audrey, her husband, Mel Ferrer, Cary and Dyan Cannon, Stanley Donen and his then wife, Adele, a great beauty who had been married to Lord Beatty, and my wife, Mary, and me. Audrey served enormous Idaho-type baked potatoes, and everybody spooned sour cream and Russian caviar from Cary's five-pound tin into them. It was as glamorous an evening as one can imagine, but it was truly boring. It wasn't anybody's fault. Nobody there was boring. Far from it. But it was just one of those terrible evenings where nobody got any conversation going. Nobody was in great humor. Cary and Dyan were arguing a bit. Mel and Audrey were arguing a bit, and Stanley and Adele were arguing a bit. The only ones who remained happily married to each other were Mary and me."

Meanwhile, *Paris When It Sizzles* had fizzled in sneak previews. Test audiences were bewildered by its offbeat humor and the cutting back and forth between the real story and the one being written for a movie script. As a consequence, Paramount fiddled with it in the editing room for a year and a half, finally releasing it to unfavorable reviews and disastrous box office in the spring of 1964. It was a less than glorious ending to Audrey's and William Holden's tenure at Paramount, where they had made some of their best movies.

Though filmed after *Paris When It Sizzles*, *Charade* reached theater screens six months earlier and turned out to be Audrey's biggest box-office hit yet, no doubt helped by the presence of Cary Grant, the most potent drawing card of all her leading men so far. Not surprisingly, *Charade* broke all records in its premiere at New York's 6,000-seat Radio City Music Hall, where Grant ranked as its "all-time box-office champion." Over the years, twenty-five of Grant's films had been shown there, for a total playing time of ninety-nine weeks.

Although Audrey Hepburn couldn't hope to come anywhere near that record, she herself was a Music Hall champion. *Charade* became the sixth of her eleven starring films to date to debut there, a stunning achievement for a span of only ten years.

chapter thirteen

ACCUSTOMED TO HER FACE

After Audrey finished *Charade* in February 1963, the whole family flew back to Switzerland to enjoy what remained of the winter season. The strain of making two movies in eight months, with no break in between, left Audrey physically exhausted and emotionally drained. Mel's working sojourn in Spain hadn't helped. They were becoming strangers to each other, and to their son, now going on three. They all needed to get reacquainted and to spend more time together.

Audrey desperately wanted to have another baby, but nature wasn't cooperating. Meanwhile, Sean had grown into a precocious charmer with expressive eyes like his mother's and sandy blond hair that eventually darkened to brown. His parents were trying hard not to spoil him and were determined to give him a multilingual upbringing. Though English was the family's language of choice, Audrey and Mel were also training Sean in French and the local Swiss-German. He could also babble away in Italian, which he picked up from nanny Gina.

In the last week of May, Audrey and Mel flew to New York on a topsecret mission. Some highly placed friends in the Democratic party had asked

Audrey to make a surprise appearance at a forty-sixth birthday party for President Kennedy at the Waldorf-Astoria Hotel. How could she refuse? On several occasions, JFK had personally telephoned her from the White House to rave about one of her performances and to tell her that he was her number-one fan.

When Audrey stood up to sing "Happy Birthday, Mr. President," no one could have known that there would be no more such celebrations after this one.

Back in Switzerland again, Audrey received confirmation of a hush-hush deal that Kurt Frings had been negotiating for months. One of the most coveted roles since Scarlett O'Hara in *Gone With the Wind*—Eliza Doolittle in the movie of *My Fair Lady*—was hers. Deep in her heart, Audrey had longed to play the part since seeing Julie Andrews do it on Broadway in 1956, but she doubted she'd ever get the chance because of her meager musical qualifications.

But Hollywood moguls often work in mysterious ways, and Jack L. Warner, one of the last of the originals still active, wanted no one but Audrey Hepburn. *The Nun's Story* being his studio's highest grosser in years ($14 million) was one reason; her top ranking in the box-office popularity polls was another. She was especially big in Europe and Japan, which should overcome their usual resistance to Hollywood musicals. Warner had spent $5.5 million just for the screen rights to *My Fair Lady* and would need to lavish at least twice that on production costs. He couldn't risk the logical choice of Julie Andrews, who had yet to make a Hollywood movie and lacked a track record at the box office.

For Audrey's services, Kurt Frings demanded $1 million plus a percentage of the profits, which sent Warner into shock. Warner Brothers had never paid that much to a star in its thirty-nine-year history. However, Kurt Frings made it relatively painless by requesting that the money be paid out over a period of ten years, which would save Audrey a bundle in income taxes.

Warner Brothers purchased the screen rights to *My Fair Lady* from the Columbia Broadcasting System (CBS), which had invested $400,000 in the Broadway stage production and subsequently became the 100 percent owner by acquiring the interests of writer-lyricist Alan Jay Lerner, composer Frederick Loewe, and director Moss Hart. As a condition of the film deal, Jack Warner had to promise CBS 50 percent of gross revenues above $20 million, which made it his studio's biggest financial gamble ever. Playing it close to the vest, Warner appointed himself the producer, the first time that he became personally involved in every detail of a movie, from the casting on down.

Warner offered Cary Grant the role of Professor Henry Higgins, but Grant felt he could never equal Rex Harrison's performance on the stage and refused. When Laurence Olivier, Richard Burton, and Peter O'Toole all rebuffed Warner for the same reason, he begrudgingly hired Harrison, who had been branded "box-office poison" after a string of Hollywood flops for 20th Century--Fox circa 1946–49. Because of his tarnished film record, Harrison had to settle for a flat fee of $200,000, peanuts next to Audrey's deal despite a role of equal importance.

To compensate for Harrison's alleged weakness at the box office, Warner tried to coax James Cagney, once one of the studio's biggest draws, from retirement to play Eliza's irrepressible father, Alfred P. Doolittle. The casting wasn't as loony as it might seem; though Cagney excelled at acting gangsters and tough guys, he was also a masterful song-and-dance performer. But he also hated Jack Warner's guts for harsh treatment over the years and rejected the offer, causing Warner to fall back on the Broadway production's Doolittle, Stanley Holloway.

Since Warner Brothers had not been a major force in musicals since the glory days of Busby Berkley in the 1930s, Jack Warner wanted to borrow the sovereign Vincente Minnelli from MGM to direct *My Fair Lady*. Minnelli was also the personal choice of Lerner and Loewe, with whom he made the Oscar-winning *Gigi*. But the deal fell through because Warner refused to give Minnelli the same kind of lucrative percentage arrangement that Minnelli enjoyed at MGM.

Ironically, the job landed in the lap of George Cukor, whose direction of Minnelli's ex-wife Judy Garland in a *A Star Is Born* had made it one of Warner Brothers' few musicals of distinction in recent years, even though it bombed at the box office. By comparison to Minnelli, Cukor agreed to work cheap, a flat fee of $300,000 and no "points" (percentage of the profits).

The switch worked to Audrey's advantage

because Cukor had a well-deserved reputation as a woman's director (most notably with Katharine Hepburn, Greta Garbo, Joan Crawford, and Judy Holliday). Minnelli had a more visual flair and a greater command of camera technique, but he tended to treat his actors (male and female) as though they were just part of the scenery. Cukor, of course, had been longing to work with Audrey for years, ever since losing out on the chance to direct her in her Broadway debut in *Gigi*.

Audrey knew she'd need all the help she could get in portraying Eliza Doolittle. Besides the singing demands of the role, she had to portray a woman who ranked lower down the social scale than most she'd acted in the past. She'd have no problem with the "lady" that Eliza eventually becomes under Professor Higgins's tutelage, but could she make a convincing grubby street peddler with a shrill Cockney accent?

After Natasha Rostova, Rima, and Holly Golightly, Eliza Doolittle was Audrey's fourth film role where she had to contend with preconceived notions of a literary character. Of the four, Eliza probably had the widest public awareness. Starting with the original production of George Bernard Shaw's *Pygmalion* in London in 1914 starring the legendary Mrs. Patrick Campbell, Eliza had been captivating audiences for half a century, most vividly in the 1938 movie of the play with Wendy Hiller and then in 1956 as the musicalized *My Fair Lady*. Gertrude Lawrence and Lynn Fontanne were other celebrated Elizas in *Pygmalion* on the stage.

As adapted by Lerner and Loewe, the musical

was uncommonly faithful to George Bernard Shaw's original play but used the happier romantic ending that Shaw approved for the 1938 film. (GBS died in 1950 at age ninety-four.) Lerner also wrote the screenplay, but would have slight input into the actual filming. He was furious with Jack Warner for not hiring Julie Andrews, whom he had personally selected for Eliza on Broadway after admiring her work in the British import *The Boy Friend.*

At the insistence of CBS board chairman William Paley, Warner hired Cecil Beaton to re-create the look of the original Broadway production, for which Beaton had designed the costumes and Oliver Smith the sets. Since then, Beaton had won an Oscar for his work with Vincente Minnelli on Lerner and Loewe's *Gigi,* one of the rare supermusicals produced originally for the screen instead of the stage, so Warner had no reason to dispute his qualifications.

Beaton tried to persuade Warner to film the movie in London for greater authenticity, but the latter refused to budge from the Burbank studios, where he could better control expenses. George Cukor sided with Warner. "The English are always breaking for cups of tea," he argued.

Because of the vastness of the production, Audrey was warned to expect a minimum of seven months residency in Los Angeles. For the duration, the Ferrers leased a Mediterranean-style villa high up in the hills of Bel Air, complete with swimming pool, tennis court, and a spectacular view all the way to the Pacific Ocean on a smogless day. The house came equipped with a staff of servants, augmented by Gina, Sean's Italian nanny.

In order to keep Mel close to her all those months, Audrey applied pressure at Warner Brothers to get him some work that overlapped with hers. Richard Quine, director of *Paris When It Sizzles*, came through with a featured role for Mel in *Sex and the Single Girl*, which used just the title of Helen Gurley Brown's nonfiction best-seller for a romantic romp about a respected authority on sexual matters accused of being a virginal fraud.

The side-by-side working arrangement was another severe test of the Ferrers' marriage. How does a husband cope with his wife earning a million dollars plus for *My Fair Lady* while he's working nearby in dreck for a flat fee of $35,000? Though Mel might have felt insulted, the pay was commensurate with what two bigger stars were receiving for similar featured roles in *Sex and the Single Girl*. Henry Fonda got $100,000 and Lauren Bacall $50,000. The big bucks were reserved for the top-billed principals: $750,000 for Natalie Wood and $400,000 for Tony Curtis.

The Ferrers arrived in Los Angeles in the early summer of 1963, allowing Audrey six weeks of preparation before *My Fair Lady* started filming. Except on the weekends, she spent the better part of every day shuttling back and forth between teachers and trainers. She took singing lessons from Susan Seton and also practiced with pianist Andre Previn, the movie's musical director. Hermes Pan, Fred Astaire's longtime associate and her friend since *Funny Face*, helped her brush up on her dancing skills. To perfect Eliza Doolittle's Cockney accent, she studied with Peter Ladefoged, a professor of phonetics at the University of Southern California.

Audrey adored the costumes designed by Cecil Beaton, but insisted on sending copies of his sketches to Hubert de Givenchy in Paris for a second opinion. Givenchy not only gave them his blessing, but flew to California to help with the fittings. It seemed the least he could do, given Audrey's contributions to his success. She had never demanded compensation for the use of her name and photographic likeness in the marketing of Givenchy's L'Interdit perfume. Friends claim she was too much a lady to even ask for a discount on clothes she bought for her personal wardrobe.

George Cukor agreed to Audrey's demands for filming the scenes in strict continuity so that she could grow into her role. She knew that the first half of *My Fair Lady* would be the most difficult for her to bring off because she had nothing of her own persona to contribute to the "deliciously low, horribly dirty" side of Eliza Doolittle. She wanted to do those scenes while she was still fresh and had all her strength. After that, the glamorous Eliza should be smooth sailing.

To be transformed into the unwashed churl, Audrey had to report to the studio by six in the morning to be dirtied up. Manufactured grime was painted on her face and dabbed under her fingernails and on her outer ears. Her hair had to be treated with a mix of absorbent clay and petroleum jelly to create a matted texture. Fortunately there was no need to smell bad, so she could stick with L'Interdit rather than *eau de sueur*.

In those guttersnipe scenes, Audrey also dispensed with her usual eye makeup. Without it, she had "no eyes," or so she claimed. She laughingly told Cecil Beaton that the so-called most beautiful eyes in the world were the creation of her longtime makeup adviser Alberto di Rossi.

Beaton was amazed by his first view of Audrey in that raw state. "Without the usual mascara and shadow, Audrey's eyes are like those in a Flemish painting and are even more appealing—young and sad. Yet it was extraordinary to see that simply by painting her eyes she has become a beauty in the modern sense," he noted in his diary.

Like others before him, Beaton realized that Audrey's square face would present problems, especially as the scruffy Eliza in squat straw hats. They decided not to bother with it, so Eliza's transformation into a beauty would be even more startling. For the latter, Beaton designed upswept hairdos and tall hats that gave her a more angular look and brought out her exquisite bone structure.

The white ball gown that Audrey wears in her first appearance as the transformed Eliza was a genuine antique that Beaton brought over from England. "In that absolutely sublime dress, with my hair dressed to kill, and diamonds everywhere, I felt *super*! All I had to do was walk down the staircase in Professor Higgins's house, but the dress made me do it. Clothes, like they say, make the man, but in my case, they also gave me the confidence I often needed," she recalled.

When *My Fair Lady* started filming in August, Audrey found herself caught in the middle of hostilities between Cecil Beaton and director George Cukor. Although Cukor was supposed to be boss, Beaton had to be consulted on everything concerning the costumes, decor, and overall look of the movie. A renowned photographer in addition to his other talents, Beaton also had an assignment to take exclusive stills for major magazines like *Life* and *Vogue*. He needed to be on the set all the time, especially around Audrey. Magazine editors weren't much interested in devoting covers and/or layouts to Rex Harrison or anyone else in the gifted but unnewsworthy supporting cast.

Beaton hovered around Audrey like a mother hen, fussing with her hair, makeup, and costumes until he soon drove Cukor wild. Cukor probably wasn't as upset by Beaton's devotion, which obviously was to Audrey's advantage, as he was by Beaton himself. Both men were gay, but extreme opposite types: Cukor ultraconservative and closeted, Beaton an effeminate dandy. Through mutual friend Greta Garbo, they'd been acquainted for years, but they were too disdainful of each other's lifestyles to get along harmoniously. Beaton had also once appropriated a boyfriend of Cukor's, which didn't help matters.

Audrey welcomed Beaton's attentiveness, but eventually had to discourage some of it when she realized how much it upset Cukor. Of the two men, the director was the one she needed most to deliver the performance that was expected in return for her million-dollar fee. The bickering that often erupted between Cukor and Beaton rattled her nerves and stretched the limits of her patience.

One day while Beaton was snapping pictures of Audrey working in a scene, Cukor ordered one of his assistants to ask him to leave. In future, Beaton would have to shoot Audrey during her breaks or arrange sittings in the studio portrait gallery. Beaton was outraged, but had to comply because Cukor outranked him.

Probably because of her insecurities about the role, Audrey seemed to be emulating Greta Garbo by isolating herself at the studio. Her dressing bungalow had a white picket fence around it with a "Positively Do Not Disturb" sign on the door. Visitors were restricted to Mel, Sean and his nanny, a secretary, and the requisite hair, makeup, and wardrobe people.

When she was working on the set, Audrey insisted on unobstructed sight lines. Because she was easily distracted, nobody could enter those points where she might have to look while the cameras were grinding. To make things easier, George Cukor ordered the erection of black screens which had peepholes for the technicians to look through.

Except for Cecil Beaton, who had to be tolerated, Audrey didn't want to be distracted by still photographers. The two assigned to providing the everyday coverage used for publicity and advertising had to wear black clothing and hide behind or under furniture to prevent Audrey from spotting them.

During the filming, Audrey had a cordial but cool relationship with Rex Harrison, who came to *My Fair Lady* directly from a punishing experience working opposite Elizabeth Taylor and Richard Burton in the troubled and long-delayed *Cleopatra*. Since Harrison had already given 1,006 performances as Professor Higgins on the stage in New York and London, he would have preferred making the movie with Julie Andrews rather than Audrey, who had no experience in her role and was likely to the turn the movie into another *Cleopatra* in terms of production problems.

Happily, that didn't happen. In fact, the freshness that Audrey brought to her interpretation of Eliza challenged Harrison into giving a more touching and animated performance rather than a mere carbon copy of the original, which would have been disastrous for the movie.

In George Cukor, Audrey had the good luck of getting one of those rare directors who knew exactly when to cut away with the camera and save an actor from an unconvincing performance. He had the eye of a hawk and noticed from the first day that Audrey could only be pushed so far into conveying the guttersnipe Eliza. Whenever she seemed to be having problems with her coarse accent or grimy looks, Cukor would immediately cut to a shot of Rex Harrison's reaction. Harrison would look so appalled at Audrey's ugly duckling that the audience would come to believe in it too. It was a shrewd device for marking time until the second half, when Audrey could easily handle Eliza the glorious swan.

As the director did many times in the past, most notably with Katharine Hepburn and Spencer Tracy, Cukor also had to find a common ground been Audrey's and Harrison's very disparate talents. He worked more like a stage director than a film maker, giving slight attention to the camera crew and concentrating on his two stars. Although he was never short of instructions and advice, he also encouraged them to improvise. "Feel totally free," Cukor often said. "Whatever you do, the camera will follow you, so do what you like."

At Harrison's insistence, Cukor agreed to shoot his musical numbers live, meaning that the singing would be recorded at the same time as the filming. Usually the actors would just mouth the words and then dub them in later, which made it easier for the sound technicians to balance the voices with the orchestra and to wipe out extraneous noises.

That worked fine for Rex Harrison, who, of course, wasn't a trained singer but had developed a unique half-spoken style of singing in *My Fair Lady*. But it immediately showed the limitations of Audrey's vocal talents, although George Cukor and associates refrained from telling her for fear of causing a nervous breakdown.

In Audrey's numbers with Harrison, Cukor was reluctant to stop for retakes, because the actor got angry. In Audrey's solos, the director could follow the usual procedure by having her just mouth the words and then sending her to the recording department to do the actual singing. Audrey was determined to get it right, spending hours and often days recording and rerecording every number.

But without telling her, Jack Warner ordered Ray Heinsdorf, head of the studio's music department, to hire someone to dub Audrey's singing voice. From a very limited field of such professionals, Heinsdorf chose operatically trained Marni Nixon, who in the past had proven her versatility by dubbing for actresses as different as Deborah Kerr in *The King and I* and Natalie Wood in *West Side Story*.

Needless to say, Audrey was devastated when George Cukor broke the news. To comfort her, he promised to try to salvage the best bits of her recordings and splice them into the new tracks made by Marni Nixon. But in the end, about 95 percent of the singing was Nixon's. As the gentlemanly Cukor later explained, "Marni did it prettily, and then we mixed in some of Audrey's parlando moments, which were more recitation than singing."

On November 22, Audrey was working on the Covent Garden set in the jubilant "Wouldn't It Be Loverly" production number when word flashed around the studio that President Kennedy had been assassinated in Dallas. Like everybody else around her, Audrey broke down in tears and couldn't continue. Memories of JFK's beaming face as she sang "Happy Birthday" to him only six months before flashed through her mind.

For all her outraged feelings, Audrey took charge as everybody milled around speechless.

Snatching a bullhorn from the hands of one of the assistant directors, she quaveringly announced: "The President of the United States is dead. Shall we have two minutes of silence to pray or do whatever you feel is appropriate?"

Audrey removed the straw hat she'd been wearing in the scene and bowed her head. After the pause, she continued: "May he rest in peace, and may God have mercy on his soul."

Jack Warner, a rabid Republican who'd contributed heavily to Richard Nixon's campaign against JFK in the 1960 election, wanted work to continue. But Audrey, along with everybody else in the studio that day, quietly walked off the job and went home.

The days of national mourning that followed made for one of the bleakest times in Audrey's experience, intensified by the problems she was having with *My Fair Lady* and on the domestic front. Sean had a nasty case of the flu, with high fever. Mel, having finished his movie, was without work and seemed to resent the fact that Audrey was working. They were constantly bickering, fueled by her fear that while he had time on his hands he might be philandering.

As *My Fair Lady* dragged on, Audrey's strength began to fail. Since the beginning of filming, she'd lost eight pounds, twice as much as she usually did while working. George Cukor finally arranged to shoot around her for a week while she stayed home in bed and got as much sleep as possible. She returned replenished, enabling Cukor to complete *My Fair Lady* just a few days before Christmas.

By then, Jack Warner had expended $17 million on the project, a new record high for a Hollywood-based production. The perfectionist George Cukor was badgering him to spend even more by reshooting the big Ascot Gavotte production number. Warner finally shut him up by destroying the set with a bulldozer so it couldn't be used again.

The Ferrers left immediately for Burgenstock. Audrey was determined to gain back the weight she'd lost and to take a long vacation. She was also praying for another pregnancy. She told Kurt Frings to keep her calendar clear until October, when she'd promised Jack Warner to make a limited publicity tour for the American and European premieres of *My Fair Lady*.

Mel, meanwhile, was developing plans for another joint project. While working for Samuel Bronston in *The Fall of the Roman Empire*, he'd interested the Madrid-based producer in a historical epic about Queen Isabella of Spain, to be filmed in giant screen Cinerama. Audrey would, of course, play the title role, with Marcello Mastroianni as Ferdinand V. Mel would portray Christopher Columbus, in addition to directing the movie.

Bronston, a Russian-born promoter who allegedly received his financing from Mafia sources loved the idea and assigned Philip Yordan, his American scriptwriting associate, to develop it. The project eventually died when Bronston's profligate spending on films that proved box-office bombs caught up with him and he went bankrupt.

Instead of resting in Burgenstock as she intended, Audrey started traveling around Europe with Mel while he worked to keep his own career going. With nobody chasing him with offers, he turned to packaging his own. The first actually to get made was *El Greco*, a biopic of the sixteenth-century Greek who became Spain's revered artistic genius. Mel produced the movie and also acted the title role, with the Italian Rosanna Schiaffino as leading lady. Following that, he served as producer on *Every Day Is a Holiday*, a bullfighting musical starring Marisol, Spain's sixteen-year-old singing and dancing phenomenon.

Mel was getting his financing from various European, American, and Asian distributors, who would later handle the movies. Most of the production took place in remote parts of Spain and Italy, where the Ferrers had to rough it. Although Audrey had no business reason for being there, she felt that for the sake of marital harmony it was her turn to take a backseat to her husband. No doubt she also didn't trust him alone in the company of some of his female associates, especially the reputed sex kitten Marisol.

In August 1964, like a thunderbolt from out of nowhere, Audrey received word that her father had died. By this time she had not heard from Joseph Ruston or seen him in the quarter of a century since the outbreak of World War II—a sad but weird state of affairs, considering that his daughter had become world famous.

"I was so distraught," Audrey recalled. "I realized how much I cared about my father. I'd always cared, obviously. I just couldn't bear the idea that I would never get the chance to see him again. I cursed myself for not having made more of an effort while he was alive, but his silence had me convinced that he didn't want to see me."

Happily, she would still get the chance: "Mel said to me, 'Maybe it's not true. Did it ever occur to you that he's still alive?' Mel went about finding him and discovered that he was still living in Dublin, and we went to see him."

When the Ferrers arrived in Dublin, someone at Aer Lingus had tipped off the press and there were several reporters and photographers waiting in ambush. Mel got angry and refused to divulge the reason for their visit. Audrey was a bit friendlier, claiming it was her first trip to Ireland and a weekend holiday for sightseeing. The couple got into a waiting limousine and were whisked away before reporters could ask any more questions.

The need for secrecy may have had nothing to do with Joseph Ruston's fascist past. Just the fact that Audrey Hepburn had a father living in Dublin was likely to earn him local celebrity that he might not have desired.

Ruston would turn seventy-five that November. He had been fifty when Audrey last set eyes on him. "He looked the way I remembered him. Older, yes, but much the same. Slim and tall. He was living in a tiny apartment, just two rooms, but not because he couldn't afford more. It was very hard to find anything bigger in that section of Dublin."

There also happened to be a Mrs. Ruston.

Audrey discovered that she had a stepmother not that much older than she was, Ruston's junior by thirty years.

It must have been a very strained reunion all around. One can only guess at what actually transpired, but in an interview many years later, Audrey attributed the long separation from her father to "his sense of discretion." Presumably, Ruston feared that his fascist politics and World War II imprisonment could be used to smear Audrey's sterling reputation and cause her grief and embarrassment that she didn't need. Also, Audrey's mother would inevitably get dragged into it as well once the press started digging into Ruston's past.

Ruston turned out to be up to date on Audrey's fame and accomplishments, but didn't react like a long-lost father might. "I think he was proud, but in a very Victorian sort of way. My mother was like that too. It was a job well done, but you didn't make a lot of fuss about it," she recalled.

When Audrey happened to mention the riding accident she suffered while filming *The Unforgiven*, she got slight sympathy from her father: "He had been a great horseman in his youth, and he said to me, 'Of course you were a fool to ride a gray stallion.' He was cross with me for riding a horse that I should have known was likely to throw me."

The reunion did not achieve what Audrey might have hoped for. It was probably too late to renew a relationship that had effectively ended when she was six and her parents separated. Then or now, her aloof father seemed incapable of being able to reciprocate her love.

But a door had been reopened, and Audrey came back to visit her father from time to time over the years. Friends claim that she also started sending him generous monthly checks and took care of his every need for the rest of his life.

In October 1964, Audrey and Mel traveled to the United States for the launching of *My Fair Lady*. Warner Brothers had decided on a hard-ticket road-show release for the initial engagements, a practice that had become standard in the industry for most lengthy superbudgeted movies since *The Ten Commandments* and *Oklahoma!* circa 1955–56. It was Hollywood copying Broadway, with reserved seats sold in advance and daytime matinee and evening screenings. Bookings were exclusive, limited to a single theater in any one city, with ticket prices running five to six dollars (ordinary first-run movies charged about two dollars then).

Counting on favorable reviews, Warner Brothers intended continuing the hard-ticket policy through the annual award-giving period that started in late December and peaked with the Academy Awards in the spring. By that time, *My Fair Lady* would change strategy and go into normal broad release to capitalize on the hoped-for Oscar nominations and wins.

Audrey and Mel attended ten major premieres of *My Fair Lady*—first in Los Angeles, New York, San Francisco, Denver, Chicago, and Washington, then in London, Paris, Rome, and Madrid. For Audrey it was one of the unhappiest experiences of her career. She deeply regretted not having fought harder to do her own singing. She felt like hiding under her seat during the scenes where Marni Nixon's voice wafted from her throat.

Movie critics were quick to detect the dubbing, which forced Warner Brothers to confess to the subterfuge (Nixon, of course, did not receive billing in the credits). Gossip columnist Hedda Hopper sniped that "With Marni Nixon doing the singing, Audrey Hepburn gives only half a performance." A perplexed Jack Warner responded, "I don't know what all the fuss is about. We've been doing it for years. We even dubbed the barking of Rin-Tin-Tin."

The criticism made Audrey embarrassed, to a point that when asked about it, she answered, "You could tell it wasn't me, couldn't you? Next time I'll do my own singing." But that opportunity never came again.

chapter fourteen

CHANGE OF PACE

Despite the Hepburn-Nixon dubbing controversy, *My Fair Lady* received rave reviews and did record-breaking business. Longtime admirer Bosley Crowther of *The New York Times* stated, "The happiest thing about it is that Audrey Hepburn superbly justifies the decision of Jack Warner to get her to play the title role."

In December, the esteemed New York Film Critics voted it Best Picture of 1964, a sure-fire omen of Academy Award nominations. The New York critics also picked Rex Harrison as Best Actor, but Best Actress went to Kim Stanley for *Séance on a Wet Afternoon*. Whether Audrey figured in the final voting is unknown, because the group kept their nominations and balloting secret in those days.

By the time the Oscar nominations rolled around in February 1965, the Ferrers were in Rome, where Mel was supervising the editing and English dubbing of his Spanish-Italian *El Greco*, which 20th Century-Fox had picked up for distribution in the United States. As luck would have it, Audrey didn't know the nominations had been announced until she received a telegram from George Cukor expressing condolences over her failure to be chosen.

My Fair Lady received twelve nominations, in virtually every major category except Best Actress. Ironically, the alphabetical list in that group was headed by Julie Andrews, who after being rejected by Jack Warner for *My Fair Lady* had been snapped up by Walt Disney for *Mary Poppins*. Nominated along with Andrews were Anne Bancroft for *The Pumpkin Eater*, Sophia Loren for *Marriage Italian Style*, Debbie Reynolds for *The Unsinkable Molly Brown*, and Kim Stanley for *Séance on a Wet Afternoon*.

Not surprisingly, the news media had a field day reporting "the greatest upset in Oscar's thirty-seven years." The *Los Angeles Times* head-lined it on the front page: JULIE ANDREWS CHOSEN, AUDREY HEPBURN OMITTED. Andrews told reporters, "I think Audrey should have been nominated. I'm very sorry she wasn't." George Cukor used even stronger language: "I'm sick about it." Veteran producer Mervyn LeRoy, a frequent spokesman for the industry, commented, "I'm very disappointed. I find it very mean of Hollywood not to have at least nominated this great actress."

Hollywood's bible, *Daily Variety*, conjectured that "Hepburn did the acting, but Marni Nixon subbed for her in the singing department and that's what undoubtedly led to her erasure." Jack Warner seemed to think the writer was blaming Nixon's vocal talent rather than the deception involved. He fired back a telegram to the editor: "The next time we have some star- dubbing to do, we'll hire Maria Callas."

The other Hepburn, Katharine, sent Audrey a

telegram advising, "Don't worry about not being nominated. Someday you'll get it for a part that doesn't rate it."

Audrey would have been happy to let the controversy end there. Since she hadn't been nominated, she wouldn't have to attend the Hollywood ceremonies and be dragged into a contest with Julie Andrews on worldwide television. But Audrey didn't count on a last-minute invitation to present the Oscar for Best Actor.

Though the previous year's Best Actress should have been the presenter, Patricia Neal had just suffered three life-threatening strokes in one week, so how could Audrey refuse to substitute for her? The invite was apparently something of a consolation prize to Audrey for not being nominated; there were plenty of former Best Actress winners residing in Los Angeles who could have spared the Academy importing one from Europe.

By agreeing to attend, Audrey gave Hollywood a lesson in "good sportsmanship," said gossip columnist Mike Connolly, who claimed that her decision "has captured this town's imagination like nothing since Mary Pickford said yes to Douglas Fairbanks." He thought Audrey had real courage, considering it was likely she'd be handing the Oscar to co-star Rex Harrison, which would only add salt to the wound of not being nominated for her own performance.

Mel couldn't leave the editing of *El Greco,* so Audrey flew alone to Los Angeles for the April 5 ceremonies at the Santa Monica Civic Auditorium. George Cukor, nominated for Best Director, became her escort for the evening. They occupied seats adjacent to Jack Warner and white-haired Gladys Cooper, a nominee for Best Supporting Actress for her portrayal of Henry Higgins's mother. Rex Harrison and actress wife Rachel Roberts sat in a section nearer the stage, a row ahead of Julie Andrews and designer husband Tony Walton. TV cameras kept flashing between Audrey and Andrews in anticipation of some high drama when the Best Actress award came around. Since that was scheduled next to last, just before Best Picture, it would be a long wait.

As the evening progressed, *My Fair Lady* won Oscars for Cecil Beaton for costume design and for Harry Stradling for cinematography. Stanley Holloway, up for Best Supporting Actor for Alfred P. Doolittle, lost to Peter Ustinov of *Topkapi*, while Gladys Cooper saw Best Supporting Actress go to Lila Kedrova for *Zorba the Greek*. *My Fair Lady* had also captured Oscars for Musical Scoring, Art Direction, and Sound Engineering by the time the Directing category came around.

Since George Cukor had already won the Screen Directors Guild's annual award for *My Fair Lady*, he was considered a sure shot for the Oscar and didn't disappoint. Like all the previous *My Fair Lady* victors that night, his acceptance speech made a subtle snipe at the Academy voters for not nominating "Miss Audrey Hepburn, whose magic makes it so easy for us to win these awards."

Introduced by emcee Bob Hope, Audrey received the longest ovation of the evening as she walked onstage next, with TV viewers treated to a close-up of Julie Andrews clapping for her. Pausing only for a whispered "thank you very much," Audrey announced the Best Actor nominees, who besides Rex Harrison included Richard Burton and Peter O'Toole for *Becket*, Anthony Quinn for *Zorba the Greek*, and Peter Sellers for *Dr. Strangelove or: How I learned to Stop Worrying and Love the Bomb*.

Audrey tore open the envelope, smiled when she read the enclosed card, and proclaimed Rex Harrison the winner. When Harrison marched up onstage, he threw his arms around her and kissed her three times. He continued hugging her throughout his acceptance speech. "I feel in a way I should split it in half between us," he said, resting his Oscar on the podium.

"Hold it up!" Audrey instructed him. "Deep love," Harrison concluded, "to—uh—well, two fair ladies." "Yes!" Audrey agreed as they strolled off arm-in-arm.

The other fair lady's turn came next as Sidney Poitier announced the Best Actress nominees. When he declared Julie Andrews the winner for *Mary Poppins*, she bounded onstage with an acceptance speech that steered clear of the *My Fair Lady* controversy and thanked everybody in America for making her feel welcome: "I know you Americans are famous for your hospitality, but this is ridiculous." A month earlier, when similarly honored with a Golden Globe Award, Andrews had jokingly referred to Jack Warner as "the man who made all this possible," but now she mentioned only Walt Disney.

Backstage, press photographers were hoping

for a catfight between Audrey and Andrews, but they had to settle for a kissing match as the two women hugged and happily posed for two-shots. Clutching her Oscar, Andrews kept muttering, "I don't believe it. I don't believe it."

"I'm thrilled for her, of course," Audrey told reporters. When asked for his interpretation of the outcome, Rex Harrison said, "I wouldn't consider it poetic justice. Julie was marvelous onstage but Audrey was wonderful, too."

Meanwhile, out onstage, *My Fair Lady* had just won its eighth and most important Oscar of the night, the one for Best Picture of 1964, beating *Becket*, *Dr. Strangelove*, *Mary Poppins*, and *Zorba the Greek*. It was the first best-picture winner from Warner Brothers since 1943's *Casablanca* and also Jack Warner's first as an individual producer.

Everybody went on from there to the Motion Picture Academy Governors' Ball at the Beverly Hilton Hotel. Jack Warner lived up to his clown-prince reputation by saying that he'd voted for Julie Andrews in the Oscar balloting. In his head maybe. The voting in that category was restricted to members of the acting division.

At the party, Audrey ran into singer Eddie Fisher, a longtime admirer who'd had romantic notions about her prior to his disastrous entanglements with Debbie Reynolds and Elizabeth Taylor. Still a bit touchy about the *My Fair Lady* fracas, Audrey took Fisher's hand and asked, "Are you *still* my number-one fan?" He was.

Before leaving Los Angeles, Audrey agreed to star in William Wyler's next movie, *How to Steal a Million*, which would be produced by 20th Century-Fox. After the unfortunate *The Children's Hour*, Audrey had rejected Wyler's offer of another stark dramatic role in *The Collector* (played instead by Samantha Eggar). She couldn't very well say no again to the director who had turned her into a movie star and Oscar winner in one swoop.

How to Steal a Million, for which Audrey would earn a million dollars in salary, was Wyler's first romantic fluff since *Roman Holiday*, so perhaps lightning could strike twice. Scripted by novelist-playwright Harry Kurnitz, the movie put a sophisticated spin on the popular caper genre, dealing with forgery in the art world and the robbery of a supposedly priceless sculpture.

Audrey would portray Nicole Bonnet, daughter of a sculptor specializing in copies of great masterpieces. When a copy of Cellini's Venus lands in a Paris museum, she hires a so-called cat burglar to steal the piece before the forgery can be detected and her father sent to prison for fraud. Although the movie had few exterior scenes and could easily have been filmed at Fox's Los Angeles studios, Wyler agreed to filming it in France to accommodate the income tax situations of his two foreign-resident stars.

Besides the lure of another Paris-based production, Audrey jumped at the chance to work opposite Peter O'Toole, Wyler's choice for leading man. In the three years since his dazzling debut in *Lawrence of Arabia*, the Irish blue-eyed blond had become one of the hottest actors on the scene, with Oscar nominations for that movie and *Becket*.

At thirty-three, O'Toole happened to be three years younger than Audrey, but it wasn't enough of an age difference to be noticeable. For the sake of her romantic image, Audrey could stand some young blood after being matched with Cary Grant and Rex Harrison in her last two films.

Wyler hired Hugh Griffith, the flamboyant British character actor who won an Oscar for his performance as Sheik Ilderim in the director's *Ben-Hur*, for the role of Audrey's father. In addition, Wyler provided her with yet another opportunity to work opposite one of the screen's legendary lovers, in this case Charles Boyer, who would portray a lecherous art dealer trying to seduce her.

How to Steal a Million started filming in Paris in July 1965. Charles Lang, who'd photographed *Paris When It Sizzles* and *Charade*, was again on board at Audrey's request. Franz Planer, who had always been her favorite cinematographer, had died in 1963. (*The Children's Hour* was the last film he ever worked on.)

Hubert de Givenchy, of course, had the costume assignment, assisted in the accessory department by André Courreges. The latter's futuristic headgear and bubble sunglasses became the new looks in hats and eyewear after Audrey was seen wearing them in the movie.

Like William Holden, Peter O'Toole had a reputation as a hard-drinking swinger. Gossipmongers began wondering what would develop when he and Audrey started working together. O'Toole had a domestic situation similar to hers, an actress wife (the Welsh Sian Phillips) and a young daughter. Would that prevent them from striking up an intimate friendship? Such questions were seldom raised when Audrey worked with the older Cary Grant or Rex Harrison.

During the filming, Audrey stayed at the Hotel Raphaël while Mel remained in Switzerland with Sean. It was the height of the tourist season in Paris, so it didn't make sense for the rest of the family to leave their rustic paradise in the Alps. William Wyler granted Audrey the rare privilege of jetting home on the weekends. Stars were usually grounded during filming periods; personal traveling was not covered by production insurance.

Besides sparking rumors of marital discord, Audrey's temporary separation from her husband added fuel to the gossip about an affair with Peter O'Toole. None of it seemed true, although the Ferrers' marriage, now nearing its eleventh anniversary, had declined from the passionate heights of its early years. Mel seemed to become increasingly jealous as Audrey's career prospered and his languished. Since her million-dollar fees permitted them to live on a lavish scale that would have been impossible on his earnings, he tolerated the situation, but it must have dented his pride.

The Ferrers were also in a battle of wills over Audrey's identification with the House of Givenchy. Mel, perhaps rightly so, thought that she should be compensated for the use of her name and likeness in the marketing of Givenchy's

L'Interdit, which had not only grossed millions of dollars but was also challenging Chanel's Number Five as the world's most popular French perfume. Without telling Audrey, Mel instructed Henry Rogers, their longtime public relations counselor, to pursue the matter with Claude de Givenchy, the designer's brother and business chief.

Though the Givenchys proved agreeable to making a deal with Audrey, she exploded in anger when Mel and Rogers told her that discussions had been held without her knowledge. "Neither of you seems to understand," she said. "I don't want anything from Hubert. I don't need his money. He is my friend. If I've helped him build his perfume business, then that's exactly what one friend should do for another. If someone else offered me one million dollars to endorse a perfume, I wouldn't do it . . . but Hubert is my friend. I don't want anything. Yes, I even want to walk into a store and buy the perfume at the retail price."

What developed between Audrey and Peter O'Toole during the filming of *How to Steal a Million* could be answered only by them, but it was apparently a more relaxed and companionable association than she had with her much older leading men. Both were apprehensive about acting together because they were opposite types, Audrey a reserved lady and O'Toole an unruly leprechaun. For one of their first scenes, they spent a total of eleven shooting days supposedly hiding in a narrow closet of the art museum.

"Neither of us was Herculean or Junoesque;

nevertheless, it was a tight fit," O'Toole recalled. "We were pretty close and we talked a lot and I found I liked her a great deal."

Both tended to be gigglers, causing hell for William Wyler when one or both suddenly broke out laughing in the middle of a take. In one scene, after Audrey's guffaws spoiled three consecutive takes, O'Toole begged her to leave the set and to not even watch from the sidelines, because he could crack up just from the expression on her face. "They react on each other like laughing gas," Wyler said, "and the trouble is they're in almost every scene together."

Thanks to O'Toole, Audrey got drunk on the job for the first and only time in her working experience. One unexpectedly chilly summer's day, while they were filming a scene where Audrey had to get into a car and drive away, she began shivering, so O'Toole took her to his dressing trailer for a warming sip of brandy.

"Audrey went all roses and cream, bounced out of the caravan, radiated towards the motor car, hopped into it, and drove off, demolishing five huge lamps that were being used to light the scene," O'Toole recalled.

Despite all the merriment on the set, *How to Steal a Million* turned out to be the unfunniest comedy that Audrey had done so far. Critics blamed it on a trite script and the elephantine direction of William Wyler, who since winning eleven Oscars for *Ben-Hur* seemed to think that every movie should be treated with similar solemnity and pomposity. Audrey never worked again with Wyler. Nearly devoured alive by newcomer

Barbra Streisand during his next film, *Funny Girl*, he made only one more, the disastrous *Liberation of L. B. Jones*, before opting for retirement in 1970.

When Audrey finished *How to Steal a Million*, the Ferrers started shopping around for a new place to live. After years of renting in Burgenstock, it seemed time to set down roots with property of their own. With Sean now of school age, Audrey was also thinking of his future. Though she wanted to remain in Switzerland, her wartime memories of the Nazi occupation made her reluctant to have her son educated in the German language. That would be the case if they stayed in Burgenstock or settled elsewhere in the country's German-speaking cantons.

The Ferrers canvassed the French-speaking regions to the west and finally found their dream house in Tolochenaz, a sleepy village in the canton of Vaud. It was situated just above the town of Morges, in the mountains overlooking the midpoint of lengthy Lake Geneva. The village stood on the site of one of the earliest human settlements in Europe. Lake dwellers, with homes built on stilts, created the first Tolochenaz, a name Celtic in origin.

For two international movie stars, the place had the advantage of being within an hour's drive of the airport at Geneva, yet remote enough for privacy. It was also only twenty miles from Vaud's capital city, Lausanne, which had upscale shopping of every sort and some of the best arts and music facilities in Europe.

Tolochenaz offered most of the scenic beauty

associated with Switzerland but was unmentioned in most travel books and unlikely to draw many tourists. They seldom went beyond Morges, which has a military museum housed in a castle built by the Duke of Savoy in the thirteenth century.

About five hundred people lived in Tolochenaz, mainly families involved in farming or with the wine-producing industry in Morges. There were just two shops, a grocery and a hardware store, plus a two-room school for Sean to attend when the time came. Audrey wanted him to have as normal a childhood as possible. Private boarding schools could wait until he was older.

Another important reason for Audrey's attraction to the area was its proximity to the home of her great friend Doris Brynner, who lived with actor husband Yul about twenty miles away on a magnificent estate overlooking Lake Geneva. Involved in the Paris fashion industry before marrying Brynner, the former Doris Kleiner was Audrey's link to that world and to the international community of the rich and famous known as "The Beautiful People," of which Doris was a founding member.

The Ferrers bought an eighteenth-century farmhouse on Tolochenaz's only street, Route de Bière. Constructed from local stone that had a distinctive peach coloring, the two-story building was so spacious that the original farming owners had lived in one half and kept their cows in the other. Under the black slate roof was an enormous attic with gabled windows. The property covered an acre of grounds, including flower gardens and an orchard, and was well protected by a stone wall in front and iron fences elsewhere.

Audrey christened the house "La Paisible," "the peaceful place." With a five-year-old boy in residence, she was in no hurry to redecorate it into a candidate for the pages of *House Beautiful*. She brought all their belongings from the Burgenstock chalet and sent for the countless items that she'd purchased in her travels over the years but had left with her mother or friends for safekeeping. Slipcovers were ordered for the best furniture. "A house isn't a home if children and dogs can't go into the main room," she told one of her new neighbors.

In addition to the Yorkshire terrier Assam of Assam, the Ferrers now owned Mouchie, a German shepherd trained from puppyhood to be a companion and guard for Sean. Unhappily, Mouchie became overprotective of Sean, barking or snapping at everybody else, so he was put up for adoption and replaced by an Australian sheepdog with a sweeter disposition.

Audrey encouraged Sean to make friends with the local children and to bring them home to play. Their merry voices and loud games were music to her ears. She was never more than a few yards away, puttering in the garden or playing with the dogs.

For those times when the cold and snow in Tolochenaz became too much, the Ferrers also bought a villa near Marbella, on the Costa del Sol, Spain's equivalent of the French Riviera. The resort town had some of the finest sand beaches on the Mediterranean. Though the official season ran from mid-June to mid-September, the weather was sunny and mild most of the year; the Ferrers could go there in winter without having to contend with mobs of tourists.

Something about their new domestic arrangements must have agreed with Audrey and perhaps her husband as well. In December, she was pregnant again. She made an early New Year's resolution to really take it easy this time to avoid another miscarriage. No work and not much play either. She was prepared to spend the whole nine months in bed at La Paisible if necessary.

But a month later, Audrey developed abdominal pain and landed in the hospital in Lausanne. Doctors found an ectopic pregnancy and wished her better luck next time. Audrey's despair was worse than usual. Like many women past thirty-five, she wondered, at going on thirty-seven, how many chances she had left before she reached the dreaded forty, generally the end of the childbearing years.

During Audrey's recuperation, Kurt Frings kept bombarding her with scripts and development deals, hoping to cure her blues by getting her back to work. His top recommendation was an offer from MGM to team with Richard Burton in a musical remake of *Goodbye, Mr. Chips*, the 1939 tearjerker with Robert Donat and Greer Garson about an English schoolmaster who devotes his life to his students. But Audrey thought it was too soon after *My Fair Lady* and didn't want another musical, even if permitted to do her own singing. It turned out a wise decision. When finally produced three years later with

Peter O'Toole and Petula Clark, *Chips* proved a critical and box-office disaster.

By this time, sneak preview reactions to *How to Steal a Million* were not encouraging, with the film threatening to be as detrimental to Audrey's career as Wyler's *Roman Holiday* had been beneficial. For her next project, it seemed imperative that she should try something that was completely different for her and also more in touch with the liberated cinema of the so-called Swinging Sixties.

Stanley Donen, now working on his own since marriage and fatherhood led Cary Grant to retire from film making, offered a possible solution to the quandary when he sent Audrey a script entitled *Two for the Road*, an original written directly for the screen by Frederic Raphael. Audrey was immediately impressed because Raphael had just won an Oscar for writing *Darling*. In addition, that movie's star, Julie Christie, had matched Audrey's *Roman Holiday* feat by winning the Best Actress Oscar with her first major role.

But after reading *Two for the Road*, Audrey had serious doubts about doing it. For the first time, she would portray a married woman experiencing husband problems—while Audrey was experiencing her own husband problems in real life. There were also moments of sex and nudity that she thought would offend those who still cherished her portrayal of Sister Luke in *The Nun's Story*.

Stanley Donen and Frederic Raphael traveled to Tolochenaz to try to talk Audrey into it, discovering that her main resistance came from a fear of letting go of the genteel image that had been serving her well through fifteen years of starring roles. Once Donen and Raphael convinced her that they had a serious, non-exploitative film in mind, Audrey accepted.

"From that moment on," Frederic Raphael recalled, "she became a totally committed and honorable member of the cast, without conceit or self-importance. By 'honorable' I mean that having agreed to do the film, she did not ask for changes or betray the idea to which she had agreed. The absurdity of the belief that film actresses are inferior to those who appear on the stage was never more plainly revealed than by Audrey."

For Audrey's co-star, Donen and Raphael selected Albert Finney, another of Britain's ascendant angry young men. Audrey approved Finney like a shot because she'd already heard lots about him from Peter O'Toole, one of his closest friends since they'd studied together at London's Royal Academy of Dramatic Art. Ironically, O'Toole got the lead in *Lawrence of Arabia* only after Finney rejected it because of his preference for working on the stage. Instead of *Lawrence of Arabia*, Finney chose to do *Billy Liar* and *Luther* in London's West End, both winning him great acclaim, the latter twice when it traveled to Broadway.

Audrey had also admired Finney's film work in *Saturday Night and Sunday Morning* and *Tom Jones*, which won the Best Picture Oscar for 1963. He received an Oscar nomination for his performance in that box-office blockbuster, which finally landed him alongside O'Toole as one of the hottest personalities in international moviemaking. For the record, Finney happened to be four years younger than O'Toole. While Finney's name suggested another Irishman, he was born in Lancashire in northern England.

As might be expected in a script by the author of *Darling*, *Two for the Road* was practically revolutionary for an Audrey Hepburn movie, with the story flashing back and forth in time to reflect what's going on in the minds of the two leading characters. In the past, Audrey had always insisted on working chronologically so she could grow with her characterizations, but here it would be impossible for lack of a clear-cut linear plot.

Audrey and Finney were cast as Joanna and Mark Wallace, getting ready to celebrate their twelfth wedding anniversary by driving from their home in London to the French Riviera in their convertible sports car. He's a successful architect, and she's a devoted housewife who's learned to cope with his philandering and egomania. During their three-day road trip, we get glimpses of their life together, from the time they first met to current squabbling that suggests they might be better off divorced.

After directing Audrey at her chicest in *Funny Face* and *Charade*, Stanley Donen decreed that she would have to do without Givenchy this time. Joanna Wallace would never have been able to afford Paris couture, so Audrey's wardrobe would be selected ready-made from department stores or boutiques in the character's price range.

Audrey got nervous, because Givenchy knew

her physical faults and how to conceal them. To break down her resistance, Donen took her on a shopping trip to London and Paris so they could pick the clothes together. Donen invited Ken Scott, one of the trendy London designers of the time, to come along as their fashion consultant. In the end, most of the choices came from London's Mary Quant (her miniskirted mod fashions had become the dominant look of the 1960s) and Paris's Michele Rosier and Paco Rabanne.

After the clothes were delivered, they were sent for customizing to Lady Claire Rendlesham, a London fitter whom Audrey had known for years. Separates, rather than dresses, predominated. Body-hugging tops needed to be padded at the bust. Waist lines of slacks and jeans were altered to camouflage Audrey's wide hips.

Stanley Donen also persuaded Audrey to go for a softer and sexier look. He wanted her to wash and arrange her long hair herself, wearing it hanging loose or tied in a ponytail. Her longtime makeup artist, Alberto de Rossi, gave her new eyes, or at least thinner brows than she'd ever sported before.

Production of *Two for the Road* started in July 1966. Because of the expected hot weather, as well as the many changes of location involved, Audrey and Mel decided that he would stay with Sean in Tolochenaz for the duration. Audrey would be unable to fly home on the weekends because she appeared in nearly every scene and would be too pooped to do any extra traveling.

Though it might have seemed that Mel had been reduced to a glorified baby-sitter, he was also involved in preparations for Audrey's next movie. Via agent Kurt Frings in Los Angeles, the couple were close to a deal with Warner Brothers for the filming of the Broadway stage hit *Wait Until Dark*, with Audrey as star and Mel in the producer's chair.

Audrey met Albert Finney for the first time during rehearsals for *Two for the Road* at the Boulogne Studios in Paris, where some of the interior scenes were being filmed. It was a case of immediate mutual attraction. Seven years younger than Audrey, Finney oozed sex appeal, but in a more virile way than Peter O'Toole. He had a brilliant intellect, balanced by a boyish sense of mischief. Audrey found him irresistible.

Finney, who came from a scruffy lower-class background, was overwhelmed by Audrey's regal aura and unaffected chic. She was also the first international superstar that he'd ever been teamed with, and no doubt visions of a romantic conquest danced in his head. Not solely for his acting skills was Albert Finney known as the next Richard Burton.

With Audrey's husband in Switzerland and Finney unattached (divorced in 1961 from actress Jane Wenham), there was no one around to deter them from becoming pals: "We got on immediately," Finney recalled. "After the first day's rehearsals, I could tell that the relationship would work out wonderfully. Either the chemistry is there, or it isn't. I find I can have very good rapport with an actress I am working with, but occasionally there's an absolute attraction. That happened with Audrey. Doing a scene with her, my mind knew I was acting but my heart didn't, and my body certainly didn't!

"Performing with Audrey was quite disturbing, actually," Finney continued. "Playing a love scene with a woman as sexy as Audrey, you sometimes get to the edge where make-believe and reality are blurred. All that staring into each other's eyes—you pick up vibes that are decidedly not fantasy."

Audrey told an interviewer at the time, "I love Albie. Oh, I really do. He's so terribly, terribly funny. He makes me laugh like no one else can. And you can talk to him, really *talk*. He's serious, too, completely so about acting, and that's wonderful. Albie's just plain wonderful, that's all there is to it."

As the filming slowly snaked southwards from Paris to Saint Tropez, a clear attraction developed, flamed by the first explicitly sexual scenes that Audrey had ever acted. In one, she and Finney were in bed together apparently naked under the sheets. In another, the couple went skinny-dipping in the Mediterranean.

Always self-conscious about her scrawny figure, Audrey was forced by the dictates of the script to parade in swimsuits or less in front of Finney, the director, and all the technicians on the set. But once her shyness wore off, she seemed liberated, both in her performance and in her public socializing with Albie.

After work, the couple usually dined together at one of the local bistros and then went on to a bar or discotheque. Actor William Daniels, who played a nerdy American tourist in the film, recalled that they seemed like a couple of teen-agers together—laughing, chattering, flirting, and holding hands. It was completely open and spontaneous.

One weekend, Mel Ferrer came to visit, which put a temporary damper on things. "Audrey and Albie had developed this wonderful thing together, a sort of private vocabulary of jokes and references that shut everybody else out," an actress in the film recalled. "When Mel turned up, they got rather formal and a little awkward with each other, as if they were afraid of being found out."

Finney seemed to make a new woman of Audrey. She had always kept to herself during production, but now she hung out with the other actors and even engaged in horseplay on the set. Stanley Donen, in the nearly ten years since first directing Audrey in *Funny Face*, noticed a remarkable change. "I saw an Audrey I didn't even know," he recalled. "She overwhelmed me. She was so free, so happy. I never saw her like that. So young! I guess it was Albie."

Eventually, the closeness between Audrey and Finney reached the gossip tabloids, courtesy of 20th Century–Fox's publicity department, which prayed for another headline bonanza like the one it helped to create with the Taylor-Burton *Cleopatra*. This one, however, never developed much sizzle, probably because the conservative mainstream media had more respect for Audrey Hepburn than they did for Elizabeth Taylor. Audrey had the image of a lady and would always be painted in those terms, while Taylor was the perennial wanton.

Like most relationships that flare up during the filming of a movie, Audrey's with Albert Finney really had no place to go when they finished *Two for the Road*. Audrey had a husband and child to consider, as well as a career that paid her a million dollars a picture. Other than attraction, which tends to die quickly when two people part, she had no common bond with Finney. Having earned enough from *Two for the Road* to keep him comfortable awhile, he was returning to stage acting in London with a two-year contract for repertory work with the esteemed National Theatre.

The Ferrers ignored the rumors of marital problems and resumed their life together. At Christmas, Audrey immersed herself in helping six-year-old Sean prepare for the local church's holiday pageant. Besides having to dress up as a sheep in the Nativity scene, Sean was to recite a poem in a later part of the program. Because he was the youngest of the children selected, his recitation would come first, so Audrey drilled him for weeks to ease his anxiety.

As she recalled, "Our little boy stood up straight as a die, opened his mouth, and in a loud French voice recited this little French poem, hands by his side. And he spoke good and loud as I'd asked him to. And he did fine. And his father and I were absolute wrecks because to the very last line we were afraid he would forget, or lose his confidence. But he didn't. He did us proud. It was a big thrill."

By this time, negotiations had been concluded with Warner Brothers for Audrey's next movie, *Wait Until Dark*, with Mel serving as the producer. Audrey received her usual $1 million plus a percentage. Reluctant to take Sean out of school in Tolochenaz, the couple left him under Granny van Heemstra's supervision when they departed for the United States in January 1967 to prepare for the filming.

chapter fifteen
PARTNERSHIP DISSOLVED

The role of Susy Hendrix in *Wait Until Dark* was another digression for Audrey Hepburn, her first suspense shocker and her first attempt at portraying a physically handicapped person. Permanently blinded in an accident and often left alone during her photographer husband's business traveling, Susy ends up being terrorized by three murderous thugs who break into her apartment believing that a fortune in illegal drugs has been hidden there.

Written by British dramatist Frederick Knott (*his Dial M for Murder* had been filmed by Alfred Hitchcock), *Wait Until Dark* had already been a hit on Broadway with Lee Remick and in London's West End with Honor Blackman. Jack Warner paid a million dollars for the screen rights, with Audrey specifically in mind for the lead. Despite the dubbing brouhaha, *My Fair Lady* had been the biggest hit in Warner Brothers' history (with worldwide rentals of $65 million thus far), so he wanted Audrey back for a project that seemed even better suited to her talent.

Not long after purchasing the rights to *Wait Until Dark*, Jack Warner got an irresistible $33 million offer from Seven Arts Productions to buy his one-third interest in Warner Brothers

Pictures. Audrey's movie and his personal production of *Camelot*, Lerner and Loewe's successor to *My Fair Lady*, would mark the end of his forty-four-year reign as head of the studio. In the summer of 1967, he would become honorary chairman of Warner Brothers and just one of many independent producers on the lot.

But in the meantime, Jack Warner was still boss, and giving the Ferrers a difficult time over Englishman Terence Young, their choice for director of *Wait Until Dark*. Warner wasn't impressed by the fact that Young had directed the first three James Bond blockbusters: *Dr. No*, *From Russia With Love*, and *Thunderball*. All that concerned him was Young's reputation for going far over budget. Warner thought the director seemed to have no respect for money, which Warner, a heavy gambler himself, attributed to Young's fondness for the casinos of the French Riviera.

Jack Warner proposed Sir Carol Reed in place of Terence Young, but the Ferrers were adamant. Mel and Audrey had entered into an agreement with Young for additional collaborations, starting with a remake of *Mayerling*, which the Ferrers had done on television in 1957.

Since Audrey never enjoyed working in the Hollywood studios, Mel tried to persuade Jack Warner to shoot *Wait Until Dark* in Paris or Rome, where she always felt more at ease. Except for a few street exteriors in New York's Greenwich Village, the action took place indoors and could easily have been filmed in a studio anywhere. But Warner wouldn't agree, because

335

the WB plant in Burbank, once one of the busiest in the industry, was underutilized and facing closure if it couldn't attract more activity.

The casting of the other main roles in *Wait Until Dark* became more difficult than with any of Audrey's previous films. Though she portrayed a married woman, the husband was only a secondary character appearing in a few scenes. The chief male role was the leader of the menacing thugs, a raging psychopath who would have everybody in the audience despising him for threatening the life of a helpless blind woman.

None of the big-name Hollywood stars would risk taking such an unsympathetic part. It finally went to Alan Arkin, a respected stage actor who'd just been Oscar-nominated for his movie debut in *The Russians Are Coming! The Russians Are Coming!* Richard Crenna and Jack Weston were signed to portray Arkin's slimy cohorts. Jack Warner's longtime protégé, Efrem Zimbalist, Jr., who never quite made it as a movie star but became a TV name in the studio's *77 Sunset Strip* series, got the token role of the husband.

Filming of *Wait Until Dark* started in New York to get the few exteriors out of the way and to enable Audrey to experience firsthand what it meant to be blind. Before leaving Switzerland, she'd taken counseling from an eye specialist in Lausanne, who recommended her to the training program at Manhattan's famed Lighthouse for the Blind. The Lighthouse permitted Audrey to attend classes and also arranged for her to spend time with Karen Goldstein, a blind college student enrolled there. Director Terence Young insisted on tagging along because he needed to know as much about blindness as Audrey did if her pretending was to be accurate and convincing.

At the Lighthouse, Audrey and Young had to wear black shields over their eyes until they became acclimated to what it was like in the world of the visually impaired. Bit by bit, Audrey learned how to depend on hearing and touch rather than sight. She look lessons in Braille and how to walk with a stick. She became adept at applying makeup and fixing her hair without help from a mirror. At the end of every visit to the Lighthouse, she counted her blessings for being able to return to a seeing world.

A pitched battle developed over whether Audrey should wear contact lenses during the actual filming. She considered them an actressy prosthetic device and believed she'd learned enough at the Lighthouse to be able to convey blindess without artificial help. But after screen tests were made both ways, Jack Warner and Audrey's longtime cameraman Charles Lang insisted on the contacts. Without them, Audrey's eyes were just too alive and expressive to simulate the blank look that accompanied blindness.

Audrey was furious, but gave in. In 1967, contact lenses were less wearer-friendly than they are today and a terrible nuisance to put on and remove. Throughout the filming she had to endure constant itching and soreness, though she would have been the first to admit that the suffering was preferable to being sightless.

When production of *Wait Until Dark* shifted

to California, the Ferrers stayed in one of the largest bungalows at the fabled Beverly Hills Hotel and flew over two servants from their home in Tolochenaz to cook and take care of them.

Jack Warner fumed at the extravagance and got even angrier when Audrey insisted on ordering her film wardrobe (again too ordinary for Givenchy!) from the same European boutiques that supplied her clothes for *Two for the Road.* Audrey's tailoring friend in London, Lady Rendlesham, was retained to make the selection and do the customizing (a mammoth job because each item had to be purchased in triplicate to protect against accidents during production). Lady Rendlesham's bill alone, including the cost of her shopping trips to Paris and Rome, was enough to keep Jack Warner in Cuban cigars for the rest of his life.

Warner kept questioning the Ferrers' expenditures, but directed all his blasts at Mel, the film's producer, rather than at Audrey, for fear of affecting her work. Warner blew his stack when she and Terence Young insisted on a daily schedule similar to the one both were accustomed to in European studios, with work starting at noon and ending at eight in the evening, with a tea break in the late afternoon. Mel authorized the building of a replica of an English tea garden next to Audrey's dressing quarters for the cast and crew to gather when refreshments were served.

Jack Warner went berserk because the later working hours meant paying the unionized workers huge overtime. But after much fighting with Mel, the best concession Warner could get was a one-hour change, starting at eleven instead of noon and ending at seven instead of eight.

As the weeks of filming *Wait Until Dark* ticked by, Audrey became a nervous wreck, worn down both by the demands of the most difficult role of her career and by personal despair. Regardless of surface appearances, she and Mel had reached the breaking point in their marriage. The only thing keeping them together was Sean. Audrey missed him so terribly that she was running up hundred-dollar-a-day telephone bills to Switzerland just to hear the sound of his voice.

During the working day, pretending to be a terrorized blind woman helped her to forget some of her problems. Co-actor Richard Crenna recalled a difficult scene where chief villain Alan Arkin waved a burning candle under Audrey's nose: "For some reason, it wasn't working for Alan, and it was a moment where Audrey had to become hysterical. Again and again they tried to get a take, but it still wasn't working for Alan. He was either blowing lines or blowing the action. But at no point did Audrey visibly show or articulate her impatience to him as an actor, because she sensed that he was trying.

"This continued for almost an entire day, during which Audrey was required to scream and holler; very emotional stuff. That, to me, showed what true professionalism was. I'll always remember that vividly. I would have jumped up and down on Alan's head."

During the filming, Audrey lost nearly fifteen pounds, which might have been due to her marital worries. But Terence Young thought differently: "The role was probably the most rigorous that Audrey ever played. She worked herself so hard that you could see the pounds rolling off her each day."

At Easter, Audrey's mother brought Sean over from Switzerland to spend the spring school recess with his parents. Mel arranged the shooting schedule so that Audrey could have some time off. It was hard to tell who was having more fun when Audrey took Sean, going on seven, on his first trips to Disneyland and Knott's Berry Farm. Gadding about Los Angeles in a chauffeured Rolls-Royce, they also shopped for toys, lunched at the Farmer's Market, visited the set of a TV western series, and watched the surfers at Malibu.

It ended all too soon. After Sean and his granny left for Switzerland, Audrey began counting the days when she could go back herself. Mel, in his producer's capacity, would remain in Los Angeles to supervise the editing and the recording of the background music. By now, Henry Mancini was Audrey's composer of choice, having previously contributed to *Breakfast at Tiffany's*, *Charade*, and *Two for the Road*.

When she could spare the time, Audrey was also doing press interviews for *Two for the Road*, which 20th Century–Fox would release that summer. She laughed away questions about her relationship with Albert Finney and tried to create the impression that her marriage of nearly thirteen years had never been happier or more solid.

But few with access to the Hollywood grapevine believed her. During the casting of the movie, there had been a score or more of beautiful young actresses parading through Mel's private office to audition for the small but indelible role of the drug courier who ends up a corpse hanging in a closet. This resulted in the inevitable rumors that Mel was philandering.

Audrey and Mel were also at loggerheads over career matters. She wanted to make fewer films, spend more time at home, and have more children. But Mel's career had become so entwined with hers that if she cut back, he might find it hard getting work on his own.

"Mel would have had his wife solidly booked five years in advance if she'd let him," a friend of the couple said.

Nearly thirty-eight, Audrey was just two years away from the dreaded forty, which in her case carried a double whammy. Besides being a theoretical limit for childbearing, it also was the point at which a romantic star actress became branded as over the hill. It was an unfortunate reality of the profession that the choice roles, especially in movies and television where the encroachments of age were harder to conceal than on the stage, usually went to women in their twenties or early thirties.

Critical acclaim for *Two for the Road* that summer suggested that Audrey might be able to continue in romantic leads a bit longer than other actresses her age. Many reviewers said she had never looked fresher or more relaxed, perhaps because of the influence of her costar, Albert Finney. The movie was a moderate success, doing bigger business abroad than in the United States, where it was unfortunately categorized as an art film and lost the mass audience. The title song by Henry Mancini and Leslie Bricusse became another of Audrey's musical signatures.

Back in Switzerland after finishing *Wait Until Dark*, Audrey tested pregnant again. Whether planned or not, her condition couldn't have come at a worse time in her marriage. Friends hoped that for Audrey's sake, the pregnancy went well and that she would at least have another baby to show for all she'd had to put up with. But a month later she miscarried again and all but gave up hope of having more children.

Meanwhile in Los Angeles, Mel and Terence Young completed the editing of *Wait Until Dark* and screened it for Jack Warner to get his opinion. Warner liked everything but the climactic encounter between the blind woman and the psychopath in the darkness of her apartment. Warner quibbled with the cutting and insisted on a sneak preview to gauge audience reactions. During the showing at a 900-seat theater in Glendale, the disputed scene left the capacity crowd gasping and shrieking with fright, so Warner gave it his blessing.

Wait Until Dark premiered in November to record-breaking grosses at New York's Radio City Music Hall (the ninth of Audrey's sixteen starring films to date to open there). The sound of 6,000 patrons reacting to the frightening finale was something astonishing to hear. The movie did big business everywhere, eventually bringing Warner Brothers worldwide rentals of $16 million and a profit of $10 million on its investment. It also seemed to be the determining factor in Audrey Hepburn being voted the industry's Box-Office Queen for 1967, her fourteenth anniversary as an international star.

Although it wasn't planned that way, *Wait Until Dark* became Audrey's last movie for nearly a decade. But at the time of its completion, she and Mel were planning *Mayerling* as their next project, with Terence Young again as director. Mel spent most of the summer of 1967 in Paris and Vienna implementing the production, which would be co-financed by MGM and Gaumont and partially filmed on location on the historical sites in Austria.

While Audrey and Mel had co-starred in *Mayerling* on television, he was not destined to be cast as leading man this time. For the role of Prince Rudolph, MGM insisted on Omar Sharif, star of its phenomenally successful *Dr. Zhivago*. Audrey thought he would be ideal. The Egyptian-born actor had become one of the most smoldering sex symbols since Rudolph Valentino.

But Audrey's latest miscarriage left her in a desolate mood, and the separations from Mel while he organized *Mayerling* didn't help matters. Since they'd been at each other's throats throughout the filming of *Wait Until Dark*, Audrey finally decided that it would be unwise to work with her husband so soon again. Surprisingly, Mel reacted rather calmly and perhaps spitefully as well. He selected Catherine Deneuve as Audrey's replacement.

Though it had been her own decision to give

up the role, Audrey suddenly felt like a withered reject. Deneuve was fourteen years younger, and one of the few up-and-coming stars to challenge Audrey's supremacy as a great beauty and fashion designer's dream.

During Mel's involvement with *Mayerling*, Audrey stayed at home with Sean in Tolochenaz or at the family's villa in Marbella. The separation became an official one in September 1967, when the couple announced their decision to live apart after thirteen years of marriage. Oddly enough, there was no mention of a divorce.

The news came as a shock to everybody but those who knew the Ferrers intimately and had been pessimistic about the marriage from its start. "Although Audrey loved acting, she wanted to work less and spend more time in private with Mel and Sean. She was filled with love. Mel was filled with ambition, for his wife and for himself," said Henry Rogers, the couple's longtime public relations representative.

Yul Brynner, then recently separated from wife Doris and perhaps being a bit tactless, given her close friendship with Audrey, told a reporter, "I don't know how Audrey put up with it for so long. But then, I suppose, she was so desperate to make it work, and she is so sweet, loyal, and human. I'm sure that, above everything, Mel was jealous of her success, and he could not reconcile himself to the cold facts of life. She was much better than he in every way, so he was taking it out on her. Finally, she couldn't take it any longer. God knows, she did everything a woman could do to save her marriage."

It turned out to be an unusual separation. Just days after announcing the split, the couple were spotted strolling arm in arm in Tolochenaz. Divorce seemed the least likely thing on their minds. However Mel felt, Audrey certainly wasn't pushing for one.

Years later she recalled: "When my marriage to Mel broke up, it was terrible; more than that, it was a keen disappointment. I thought a marriage between two good, loving people had to last until one of them died. I can't tell you how disillusioned I was. I'd tried and tried.

"I knew how difficult it had to be, to be married to a world celebrity, recognized everywhere, usually first-billed on the screen and in real life. How Mel suffered! But believe me, I put my career second. Finally, when it was clear it was ending, I still couldn't let go."

Audrey remembered her parents' divorce and her mother's unlucky first marriage. Now it was happening to her, but she couldn't accept it. She seemed to believe that love was made in heaven, or Hollywood's version of it, with nothing but kisses and happy endings.

She went into self-imposed exile with her son at La Paisible, rarely venturing further than the village shops. She told Kurt Frings to stop sending her scripts and badgering her with job offers. She didn't care if she never worked again. She certainly didn't need to. She had millions stashed in Swiss banks.

To escape the worst of the winter, Audrey took Sean to Marbella to spend the Christmas holidays. During their stay, she found companionship with Prince Alfonso de Bourbon-Dampierre, one of several pretenders to the Spanish throne, whom she'd known casually for years. They were often observed holding hands or dancing cheek to cheek in restaurants and nightclubs. Gossip tabloids reported them celebrating New year's at the poshest hotel in Madrid, where they allegedly shared a suite of rooms.

"They were obviously completely happy in each other's company," *France Dimanche* reported.

In February 1968, the actors' branch of the Academy of Motion Picture Arts and Sciences had a hard job deciding which of Audrey's two highly acclaimed performances of 1967 should be nominated for an Oscar. Probably because of the faulty belief that stark drama is more difficult to play than romantic fluff, she got it for *Wait Until Dark* instead of *Two for the Road*.

Audrey found herself again competing for Best Actress with the other Hepburn, Kate being nominated for *Guess Who's Coming to Dinner*. The three other candidates were Anne Bancroft for *The Graduate*, Faye Dunaway for *Bonnie and Clyde*, and Dame Edith Evans for *The Whisperers*.

After five Best Actress nominations and just one win, Audrey had enough experience to think that she didn't have a prayer this time. She saw no reason for attending the televised ceremonies, but couldn't refuse when Gregory Peck, currently serving as president of the Motion Picture Academy, begged her to hand out the Best Actor award. Elizabeth Taylor, the previous year's top actress (for *Who's Afraid of Virginia Woolf?*)

should have been the presenter but was stuck in Italy filming *Boom!* with hubby Richard Burton.

Although Mel Ferrer had produced *Wait Until Dark*, it was decided that he would not accompany Audrey to Los Angeles for the Oscar presentations. If she *did* happen to be a winner, they knew the press corps would make a circus of it, photographing them together and asking embarrassing questions about a possible reconciliation.

Four days before the scheduled April 8 ceremonies, tragedy struck in Memphis, Tennessee, with the assassination of civil rights leader Dr. Martin Luther King, Jr. When the funeral was hurriedly set for the day after the Oscars, a contingent of black stars headed by Sammy Davis, Jr. and Sidney Poitier threatened to boycott the show if it was held while Dr. King was still lying in state. Gregory Peck and his board of directors voted a two-day delay (the first in Oscar's history) and also canceled entirely the lavish Governors' Ball that always followed the event.

But the show must go on, and it did on April 10 after a brief speech by Gregory Peck in which he eulogized Dr. King and noted that two of the five films nominated for Best Picture dealt with racial issues. "We must unite in compassion if we are to survive," Peck said.

Since the top awards are traditionally reserved until last, with actors preceding actresses this year, Audrey was still in the running when she swept on stage to announce the male nominees and the selection of Rod Steiger for *In the Heat of the Night*, one of the two movies cited in Gregory

Peck's opening speech. Ironically, Steiger had chosen that role in preference to the one eventually played in *Wait Until Dark* by Alan Arkin, whose performance failed to get even an Oscar nomination.

Audrey wasn't surprised when presenter Sidney Poitier read the list of female nominees and proclaimed the winner to be Katharine Hepburn, for her portrayal of his prospective mother-in-law in *Guess Who's Coming to Dinner*. With Hepburn working in Europe, close friend George Cukor accepted the Oscar. Insiders attributed Hepburn's victory to a sympathy vote for her co-star and longtime companion, Spencer Tracy, who died soon after making the film and had been a posthumous nominee for best actor.

Although the elder Hepburn now had two Best Actress Oscars to her credit and would eventually win two more, Audrey still had just the one for *Roman Holiday* and stood no chance of even being nominated again if she didn't go on making movies. Yet that thought probably never crossed her mind. The prospect of winning awards had never been a motivating force in her career.

Obviously, work had slight appeal to Audrey while her marriage dangled on the thin line between separation and divorce. While the latter seemed inevitable, there were two extremely painful matters to consider: Sean's custody and the division of community property. Since most of the Ferrers' wealth came from the millions that Audrey earned from film contracts, she stood to lose a fortune in the financial settlement.

A great consolation to Audrey during this

period was Doris Brynner, who resided twenty miles away and was in the midst of a similarly bitter separation from husband Yul. The two women had become almost like sisters, Audrey being the elder by four years. Born in Yugoslavia, Doris was the luckier of the two during World War II. Prior to its outbreak, her Jewish family fled to Chile, where she lived until landing in Paris in the 1950s in the entourage of Chilean nabobs Arturo and Patricia Lopez. Her society connections and fashion sense led to an executive job with the design house of Pierre Cardin, where Audrey first met her. She was among the match-makers in Doris's romance with Yul Brynner, then one of the highest-paid actors in the world. The couple were married in 1960 and had a daughter, Victoria, in 1962, two years after Audrey had given birth to Sean.

As Mrs. Yul Brynner, Doris crested to the top of international society. Like Audrey, she was considered one of the best-dressed women in the world, but in her case favoring Balenciaga, Dior, and Chanel over Givenchy. She was also as devoted to her Yorkshire terriers as Audrey was to hers. Doris was the more extroverted and socially engaged of the two. She loved to give parties and dinners. Her close friends were the crème de la crème, including several Rothschilds, Prince Rainier and Princess Grace, Fiat's Gianni Agnelli, the Duke and Duchess of Windsor, Loel and Gloria Guinness, French industrialist Paul-Louis Weiller, the Maharani of Jaipur, Italian tycoon Bruno Paglai and his wife, Merle Oberon. Now that Audrey was on her own, Doris kept drawing her more and more into that circle to make sure she didn't turn into a self-pitying recluse.

In the spring of 1968, Mel moved to Los Angeles to restart a career independent of his wife's. Nearing fifty-one, he knew that his days of starring roles were numbered, but there seemed to be plenty of work in movies and television, both as a supporting actor and as a director. He seemed to go Hollywood in a big way, renting a mansion in Beverly Hills and courting considerably younger women. Needless to say, Audrey disapproved, not only of Mel's carousing, but also of the drain on their joint bank account.

That summer, she had promised to permit Sean to spend his school recess with Mel in California. She changed her mind when friends hinted that Daddy's swinging lifestyle might not be the best environment for an eight-year-old boy. Audrey got so perturbed that she neglected to tell Mel that Sean wouldn't be visiting. He flew all the way to New York's Kennedy Airport to meet his son's connecting flight from Geneva, only to find him not on it. A message from Audrey at the transfer desk told him of her decision.

Audrey finally relented when Mel promised to behave himself while Sean stayed with him. But by that time, most of Sean's vacation had elapsed, so he ended up spending only one week with his father instead of six.

Meanwhile, attorneys were trying to work out a divorce settlement that would satisfy both spouses, a seeming impossiblity with millions of dollars at stake. Bank accounts and investment portfolios had to be divided, along with the houses in Tolochenaz and Marbella. Hardest to assess were the percentage deals that Audrey had on many of the movies she made during the marriage, which would continue to generate income for years to come.

An official announcement of the divorce finally came on November 21, 1968, two months after the fourteenth anniversary of the marriage. As might be expected of a Swiss-negotiated arrangement, the details were never made public, but the grounds for divorce were probably nothing more sensational than incompatibility.

Some of the couple's intimates claim that Mel came out of it a very wealthy man, Audrey a sadder and wiser woman, but still a multimillionaire. She also got the house in Tolochenaz and, more importantly for her, full-time custody of Sean. Mel received unlimited visitation rights but couldn't take the boy outside Switzerland without his mother's permission or for longer than two weeks twice a year.

The divorce hit Audrey very hard. To her, it seemed a public admission that she had failed at marriage and as a woman. It also shattered some of her hopes for the future. Fast approaching forty, she knew the odds were against her becoming second-time lucky in love or having more children. But fortunately, she had recently met a man who might prove the Prince Charming that Mel Ferrer had failed to be.

chapter sixteen

PSYCHIATRIST'S WIFE

That June of 1968, some of Audrey's jet set friends in Switzerland persuaded her to join them on a cruise around the Greek islands in the Aegean Sea aboard the yacht of French tycoon Paul-Louis Weiller and his blue-blooded wife, Princess Olympia Torlonia. It promised to be exactly the sun-baked diversion that Audrey needed from the nerveracking divorce proceedings. She left Sean with her mother and the staff at La Paisible while she was away.

During the voyage, Audrey found herself being wooed by a handsome dark blond Italian, Dr. Andrea Mario Dotti, a prominent psychiatrist-neurologist and also a professor at the University of Rome. When they were first introduced, he didn't exactly endear himself to Audrey with his account of a previous meeting when he was only fourteen years old. Standing in a crowd watching the street filming for *Roman Holiday*, he'd stepped forward during a break to shake her hand and wish her luck. He told Audrey that he felt a mad passion and rushed home to tell his mother that he'd just met a beautiful movie star who would become his wife one day!

Audrey had to confess that she couldn't remember the split-second meeting of sixteen years ago. But once she adjusted to the fact that Dotti was no longer a boy but a thirty-year-old charmer, the nine-year age difference didn't seem an obstacle to their becoming better acquainted.

A shipboard romance developed. Repressed for years in her marriage, Audrey relaxed in Dotti's company. Outrageously romantic and attentive, Dotti had "playboy" written all over him, but Audrey didn't care. She just wanted diversion, though by the end of the cruise she'd also fallen in love.

"Do you know what it's like when a brick falls on your head?" she said later. "That's how my feelings for Andrea first hit me. It just happened out of the blue. He was such an enthusiastic, cheerful person, which I found very attractive. And as I got to know him, I found he was also a thinking, very deep-feeling person."

The age gap worried her, but not enough to change her feelings. "I had lived nine years longer than Andrea, but that didn't make me more mature," she said. "Intellectually, he was older than I. His education and his work in psychiatry had matured him way beyond his years. Also, we were very close emotionally. So we met somewhere between his thirty and my thirty-nine! Even so, I always knew that in time he would be forty to my forty-nine, and in the beginning, I wondered if the physical changes would eventually make a difference."

After the Aegean cruise, Audrey and Andrea kept in contact by telephone. When the Ferrer divorce became official, they started exchanging visits to her home in Tolochenaz and his in Rome.

The son of divorced aristocrats and raised in Italy's high society, he lived with his mother, the former Countess Paola Dotti, and his journalist stepfather, Vero Roberti, in a three-story villa overlooking the Tiber. With his wealth and position, he was obviously not someone trying to advance himself on Audrey's fame and money.

Audrey was delighted by the immediate rapport that developed between Dotti and Sean. She never would have continued the relationship if Sean had showed signs of resentment or rejection. If she ended up marrying Dotti, her custodial rights meant that Sean would be spending more time with his stepfather than he ever would with his actual one.

As marriage became more of a possibility, Audrey had other dilemmas to consider. Could an international movie star be compatible with a psychiatrist-teacher who couldn't leave his obligations to chase around the world with her? Would she be able to adjust to being married to an Italian and all that entailed, a completely different lifestyle and residency in Rome, where the climate had always affected her delicate health?

There was also the question of Dotti's Catholicism. Though his own parents had been divorced, church law prohibited marriage to a divorced person. To be married in the church, Audrey and Andrea needed permission from the Vatican, which seemed more trouble than it was worth, because one of the requirements would be Protestant-reared Audrey's petitioning the Vatican to declare her first marriage null.

As Audrey and Andrea became less secretive about their courtship, they began spending weekends with socialite friends Lollo Lovatelli and his wife, the Countess Lorean Gaetani, at their estate on Isola del Giglio off the coast of Tuscany. At Christmas, Audrey and Sean celebrated the holidays with Andrea and his relatives in Rome.

It seemed to be a test of whether a movie star would be accepted in a patrician family consisting of doctors, bankers, writers, and sociologists. But the daughter of a Dutch baroness wasn't the typical Hollywood product, and she charmed everybody with her grace, humor, and unpretentiousness. They were also impressed by her upbringing of eight-year-old Sean, who seemed exceptionally bright, had perfect manners, and could speak Italian like a native.

In the excitement of the Christmas season, Andrea proposed marriage and Audrey accepted. To seal the engagement, he gave her a solitaire diamond ring from Gianni Bulgari, Elizabeth Taylor's favorite jeweler. At a small reception for the press, Andrea's mother, Paola Dotti Roberti, gushed that "Audrey will be an ideal daughter-in-law. She is such a delicious person, a dream. The age difference doesn't matter. She has become so much the perfect woman for Andrea that, for us, she doesn't have any age." It wasn't the most tactful thing to say, but she said it anyway to rebut some of the snide gossip that was circulating at the time.

Realizing that they would be hounded by the paparazzi until the wedding took place, the lovers decided to arrange one as soon as possible. With help from some of Audrey's friends back in Switzerland, the date was set for January 18, 1969, in the town hall of Morges, near Tolochenaz. A civil ceremony conducted by the town registrar would skirt the problem of getting Vatican approval for nuptials in the Roman Catholic faith.

Since tradition said that Audrey couldn't wear white as a second-time bride, Hubert de Givenchy designed her a long-sleeved mini-dress in pink jersey, with matching tights to show off her shapely legs and a foulard bonnet to protect her head from the expected snow or sleet. The wedding attendants were hurriedly assembled from the couple's friends, with Doris Brynner and Capucine serving as witnesses for Audrey, and their Greek islands cruise host, Paul-Louis Weiller, and painter Renato Guttoso for Andrea.

Baroness Ella was escorted by her grandson. Though Sean got on well with his new stepfather, who could tell what went on in the boy's mind as he watched Mummy marry someone twenty-one years younger than his own father.

There was no honeymoon in the traditional sense. The newlyweds stayed in Tolochenaz for a week before returning to Rome to find a place to live. But Audrey had no intention of giving up her beloved La Paisible, which would be used as a weekend and summer retreat. The rest of the time, the house and its staff would be supervised by the Baroness van Heemstra, now residing there year-round in an attic apartment that her daughter built for her.

Ironically, Audrey now had claim to a title

herself as Countess Dotti (handed down from Andrea's father), but neither she nor her husband wanted to be branded as nobility in an egalitarian society. They insisted on the usual *signora* or *signori*, leaving the honorifics to the snobs and phonies, of which the Italian *dolce vita* set had more than its share.

While hunting for a residence in Rome, the Dottis stayed in his mother's villa in the ancient quarter of the city. With money no object, the couple soon found something nearby—a huge rooftop apartment overlooking the Tiber, with panoramic views of Rome in every direction. It had twelve rooms and an outdoor terrace, giving Sean plenty of play space.

Legend had it that four hundred years ago a cardinal's mistress had lived there. Audrey filled its high-ceilinged spaces with a mixture of antique and modern furniture. Paintings, books, and bric-a-brac abounded, culled from wedding gifts and treasured things that Audrey and Andrea had collected separately over the years.

With Sean attending a private bilingual school during the day, Audrey had lots of adjusting to do in her new life as a Roman housewife. For the first time, she had a husband who went to work early and was gone all day, either seeing patients or teaching. Never a late sleeper, she would putter around the apartment in the mornings and go shopping or meet friends for lunch in the afternoons.

Though her face was known to millions worldwide, Audrey could put on dark glasses and stroll around Rome's streets without being pestered.

She favored the antique shops of Via del Babuino and the chic boutiques of Via Frattina and Via Condotti. By midafternoon, she would usually be tired enough to happily indulge in the Roman custom of a two-hour siesta.

In the evenings, Andrea insisted on going out. The couple's only contact with the world of the movies was through attending them. They often caught an early show at one of the small second-run and revival cinemas in the Piazza Barberini and then joined friends at a restaurant or nightclub. It was a new and rejuvenating existence for Audrey, who'd usually been in bed by ten in Tolochenaz.

The Dottis mixed with artists, writers, college professors, most of them as young and hip as Andrea. In their company, Audrey became more outgoing and gregarious than she'd ever been in her life. She drifted from Givenchy couture to the latest Italian mini-minis. She cuddled with Andrea at the movies and held him tightly when they went dancing at the discos.

Although Audrey didn't want to be bothered by journalists and photographers, she tried to be cordial when they didn't approach her in packs. One night in a restaurant she told a reporter, "I'm in love and happy again. I never believed it could happen to me. I'd almost given up. I don't care if I never make another film. After all, I worked nonstop from my early teens, when I started training for the ballet, until I was thirty-eight. I feel a need to relax. Why should I resume work and the life I rejected when I've married a man I love, whose life I want to live?"

On May 4, Audrey turned forty, and not too many weeks later tested pregnant. A joyous occasion for her as well as for Andrea, who'd often said he wanted to have "lots and lots of children." But given Audrey's age and long history of miscarriages, the main chance of that happening seemed to be through the baby turning out twins, triplets, or whatever.

This time, doctors were recommending delivery by cesarean section, which was safer for an older mother as well as for the baby. But in the first two or three months of pregnancy, they saw no reason for Audrey to make any drastic changes in her lifestyle. They urged her to just relax and have fun, which she tried to do. As soon as Sean's school recessed for the summer, the family divided their time between a luxurious beach club at nearby Lido di Roma and weekend trips to the Lovatelli estate on Isola del Giglio. The latter was a tiny version of not-too-faraway Elba Island, the rocky site of Napoleon's first exile in 1814–15.

By autumn, Audrey was becoming unnerved and fearful about the impending birth. With Sean back in school and Andrea involved with his work, she had nothing to occupy her but her worst fears and memories of past miscarriages. Finally, she decided to emulate her friend Sophia Loren, who had recently given birth to her first child after many more miscarriages than Audrey ever had. Loren attributed her success to spending the whole nine months of her pregnancy in bed.

Though Audrey had already let several months

go by, she decided to try bed rest for the remainder of her term. But she chose to do it at La Paisible in Tolochenaz rather than remaining in Rome. One reason was mistrust of Italian doctors and hospitals, which were rated among the worst in Europe. Also, her one successful pregnancy had been in Switzerland and she wanted the same gynecologist, Dr. Willy Merz, taking care of her.

Because of the cesarean delivery, the date could be fairly accurately predicted and was figured for early in February 1970. That would be five months short of ten years since Sean's birth in July 1960.

Audrey would be in confinement at La Paisible for six months, not the best marital arrangement when your husband works in Rome. Andrea could only be with her on the weekends, provided that flights into Switzerland weren't canceled by ice or snow.

Unfortunately for Audrey, Andrea Dotti seemed to have some of the typical markings of an Italian Casanova who lived by the double standard. While his wife was away, Andrea apparently didn't see anything wrong in going out with other women. Had he not been "Audrey Hepburn's Husband," his philandering might have caused not a ripple. But when he was spotted partying with gorgeous women in discos and nightclubs, the gossip tabloids had a field day headlining Audrey's "betrayal" while she awaited the birth of their first child.

News travels fast, and it wasn't the kind that Audrey wanted to hear in her already anxious and delicate condition. The situation got progressively more disturbing as Andrea became involved with a delectable twenty-year-old fashion model named Daniela, a princess of Rome's high life who'd made lots of lurid headlines with romances with Rolling Stone Brian Jones and the French rock star Antoine.

The gossip press delighted in mentioning that Daniela was young enough to be Audrey Hepburn's daughter. The affair reached ridiculous heights when Andrea tried to defend himself by claiming to reporters that his only interest in Daniela was as a psychiatrist treating her for drug addiction. That confused matters even more, because Daniela had no record as a junkie.

It's easy to imagine the rage that Audrey must have felt. Whether she confronted Andrea about the situation is unknown, but he was still keeping company with Daniela at the time he flew to Switzerland for the final days of his wife's accouchement.

Audrey got her wish for another son, born on schedule and without complications on February 8, 1970, at the cantonal hospital in Lausanne. Weighing in at seven pounds and eight ounces, the baby was called Luca, a name that had been handed down in the Dotti family for centuries, most recently to one of Andrea's brothers.

Audrey was overjoyed. After almost ten years of broken hopes, she had another child and at the same time had kept her promise to her husband to give him a male heir. Andrea had been raised in the typical old-world belief that he had to produce at least one son to perpetuate the family name.

Back in Rome again, the newly expanded family had a lot of adjusting to do. Audrey worried over Sean's acceptance of his baby brother. But the almost ten-year age difference between the two seemed to lessen the chances of problems. No longer tied to his mother's apron strings, Sean was too engaged with school and friends to be jealous. Audrey probably had more to be concerned about in Sean's relationship with his stepfather, since Luca was obviously going to be Andrea's pet.

Now painfully aware of her husband's chasing tendencies, Audrey started keeping him on a short leash. There was no renewal of the Daniela situation, or at least no public evidence of it. Andrea Dotti seemed to be behaving normally, concentrating on his work and spending all his spare time with Audrey and the boys.

By this time, three years had elapsed since the making of Audrey's last movie, *Wait Until Dark*. Partly by choice and partly because of circumstances beyond her control, she had no work on the horizon. She would only consider offers that wouldn't take her away from home and family, which meant a Rome-based project or nothing. That wasn't as restricting as it might seem, because Rome was still Hollywood-on-the-Tiber for major international co-productions.

But Audrey was also past forty and had to face the fact that she, as well as rivals like Elizabeth Taylor (thirty-eight), Leslie Caron (thirty-nine), and Jean Simmons (forty-one), were now past the age that the juicy star parts were being written for. The current favorites were Jane Fonda (thirty-three), Vanessa Redgrave (thirty-three), Faye Dunaway (twenty-nine), Julie Christie (twenty-nine), Barbra Streisand (twenty-eight), Catherine Deneuve (twenty-seven), and Mia Farrow (twenty-five).

It would be hard to imagine the fortyish Audrey Hepburn in any of the roles which earned Best Actress Oscar nominations for 1970: Jane Alexander (thirty-one) in *The Great White Hope*, Glenda Jackson (thirty-four) in *Women in Love*, Ali MacGraw (thirty-two) in *Love Story*, Sarah Miles (twenty-nine) in *Ryan's Daughter*, and Carrie Snodgress (twenty-four) in *Diary of a Mad Housewife*. Also, movies in general had shifted toward male-oriented action/adventure fare, in which women were lucky to have major roles at all.

Director William Wyler had offered to un-retire if Audrey would join him for *Forty Carats*, a comedy about a middle-aged divorcée involved with a much younger man, which had been a smash on Broadway in 1968 with Julie Harris. Though set in New York, most of the action took place indoors and could have been shot anywhere. But Columbia Pictures had a Hollywood studio to keep occupied and wouldn't agree to Audrey's demands for Cinecitta in Rome. Without Audrey, Wyler dropped out. Columbia went on to make the movie with thirty-one-year-old Liv Ullmann, which turned out a mistake because she was too young and had a seriousness inappropriate to light comedy.

Sam Spiegel, producer of epics like *Lawrence of Arabia* and *The Bridge on the River Kwai*, tried to interest Audrey in portraying one of the title roles in *Nicholas and Alexandra*, based on Robert Massie's best-seller about the fall of Russia's Romanov dynasty. But Audrey considered herself too old to portray Queen Victoria's unlucky granddaughter. The role finally went to Janet Suzman, who was Audrey's junior by ten years and ended up getting an Oscar nomination for her performance.

Instead of a career, Audrey happily settled for housewifery, determined to make her second marriage a success. She seemed to put every ounce of herself into trying to be the perfect mother and the perfect doctor's wife. Being wed to a psychiatrist turned out to be engrossing and intellectually stimulating. She wanted to learn everything she could about his field of psycho-pharmacology. She accompanied him to lectures and often went along as an observer on his visits to hospitals and mental institutions.

Audrey attacked the role of housewife with such zeal that some of her snobbier friends were appalled. "It's sad if people think that's a dull existence," she said at the time. "But 'keeping house' is in a very real sense just that. You have to be there to contribute. You can't just buy an apartment and furnish it and walk away. It's the flowers you choose, the music you play, the smile you have waiting. I want it to be gay and cheerful, a haven in this troubled world. I don't want my husband and children to come home and find a rattled woman. Our era is already rattled enough, isn't it?"

She was plain Signora Dotti now, eating as

much pasta as she wanted without growing fat. She got up early, breakfasted with Andrea and Sean before they left for work and school, did some marketing, played with Luca and the dogs (three Jack Russell terriers by this time), sometimes prepared a lunch for friends. In the evenings, which tend to start late in Rome, the Dottis had friends in for dinner or went out. Needless to say, there were always servants around to help; the Dottis couldn't have managed without them.

Inevitably, Audrey became homesick for La Paisible and wanted the whole family to spend more time together there. Rome's sweltering climate was a good excuse to stay in Tolochenaz for the whole summer with the two boys. Andrea would make flying visits on the weekends. In August, the traditional vacation period for psychiatrists, the whole family would be together.

In due time, the Dottis would go to unwind at La Paisible whenever possible. For Audrey, it was sort of a spiritual pilgrimage. The splendid old house reminded her of the country estate outside Brussels where she lived as a child with her parents before they broke up.

"You search for what made you happy when you were smaller," Audrey said at the time. "We are all grown-up children, really. Our lives are made up of childhood and adulthood, all together. So one should go back and search for what was loved and found to be real. I would rather that my children one day went back to the country, on weekends or when they want to relax, to search for a blade of grass, than for more sophisticated things which are terribly unreal and disappointing.

"I consider the house in Switzerland our real home, even more than our apartment in Rome, because it has a garden and trees," she continued. "There is something about society and life in the city that oppresses me, a procedure of obliteration. The air is polluted, the backfire of cars is reminiscent of guns, and the noise is so bad you can't hear properly. We love the Swiss privacy, and Andrea says it's the only place where he can really write the papers and reports that go with his work. In one afternoon and evening, he can accomplish more than in a week in Rome."

Although she continued to resist movie offers, in the autumn of 1970 Audrey agreed to appear in the television special *A World of Love*, a documentary about the United Nations Children's Fund being produced by Alexander Cohen for worldwide broadcast at Christmas. Hosted by Bill Cosby and Shirley MacLaine, the program also featured guest appearances by Barbra Streisand, Richard Burton, Julie Andrews, and Harry Belafonte.

It was Audrey's first volunteer work in behalf of UNICEF, though she couldn't have known that she would eventually devote the rest of her life to the organization. At the time, it was just something that seemed worthwhile doing and wouldn't take her away from home and family. Her segment was filmed in Rome to illustrate UNICEF's efforts in her adopted country.

Audrey did some additional television work for pay, with the monies to be invested in annuities for her sons. A manufacturer in Japan, long the land of her most ardent admirers, offered her $100,000 to appear in four spot commercials for "Varie," the chic foreign-sounding name for its line of women's wigs. Audrey considered endorsements undignified and at first refused. But when told that Catherine Deneuve had recently done similar ads for a rival company, she changed her mind. She insisted, however, that the commercials could never be shown outside Japan.

Audrey's second stipulation was filming in Rome, which she treated as seriously as if it were for a feature movie. Before the director and camera crew arrived from Japan, she selected some stunning outdoor location sites in and around Rome, including Lake Albano, ancient ruins on the Via Appia, and the gardens of the Rome villa of her friends the Lovatellis.

For clothes, Audrey dipped into her personal wardrobe and picked some of her favorite things by Givenchy and her Italian standby, Valentino. She asked her longtime team, the di Rossis, to do her makeup and to customize the four different wigs she had to wear. One of them would have been quite amusing to western eyes and probably another reason why Audrey didn't want the commercials shown outside Japan. The wig was in the *mitsuami* style, with plaits on each side of the face. The look was traditional for Japanese schoolgirls, who since the 1950s had been her devoted fans.

In February 1971, Mel Ferrer, now fifty-three, made another try at marriage (his fifth), this time with the thirtyish Elisabeth Soukotine, who was of Russian-Belgian descent and worked for a British publishing house as an editor of children's books. The wedding in London forced a renegotiation of Audrey's full-time custody of Sean, now going on eleven.

Immediately after the divorce from Audrey, Mel had widened the breach between them by becoming involved with a London socialite named Tessa Kennedy, which resulted in lots of sordid coverage by the London press. Audrey wouldn't permit Sean to stay with his father while that was going on. But now that Mel had a wife and seemed able to provide a fit environment, Audrey decided it would be unfair as well as unwise to deprive Sean of his father's guidance and companionship. She didn't want him suffering as she did as a child.

To start things off, Audrey agreed to sending Sean to London to attend his father's wedding ceremony. Later in the year, when Mel and his wife moved to Los Angeles, he became more demanding of Sean's company. He seemed determined to Americanize his son, who, though born a U.S. citizen, had spent most of his life in Europe.

Not surprisingly, Sean adored the casual California lifestyle, so different from his rather formal upbringing in Switzerland and Italy. He wanted to spend all his school holidays there. Audrey indulged him, despite fears of Sean turning into one of those Hollywood brats she detested.

He never gave her any problems on that score.

But in the summer of 1972, Audrey suffered momentary hysteria when Mel phoned from Los Angeles to inform her that Sean had been injured during a visit to a drive-through safari park. Disobeying orders to keep the windows closed, he reached out to pet a lion, which fortunately only clawed him instead of biting off his hand. Audrey wanted to hop on the next plane, but Mel calmed her down with assurances that Sean's wound was superficial and hardly required his mother's nursing.

In January 1974, Audrey and Andrea celebrated their fifth wedding anniversary. By that time, Andrea had resumed his playboy behavior and was often seen out in public with other women. Audrey tolerated it, but only because there seemed no alternative if the marriage was to continue.

Audrey gave evasive answers to questions about her husband's very conspicuous carousing. She told a reporter, "Andrea's an extrovert. I'm an introvert. He needs people and parties, while I love being by myself, love being outdoors, love taking long walks with my children and my dogs."

But she was heartbroken and disillusioned. Longtime friend David Niven recalled, "When Audrey married Dotti and was swept off to Rome, she was, I think, determined to be a very good wife to this very socially minded Roman. She was indeed looked upon as a wonderful wife to him, and the longer it went on, many people felt she was much too good for him and that he took incredible advantage of her and that she gamely played the wife of the social Roman and really let her career just stand still, on purpose, to be with him."

Audrey herself admitted at the time that "nobody forced me to stop working. It's what I wanted. My home gives me more happiness and pleasure than anything else. It would be terribly sad, wouldn't it, to look back on your life in films and not to have known your children? For me there's nothing more pleasant or exciting or lovely or rewarding than seeing my children grow up . . . and they only grow up once, remember."

She probably would have gone back to movie acting if the right script had come along. She deeply disappointed the great Italian director Luchino Visconti by rejecting the leading role in *Conversation Piece*. But she didn't think that she was quite ready or able to enact a matronly widow with a lover young enough to be her son. The role went instead to Silvana Mangano, the 1950s sexpot long semiretired as the wife of producer Dino De Laurentiis.

The spellbinding French star Jeanne Moreau, a year older than Audrey and facing a similar dilemma in her career, wanted to become a director and had written a screenplay with Audrey specifically in mind for one of the leading roles. Entitled *Lumière*, the drama focused on four actresses of varying ages and their intermingled lives, careers, and lovers. Audrey would have played the eldest, but she declined for the expected reason plus the need to act the part in French, which terrified her. Moreau ended up not only directing the movie but also taking the role that Audrey had rejected.

370

Ever loyal Kurt Frings had visions of teaming Audrey with his other million-dollar client, Elizabeth Taylor, and possibly Shirley MacLaine or Anne Bancroft in *Father's Day*, a comedy about three divorced mothers who invite their ex-husbands to a cocktail party on that special day. The play by Oliver Hailey was considered one of the funniest and bitchiest since *The Women*, but had flopped on Broadway because of a negative review in the *The New York Times*. Audrey was willing, but the project died for lack of interest from the major studios.

In 1975, when it was starting to look as if Audrey might never make another movie after eight years away, an original script by James Goldman, the author of the other Hepburn's Oscar-winning *The Lion in Winter*, finally induced her to take the chance. It was a sort of sequel to *The Adventures of Robin Hood*, with Robin and Maid Marian depicted as former lovers reunited in middle age.

chapter seventeen

COMEBACK

The seventeenth of Audrey Hepburn's starring film roles, Maid Marian came nearest in character, if only superficially, to Sister Luke of *The Nun's Story*. After attempting suicide when Robin Hood deserts her to join Richard the Lion-Hearted to fight in the Crusades, Marian is taken to Kirkly Abbey, where she eventually becomes the mother superior. Twenty years after he left England, Robin returns worn out and disillusioned by his experiences in the holy wars. While catching up with some of his former outlaw cronies, he idly asks whatever happened to Marian. As it turns out, she's about to be arrested as part of evil King John's scheme to deport the higher clergy from England.

Robin races to the rescue and takes Marian to hide in Sherwood Forest, where, needless to say, she sheds her wimple and love is rekindled. Robin takes up the cause of all those being oppressed by King John and the even more malicious Sheriff of Nottingham, finally killing the latter and nearly himself as well in body-smashing combat. In an ending out of *Romeo and Juliet*, Marian decides to join the fatally wounded Robin in eternity by poisoning them both.

The revisionist story had to contend with

memories and TV showings of the 1938 Technicolor epic in which Robin Hood and Maid Marian were portrayed by Errol Flynn and Olivia de Havilland at the height of their physical allure. The couple were now supposed to be middle-aged. At forty-six, Audrey could portray Marian without appearing ridiculous. "Everything I'd been offered in recent years had been too kinky, too violent, or too young," she recalled. "I had been playing ingenues since the early fifties, and I thought it would be wonderful to play somebody of my own age in something romantic and lovely."

Author James Goldman was delighted though surprised when Audrey accepted the part. "In her former roles, Audrey always played the innocent woman who had been swept up by circumstances rather than her own choices. As Marian, she seduces herself. It is Marian who chooses to go back to Robin after all these years, to give up her religious vows and return to the uncertainty and the brawling. Marian is a strong woman with a determined will and yet impulsively emotional—it's not what one expects of Audrey's image," Goldman said.

Audrey also realized that *Robin and Marian* might be her last chance at a lavish Hollywood-financed project like the ones she'd grown accustomed to throughout her career. Ray Stark, whose credits included smashes like *Funny Girl* and *The Way We Were*, was producing it for Columbia Pictures on a $10 million budget. The innovative Richard Lester, an American who first made his mark in England with the Beatles' *A Hard Day's Night* and *Help!* would direct.

An even bigger inducement for Audrey was Sean Connery as Robin Hood. One year her junior, he was one of the few contemporary stars with the charisma of her great romantic co-stars like Cary Grant, Gary Cooper, and Gregory Peck. As luck would have it, Audrey was the first female superstar to be paired with Connery since he became an international phenomenon with the James Bond 007 thrillers. His Bond women were all nonentities chosen mainly for their physical perfection. In his non-007 films he'd yet to rise higher than the ranks of Samantha Eggar and Candice Bergen.

Amusingly, Audrey's sons had threatened to disown her if she didn't sign for the movie. Sean, now a six-footer of fifteen, and Luca, a sprouting five, were crazy about movies and especially James Bond. They couldn't wait to meet Connery, and they became even more excited when Robert Shaw, one of the stars of *Jaws*, was hired to portray the Sheriff of Nottingham.

Though a fragment of Sherwood Forest still exists as parkland, the weather in England was too unpredictable for *Robin and Marian* to be filmed there. For virtually guaranteed constant sunshine, Richard Lester chose sites around Pamplona, Spain, where bulls ran free in the streets during the annual weeklong Fiestas of San Fermin. About two hundred miles northeast of Madrid, the town dated back to 1515 and had castles, churches, and stone fortifications to simulate the fabled haunts of Robin Hood in Nottinghamshire.

Originally a director of television commercials, Richard Lester worked fast and expected to shoot *Robin and Marian* in six weeks, starting in mid-May 1975, before Pamplona became packed with summer tourists. As Audrey's first movie since becoming Signora Dotti, it would be the first real test of the marriage from the standpoint of their disparate careers. There was no way that Dr. Dotti could leave his work in Rome to be with her.

With Sean due to visit in June when his school recessed, Audrey arrived in Pamplona with Luca, his nanny, and her trusted Italian friends, Alberto and Gracia di Rossi, who'd done her makeup and hairstyling over the years. There was no need for input from Givenchy. Audrey's wardrobe consisted only of sackcloth habits copied by British designer Yvonne Blake from medieval originals.

After eight years away from the movie business, the thirty-six-day shooting schedule for *Robin and Marian* came as a great shock to Audrey, who'd never worked less than three months on a film and often much longer. But in the interests of economy, all of the old-style Hollywood perks, such as personal secretaries, chauffeured limousines, and expense accounts, had been eliminated or drastically reduced. Even a canvas folding chair with Audrey's name printed on it, the traditional symbol of star status, was not provided on the set. She had to make do with one of the chairs from her compact-sized dressing trailer.

"I don't think Audrey felt very secure, nor did she get much reassurance," script supervisor Ann Skinner recalled. "It must have been nerve-racking for her. I can't remember anyone spending any time with her, taking care of her the way they used to in the big studios."

For the first time in twenty years, Audrey had no say in the selection of the cinematographer, Richard Lester's longtime associate David Watkin, who favored natural lighting and unfiltered close-ups. Not exactly the most enhancing treatment for a reigning beauty who had just turned forty-six. Because of the remoteness of the Spanish location, there could be no screenings of the daily rushes. Audrey wore out her worry beads from not knowing how she'd look on-screen in the finished product.

The fast-working Lester wasn't one of those directors who would stop for retakes, which didn't make it a happy experience for Audrey. As filming progressed, Lester also kept cutting back on the love story to favor the action scenes. Audrey kept pleading with him to save some of the best bits that James Goldman had written for her.

Anyone expecting a romance to flare between Audrey and Sean Connery was disappointed. With two sons in tow, Audrey was unlikely to be the predator, even if it had been her nature to be one. And Connery's fiery French wife, Micheline, was never far away. Having won him from his previous wife, actress Diane Cilento, she kept him on a very tight leash.

Off the set, Audrey played the doting mother

and arranged for Sean and Luca to take lessons in archery and horseback riding from the experts working on the film. "In the evenings," Ann Skinner recalled, "she rarely joined us for supper in the hotel dining room, preferring to have it in her suite with the children. Sean Connery, however, would come down every night, go in the bar, and share in the jollity with every member of the crew. But Audrey kept herself very much to herself."

During the filming, Pamplona experienced its worst heat wave in two decades. Audrey's skin broke out in splotches. Along with most of her co-workers, she also suffered from diarrhea. One day, after she had noticed Denholm Elliott, the film's Will Scarlett, making repeated visits to makeshift toilets in the woods, she offered him some of her antispasmodic pills.

"They may not be the real answer, but they're a damn good cork. I've been using them all week," Audrey told the actor.

Although Audrey's husband tried to visit on the weekends, he was often seen cruising the Roman nightlife in her absence. Newspaper accounts of his escapades were sneered at by Audrey, who told a reporter, "It's his way of relaxing. I wouldn't expect him to stay home in front of the TV every time I go away."

But Dotti's philandering had become deeply embarrassing for Audrey. No woman can stand her husband cheating on her, especially when the whole world knows. And it raised doubts about her own seductive powers. Had she grown so old and undesirable that her husband had to seek solace elsewhere?

Tony Menicucci, one of the most rabid of Rome's paparazzi, made some harsh statements to the *National Enquirer*, calling Dotti "a son of a bitch" and Audrey "a saint." He claimed that Andrea picked up women in nightclubs whenever his wife was away but behaved like an angel when she returned.

According to Menicucci, Dotti became furious in a club one night and tried to hide three women under the table when photographers found them all partying together. Menicucci also said that Dotti usually left the clubs around three in the morning, and that he drove through Rome like a madman while pursued by reporters.

Back in Rome after finishing *Robin and Marian*, Audrey got something far graver to worry about when she and Andrea started receiving mysterious telephone calls that Sean and/or Luca would be kidnapped. Snatchings of the rich and famous had become a fact of life in Rome in recent years, most notably in the case of young John Paul Getty III, who had had a portion of one ear sliced off before his family caved in to ransom demands.

The situation had become so dangerous that none of the family went out strolling in the streets anymore for fear that kidnappers would pull up in a car and snatch them away. As the threatening phone calls continued, Audrey finally decided to take the boys to Tolochenaz, where she believed they would all be safer under the protection of Switzerland's ultrastringent security code.

That wasn't as disrupting to family life as it

might seem. Sean would be returning to his boarding school near Lausanne in the fall anyway. Luca, not yet of school age, could stay with Granny Ella. Those arrangements also gave Audrey an excuse to spend more time at La Paisible as well. If it had been left to her, she would have given up residency in Rome, but her husband's career prevented it.

Not long after Sean and Luca were safely moved to Switzerland, terrorists struck again. Four masked men tried to kidnap Andrea in broad daylight as he was leaving a clinic in one of Rome's suburbs. Luckily for him, the thugs did not use chloroform to knock him out. While he grappled with them, he did enough screaming to attract two security guards from a nearby building. The kidnappers fled in their blue Mercedes and were never apprehended. Andrea suffered some cuts and bruises but was otherwise unhurt.

Audrey was aghast. She also became petrified that her turn would be next. Her love affair with the Eternal City had ended. Her marriage to a man with deep roots there might be the next casualty.

Although everyday life suddenly seemed more threatening than anything she'd experienced since World War II, Audrey set terrorist fears aside and flew to the United States in March 1976 to help with the launching of *Robin and Marian*. In the past, she'd seldom participated in the publicity and marketing of her movies, but it was now going on nine years since the release of *Wait Until Dark*. She knew that her comeback needed to be a major success in order to continue. The offers weren't exactly pouring in, with producers waiting to see how *Robin and Marian* performed at the box office. And even if it proved a smash hit, there would still be the problem of finding more roles suited to an actress on the verge of forty-seven.

Before the promotional tour began in New York, Audrey made a two-day trip to Los Angeles just to participate in the American Film Institute's Lifetime Achievement testimonial to seventy-three-year-old William Wyler, which was broadcast as a TV special by ABC.

Nearly a quarter of a century had elapsed since Audrey and Wyler made *Roman Holiday* together. Exquisitely dressed in a bright red evening gown by Givenchy, she withstood the test of time as she reminisced about the director while clips of her Oscar-winning performance at age twenty-three flashed on the screen. The years had not diminished her glamour or effervescence.

While drumbeating *Robin and Marian*, Audrey commuted back and forth between the United States, Italy, and Switzerland because she couldn't stand being separated from Andrea and the children for very long. At the end of March, Andrea joined her in Los Angeles for the Academy Awards ceremonies at the Dorothy Chandler Pavilion. As part of the hype for *Robin and Marian*, Columbia Pictures had arranged for Audrey to present the most important Oscar of the evening, the one for the Best Picture released in 1975.

Since that came at the end of the telecast,

Audrey watched most of the proceedings from the audience with Andrea. One can only guess what went on in her mind when the category of Best Actress, in which she'd figured five times in the past, came up, with Charles Bronson and wife Jill Ireland as co-presenters. The winner turned out to be Louise Fletcher as the sadistic nurse in *One Flew Over the Cuckoo's Nest,* a role that Audrey undoubtedly would have rejected if offered to her. The other nominated performances were for characters that also seemed out of Audrey's reach, whether because of age or type: Isabelle Adjani in *The Story of Adele H,* Ann-Margret in *Tommy,* Glenda Jackson in *Hedda,* and Carol Kane in *Hester Street.*

Audrey received a standing ovation when she marched onstage in a pink Givenchy dazzler to present the Best Picture award. She crisply announced the nominees as *Barry Lyndon, Dog Day Afternoon, Jaws, Nashville,* and *One Flew Over the Cuckoo's Nest,* then squealed with joy after opening the envelope and discovering the last to be the winner. She'd known the movie's co-producer, Michael Douglas, since his boyhood. He threw his arms around her and kissed her when he ran up from the audience to accept the award with partner Saul Zaentz.

The evening wasn't quite over. In honor of the two-hundredth birthday of the United States of America, senator's wife Elizabeth Taylor-Hilton-Todd-Fisher-Burton-Warner swept on stage in a red Halston strapless to lead a sing-along of "God Bless America." But Taylor seemed to have forgotten the lyrics, so Gene Kelly, one of the evening's hosts, took over as Audrey and all the other presenters and winners were herded onstage to serve as the backup choir.

Audrey and Andrea skipped the Governors' Ball and went directly to agent Irving Lazar's annual Oscar party at the Bistro in Beverly Hills. Lazar had recently seen *Robin and Marian* at a screening and predicted that Audrey would be back the next year as a winner for her performance. But that didn't happen. In fact, she was never even nominated.

With Sean Connery working in a film in Europe, the burden of promoting *Robin and Marian* fell on Audrey. For the Hollywood portion, she brought six-year-old Luca along so that he could visit Disneyland and all the other movieland sights he knew only from half brother Sean's firsthand reports.

It was also Luca's first exposure to his mother's fame. He had never seen how the public reacted to her until she took him to a gala screening of *Robin and Marian.* "Welcome back, Audrey, you've been away too long," said Jack Valenti, head of the Motion Picture Association of America, in his introductory remarks. She rose from her seat next to Luca and received a tremendous ovation that lasted several minutes.

After taking Luca back to Switzerland, Audrey flew to New York for the opening at Radio City Music Hall. *Robin and Marian* became the tenth of her seventeen starring films to date to run there. Because of a shortage of suitable films and the tremendous expense of the accompanying stage shows, the 6,000-seat theater now operated only during the summer and other peak vacation periods. *Robin and Marian* was its Easter attraction.

At the end of the first performance on opening day, a petrified Audrey reluctantly agreed to take a bow on the Music Hall's huge stage. Tears flooded her eyes as many in the audience leaped to their feet applauding and screaming, "We love you, Audrey!" She was too overcome to make a speech.

Throughout her New York visit, Audrey had bodyguards around the clock, the first time in her career that she ever felt the need for any. But times had changed, and between kidnappers and the loonies on the streets, she wasn't taking any chances. She even steered clear of autograph hunters after one accidentally spilled ink on one of her Givenchy suits.

Meeting with the press was a real trial for the naturally shy star. After taking breakfast one morning with two hundred reporters and photographers in the dining room of the St. Regis Hotel, Audrey vowed never to do it again. She also refused to do an interview on the NBC-TV morning program *Today* for fear of Barbara Walters asking too many questions about her private life, which she didn't care to share with 35 million viewers.

Because of the popularity of Audrey Hepburn and Sean Connery, *Robin and Marian* did strong business initially but faded fast, probably because the core movie audience of teenagers and young adults found it hard to relate to middle-aged romantic figures. Less than rave reviews didn't help either. While Audrey and Connery received heaps of praise, the odd mixture of tragedy and frivolity didn't. Many critics found the movie insipid and uninvolving, stripping beloved characters of all their magic.

As Pauline Kael put it in *The New Yorker*, "Connery and Hepburn are a love match. James Goldman and Richard Lester aren't." Kael thought that the writer and director were trying to "out-Kubrick Kubrick" with their carnage and brutality: "When Robin—who has survived body-smashing combat with the Sheriff—is poisoned by Marian, who has also poisoned herself, I was disgusted and angry."

Kael was one of the few who found fault with Audrey's performance, though blaming it on the script: "Hepburn, most of whose longer speeches seem to have come from a spiritualist claiming Elizabeth Barrett Browning as a familiar, has no possibility of giving a good performance. Her fragile strength is perhaps even more touching than before, and those who saw her in her most demanding role, in *The Nun's Story*, know that she can act. But all you can do here is look at her, and, when she's sententious, feel sorry about the waste."

But *Time* magazine expressed the majority opinion when its reviewer said of Audrey's work, "The moment she appears on screen is startling, not for her thorough, gentle command, not even for her beauty, which seems heightened, renewed. It is rather that we are reminded of how long it has been since an actress has so beguiled us and captured our imagination. Hepburn is unique and, now, almost alone."

If nothing else, *Robin and Marian* made it plain that Audrey Hepburn had returned, but where was she headed? She received a mild flurry of offers but nothing that appealed to her. And definitely not Joseph E. Levine's all-star World War II epic based on Cornelius Ryan's best-selling *A Bridge Too Far*. Director Richard Attenborough wanted Audrey to portray a Dutch mother of five who turns her home into a hospital for the Allied wounded. The $50 million re-creation of the Battle of Arnhem was too close for comfort to Audrey's own experience for her to want to live through it again.

The role went to Liv Ullmann, who, after *Forty Carats*, seemed to be making a career out of Audrey Hepburn's rejects. That soon happened a third time when Audrey turned down *Richard's Things*, a British TV movie written by Frederic Raphael, author of *Two for the Road*. The drama about a recent widow seduced by her husband's mistress seemed alien territory for Audrey Hepburn, though it must have been like coming home for Ullmann after her sorties into the perverse with Swedish master director Ingmar Bergman.

Audrey discovered too late a script that she adored and that made good use of her background in ballet. But since director Herbert Ross had already cast *The Turning Point* with Shirley MacLaine and Anne Bancroft, Audrey's agent, Kurt Frings, couldn't persuade him to change his mind. Audrey coveted Bancroft's role, a fading star ballerina about to be replaced by the daughter of an old friend and classmate from dance school.

Paramount wanted to team Audrey with kid star Tatum O'Neal in a tearjerker based on Fred Mustard Stewart's popular novel *Six Weeks*, the story of a divorced mother torn between a new romance and taking care of a young daughter dying of leukemia. But the fourteen-year-old O'Neal tested too mature for her role, and for lack of another name juvenile, Paramount abandoned the project. (Universal eventually filmed it in 1982 with Mary Tyler Moore and child ballerina Katherine Healy.)

Audrey also nixed the lead in a three-part TV movie based on Helen Van Slyke's novel *The Best Place to Be* because NBC wanted her to contract for its continuation as a weekly series, which was far more work than she wanted. The role of the reclusive widow forced to take over the presidency of her husband's business empire became a much-heralded comeback vehicle for the long-retired star of one of television's most popular family sitcoms, *The Donna Reed Show* (1958–66). But viewer ratings of *The Best Place to Be* were not high enough for NBC to expand it into a series.

For lack of any compelling offers, Audrey retreated to family life, moving back and forth between Rome and Tolochenaz as the need arose. "I'm not dying to film," she said at the time. "The older you get, the more you have to resign yourself to either not working or taking inconsequential or grotesque character parts.

Fortunately, I've been able to avoid that trauma by dedicating myself to my family. I may not always be offered work, but I'll always have a family."

The Dottis were approaching their tenth wedding anniversary, which made the nine-year age difference between them more of a problem than in the beginning. Audrey had never been highly sexed and on the verge of forty-nine thought marriage should be more platonic than physical. And as Andrea approached forty, the women he chased seemed to be getting younger and younger. Older women, even those as young as Audrey had been when he married her, no longer attracted him.

The relationship was tottering on divorce. Audrey wanted to spend more and more time in Tolochenaz, but Andrea preferred Rome and also needed to be there for his work. They had fallen into separate lives in different countries. While they were apart (and even when they weren't), Andrea continued to add to his notoriety as a philanderer. Hardly a week went by when a newspaper or magazine didn't run photographs showing him partying and trying to shield his face from the camera's lens.

A story in the tabloids had a friend of the Dottis stating, "It's unfortunate that the paparazzi hound Andrea. But it's also unfortunate that he gives them the opportunity. They wouldn't be able to snap those awful pictures if he was more discreet or stopped chasing, but that's as unlikely as his giving up pasta or risotto."

Publicly, Audrey put up a brave front and made

a bit of a fool of herself with her comments about the press coverage of Andrea's antics. "It's not pleasant for either of us when these pictures appear, of course it's not," she told a reporter. "We have words, just like any couple, but we have to cope with it and ignore it as best we can. Our marriage is basically happy. I can't measure it in percentages, because you can never do that with a relationship."

With Sean and Luca in school most of the year, Audrey's life assumed a lonely and depressing monotony, heightened by the lack of something to occupy her time beyond the usual domestic things. Finally, in the autumn of 1978, a shade more than three years since finishing *Robin and Marian*, she accepted an offer of the leading role in a thriller based on Sidney Sheldon's best-selling *Bloodline*. The movie belonged to a new breed of international co-productions that were financed as tax shelters by American and/or foreign interests and had varying distributors from territory to territory (in this case, Paramount in the English-speaking countries, Geria in Germany, Italy, and France).

For her customary fee of a million dollars plus a percentage, Audrey became, in effect, the box-office insurance that the producers of *Bloodline* needed to line up distributors and whet the appetites of theater exhibitors. For backup, they chose a multinational cast of stars including James Mason, Omar Sharif, Romy Schneider, Ben Gazzara, Irene Papas, Michelle Phillips, Gert Frobe, and Claudia Mori.

Audrey had insisted on some drastic changes

in *Bloodline* before she signed up. Her initial attraction to the project was its director, Terence Young, who'd guided her to an Oscar-nominated performance in *Wait Until Dark* and had long been badgering her for another collaboration. But after Young sent her a copy of Sidney Sheldon's novel to read, she was turned off by the sex and violence, which had never been major components of an Audrey Hepburn vehicle. She also knew at once that she was far too old to play the twentyish heroine.

Whether Audrey was aware of it or not, the role had already been rejected by the more suited Jacqueline Bisset, Candice Bergen, and Diane Keaton. But Terence Young assured her that the age could be upped to thirty-five without causing any major revisions in the plot. He flattered her into believing that though she was a year away from fifty, time had blessed her and she could easily pass for fifteen years younger.

As for the sex and violence, Audrey's agent, Kurt Frings, told her that for better or for worse they were necessary ingredients for a hit movie in the current marketplace. If she wanted to go on working, she would have to adjust to the times. There was no scene in the movie where she had to take off her clothes or behave in a manner contrary to her dignified, ladylike image.

Audrey finally accepted when Terence Young promised to arrange the shooting schedule so that she could stay close to home. Except for a week of locations in New York, most of the scenes would be filmed at Cinecitta in Rome, with short trips for exteriors to Munich, Copenhagen, and Sardinia.

Needless to say, Audrey wanted Givenchy to design her wardrobe and a wizard cinematographer to conceal her wrinkles. Since all her past cinematographers had either died or retired, she happily settled for Briton Freddie Young, who won Oscars for his work on *Lawrence of Arabia* and *Dr. Zhivago*. If nothing else, *Bloodline* would display Audrey Hepburn as still one of the most beautiful and best-dressed women in the world.

chapter eighteen
TENDING HER GARDENS

Elizabeth Roffe of *Bloodline* had nothing in common with any of Audrey's previous characters. In fact, like most of Sidney Sheldon's heroines, Ms. Roffe seemed to have nothing in common with any woman who ever lived, existing mainly to be victimized and terrorized until the breathless conclusion. In this instance, she's a pharmaceutical heiress being stalked by a psychopath who's already murdered her father.

Bloodline was Sheldon's third novel but only the second to be filmed, preceded by the 1977 *The Other Side of Midnight*, which turned out such a bomb that no one wanted to touch his second book, *A Stranger in the Mirror*. But Hollywood has a very short memory, and after *Bloodline* topped the best-seller lists for months, independent producers David Picker and Sidney Beckerman bought the screen rights for $1.5 million. Although Sheldon had been a successful scriptwriter before turning novelist, he preferred others to adapt his novels. Laird Koenig, author of a well-received suspenser with Jodie Foster entitled *The Little Girl Who Lives Down the Lane*, got the job for *Bloodline*.

While two of the screen's most romantic actors, James Mason and Omar Sharif, were among

Audrey's co-stars in *Bloodline*, her so-called love interest fell to Ben Gazzara. A respected graduate of Lee Strasberg's Actors Studio, he'd once been touted as "the next Marlon Brando" but, for lack of similar opportunities, never became a personality of that magnitude. Although he'd starred on Broadway in *Cat on a Hot Tin Roof* and *A Hatful of Rain*, he had had slight success in movies. He was best known for the television series *Run for Your Life*, portraying an incurably ill lawyer who vows to spend his remaining time on the run helping others. The series by the creator of *The Fugitive* aired for three seasons on NBC in 1965–68.

A year younger than Audrey, Gazzara came from an Italian-American family (his original first name was Biago) and had a reputation as being tough, temperamental, and unrelentingly ambitious. Reports of an affair erupted when he and Audrey were thrown together during the New York location filming for *Bloodline*. Audrey was traveling husbandless, and Gazzara happened to be in the midst of another of many separations from his wife, actress Janice Rule.

New York isn't the easiest place to keep a secret. Gossip was soon flying about the romance and its possible effect on Audrey's marriage. When the rumors started to get out of control, she refused to help in the publicity for *Bloodline* because interviews were becoming too personal and disquieting. "They walk in and ask, 'Is your marriage falling apart?' To start in on a person cold like that! One writer told me that if he didn't ask me about my marriage, his editor wasn't interested in the story. It's indiscreet, to say the least, no?" she complained to a friend.

Audrey's affair with Gazzara continued when the filming of *Bloodline* shifted to Munich. One night they attended Liza Minnelli's traveling concert show at the opera house and went backstage afterwards to pay their respects. As Minnelli's personal assistant Bill Thomas recalled: "I think that Audrey and Ben were having a little romance at the time. When she walked in, Audrey was dressed in a black turtleneck and black slacks and she looked incredible. In contrast, Liza had just come offstage sweating and looking like she had been through a war.

"After Audrey and Ben left, Liza jokingly said, 'That Audrey bitch was so fat!' We laughed, and then she said, 'Have you ever seen anyone thinner or more gorgeous? I felt like the ugliest stepsister in the world!' Liza was awestruck by Audrey's beauty."

Several nights later, Minnelli was invited to a midnight spaghetti party that Audrey and Gazzara gave for the cast and crew of *Bloodline*. Liza insisted on giving what turned into a rambling and very adulatory toast to Audrey Hepburn.

"In response," Ben Gazzara remembered, "Audrey got on the table and started dancing, leaping with joy. It came out of her sweetness, out of being embarrassed by the praise. I thought it was charming, better than any words. Speaking words would have made her cry. So she danced. How she danced around the spaghetti plates I don't know, but she didn't break one of them."

As in the case of Audrey's relationship with Albert Finney, the one with Ben Gazzara ended when *Bloodline* did, though this time not permanently. Friends say that Gazzara made such an impact on Audrey's emotions that she started having marriage notions if both ever shed their current entanglements.

But Audrey went back to her husband in Italy, and Gazzara regrouped with their director Terence Young in South Korea for a colossal war epic entitled *Inchon*, which was being produced by the Reverend Sung Myung Moon's Unification Church. Incredible as it might seem, the movie about the opening battle of the Korean War starred Lord Laurence Olivier as General Douglas MacArthur, with Gazzara as one of his adjutant majors.

Though Audrey had no connection with that movie, she persuaded Terence Young to hire her eldest son to work as his gofer during production. Now verging on twenty and getting restless in a Swiss university, Sean Ferrer was determined to join the family business and wanted to learn it from the ground up. Not as good-looking as either of his parents, he was more interested in pursuing a career behind the cameras than in becoming an actor.

Meanwhile, the Dotti marriage continued to unravel. In a last-ditch effort to save it, Audrey proposed a second honeymoon in the Far East, stopping off to visit Sean in South Korea and ending with two weeks in Hawaii. But the trip only inflamed their unhappy situation, and they spent more time quarreling than relaxing.

Divorce seemed the only solution, but they were reluctant to go through with it because of Luca. Now going on ten, he was deeply attached to both parents. Perhaps it was best to wait until he was older before putting him through the trauma.

By this time, *Bloodline*, retitled *Sidney Sheldon's Bloodline* to satisfy the author's ego, had opened to disastrous business and the worst reviews of any of Audrey's eighteen starring films to date. As always, critics were too fond of Audrey Hepburn to be cruel about her performance, but a few said she was starting to look her age and appeared haggard and under emotional strain. What had happened to the Hepburn spark and her obvious talent for picking scripts that turned out to be winners?

"It's a shock to see Audrey Hepburn playing a role that even Raquel Welch would have had the good sense to turn down," said the *Daily Variety* review.

As for *Bloodline* itself, a typical blast said, "It's a ghastly film, hackneyed, humorless, grubby and, worst sin of all under Terence Young's direction, so disjointed as to be a pain to follow." Others called it "trashy" and "repugnant," adjectives never before applied to an Audrey Hepburn movie.

Its only saving grace was Audrey's Givenchy wardrobe, their first screen collaboration since *How to Steal a Million* thirteen years ago. Givenchy claimed that Audrey's measurements hadn't changed since he first met her, and neither had the spare shapes and pure colors he used to adorn her thin, angular figure. In a scene filmed in the upstairs bar at Maxim's in Paris, she wore an evening gown of black velvet, trimmed in lace embroidered with rhinestones and minuscule jet beads. The day clothes, stressing the suits and dresses of a corporate executive, all had the Givenchy stamp of understated elegance.

By this time, Audrey and Hubert de Givenchy, now fifty-one, had known each other for a full quarter of a century. "I'm as dependent on Givenchy as some Americans are on their psychiatrists," she once said.

It was more than a professional relationship. "In the passage of time, our friendship deepened," Givenchy remembered. "I became her confident, I shared in all her joys and her sorrows, the good news and the bad, her marriages, the births of her children, her separations.

"What was astonishing about Audrey was that she knew perfectly how to manage her life. When she suffered—and she suffered a great deal—she kept it to herself. I sensed her in turmoil, but, naturally, I dared not ask any questions. But when she had made a decision, she would call me. Than I would say to her, as one true friend to another, 'Audrey, are you sure that's the right choice? Don't you think it will get any better?' There was nothing more that could be done, her mind was made up."

The fiasco of *Bloodline* appalled and embarrassed Audrey. If that was the sort of garbage she had to make in order to continue working, she knew she'd be better off in retirement. She certainly didn't need the money, and she had too much self-respect to want to destroy the lustrous image she'd maintained over the years. She had no wish to end up a pathetic joke, as legends like Bette Davis and Joan Crawford did in their twilight years by portraying psychopaths and ax-murderers.

But *Bloodline* seemed a hideous gravestone to a distinguished career. If there was to be a last movie, Audrey wanted it to be a good one. In the spring of 1980, she thought she'd found it when director Peter Bogdanovich approached her with a script of his own writing. Because of her association with Gershwin music in *Funny Face*, she saw an omen of good luck in the title that Bogdanovich had chosen: *They All Laughed*, from the song originally composed for Fred Astaire and Ginger Rogers in *Shall We Dance*.

Bogdanovich intended using "They All Laughed" as the theme song, but the movie would not be a musical. The romantic comedy had a premise reminiscent of *Roman Holiday*. But instead of a princess being shadowed by journalists, Audrey would portray the wife of a European multimillionaire. Her husband hires private detectives to make sure she doesn't cheat on him while she's taking a solo holiday in New York.

Audrey was charmed by the script and by Bogdanovich himself. Ten years younger than Audrey, he was a lifelong film buff who seemed to know more about her movies than she did. An actor and film critic before turning to directing, he took what he learned from idols like Howard Hawks, John Ford, and Jerry Lewis and made a trio of hits with *The Last Picture Show*, *What's Up, Doc?* and *Paper Moon*.

Bogdanovich's orbiting career suddenly went into reverse gear when he became personally and professionally obsessed with one of his discoveries, fashion model Cybill Shepherd, and tried to turn her into a great star in *Daisy Miller* and *At Long Last Love*. Those two ultraexpensive bombs lost millions. Shepherd was excluded from the director's next movie, *Nickelodeon*, which nonetheless proved another monster turkey and caused the major studios to lose interest in hiring Bogdanovich.

After three years of idleness (and a breakup with Cybill Shepherd), Bogdanovich persuaded *Playboy* publisher Hugh Hefner and independent producer Roger Corman to bankroll a modestly budgeted drama based on *Saint Jack*, Paul Theroux's novel about a Singapore pimp. The title role was played by none other than Ben Gazzara, just before he made *Bloodline*.

Gazzara was the conduit between Audrey and Bogdanovich on *They All Laughed*. Although *Saint Jack* had received some critical acclaim, it died at the box office, and the director needed a really bankable name attached to his next project if there was to be one. After he got Audrey interested, Bogdanovich succeeded in obtaining financing from Time-Life Films. The three-year-old subsidiary of the publishing giant had yet to produce a hit, but a movie starring Audrey Hepburn, who had graced more Time-Life magazine covers than any other actress, promised to be a gold mine.

Needless to say, Audrey was also attracted to *They All Laughed* by Bogdanovich's promise to cast Ben Gazzara as her leading man. To sweeten the pot, Bogdanovich insisted on hiring Sean Ferrer as one of his production assistants.

By the time filming began in New York City in the spring of 1980, the Dottis had started divorce proceedings, though no one knew how long the case would take. The courts in predominantly Roman Catholic Italy frowned on divorce and tried to make it as difficult as possible with seemingly endless paperwork, hearings, and postponements.

The working reunion of Audrey and Ben Gazzara soon rekindled rumors of an intimate relationship. Through an untimely coincidence, Gazzara's wife was also suing *him* for divorce, so columnists began citing Audrey as the cause of the breakup. To prove the absurdity of that, Gazzara admitted publicly that his fourteen-year marriage had been troubled from the beginning; he blamed the divorce totally on his own drinking, gambling, and explosive temperament.

Gazzara evaded the issue of a romance with Audrey: "We're close friends. We see each other professionally. I'd work with her anytime, anywhere, anyhow. She's a beautiful, sexy, talented woman—much more than the public gives her credit for."

Audrey had recently turned fifty-one years old. Perhaps realizing that her physical allure was diminishing and that Ben Gazzara might be her last chance at attracting a man she really fancied, she pursued him with a ferocity that amazed some of their co-workers on the movie.

Gazzara eventually became alarmed by the

intensity of her feelings. Though he had shared her feelings and the intensity of her interest did wonders for his macho reputation, he was afraid that Audrey envisioned a continuing relationship leading to marriage, which he didn't want. To discourage her, he started bringing some of his other—and considerably younger—lady friends to the set with him.

Audrey soon got the message and was emotionally shattered. But the show had to go on and it did, though she and Gazzara were barely speaking off-camera by the time filming ended.

Although no one knew it at the time, *They All Laughed* turned out to be the last theatrical movie in which Audrey Hepburn acted a starring role. It was also the first and only one in which her eldest son, Sean Ferrer, appeared. Though he had no aspirations to be an actor, as Peter Bogdanovich's production assistant he had to submit to the director's fondness for using personnel, friends, and relatives in bit parts.

Sean played a Latin gigolo named José (courting a woman in one of the many subplots). Bogdanovich's twin daughters, Antonia and Alexandra (by ex-wife Polly Platt), stood in for the children of the divorced detective portrayed by Ben Gazzara.

Despite its title, *They All Laughed* had tragedy hovering overhead. For one of the featured roles, Bogdanovich had selected *Playboy* magazine's 1980 Playmate of the Year, a dazzling twenty-year-old blonde from Canada named Dorothy Stratten. To no one's surprise, she quickly replaced Cybill Shepherd as Bogdanovich's magnificent obsession.

Since Stratten had never acted before, the director encouraged her to hang around the set and learn how a great star like Audrey Hepburn did it. The two women became fast friends, and Audrey taught the younger what she could about discipline and technique, though it became obvious that Stratten was a natural who could become the next Marilyn Monroe with the right opportunities.

But before Bogdanovich had even finished the editing of *They All Laughed*, Stratten's estranged husband, a part-time pimp named Paul Snider, became jealous of the affair, fatally blasted her in the face with a shotgun, and then took his own life. The incident and Bogdanovich's own anguish over it put another pall on his career, which has never fully recovered.

With her murder in August 1980, Dorothy Stratten suddenly became the star of *They All Laughed*. When the movie was finally released, Audrey Hepburn and the other leads might have been bit players for all the attention they received from a news media mainly interested in the murdered blonde and her one chance at screen immortality. The public didn't want to be reminded and stayed away in droves, making *They All Laughed* an even bigger flop than *Bloodline*.

Audrey now seemed to be batting zero for three in the five years of comeback attempts that started with *Robin and Marian*. Job offers weren't exactly pouring in, though at fifty-one she was at least twenty years too old for the leading roles being written for women (which weren't numerous in any case).

Kurt Frings had the bright idea of re-teaming Audrey with Gregory Peck in a sequel to *Roman Holiday*, with the princess now a queen and the reporter a rich best-selling novelist. It would be another spin of the *Robin and Marian* concept, only this time Audrey would have a daughter and Peck a son who fall in love and marry. But the project never got anywhere because of legal complications over rights to the original material.

In an interview, Audrey seemed to be putting the industry on notice that she was available for any good role that came along. "As the years go by, you see changes in yourself, but you've got to face that—everyone goes through it. I can't be a leading lady all my life. That's why I'd be thrilled if people offered me character parts in the future. I won't resent it. Either you have to face up to it and tell yourself you're not going to be eighteen all your life, or be prepared for a terrible shock when you see the wrinkles and white hair," she said.

With no work to occupy her, the children no longer requiring her full-time attention, and a divorce still meandering through the Italian courts, Audrey began suffering from loneliness and depression. Concerned women friends kept telling her she needed a new man in her life. Actually, she had already met a likely candidate in New York while filming *They All Laughed*, but she was too upset by the unpleasantness with Ben Gazzara to realize it at the time.

His name was Robert Wolders. He took her out to dinner one evening to ask her to participate in a television documentary about his late wife, the exotic movie beauty Merle Oberon, who had died seven months ago. Audrey had known Oberon through their mutual friend Connie Wald, the widow of producer Jerry Wald, and of course had acted Oberon's original role in the remake of *The Children's Hour*.

Audrey and Wolders ended up talking for several hours, both sensing an immediate rapport but not pursuing it. Audrey could see that he was still deeply upset over Oberon's death, while he had become aware of her despair and anxiety over her pending divorce. In the months that followed, a telephone relationship developed as Wolders kept calling Audrey in Europe with the latest news on his TV project (which never did get produced). Audrey found him a sympathetic ear and began phoning him with her own news and problems. Soon they were chatting almost every day.

Seven years Audrey's junior, Rob Wolders had been born in Holland. Bizarrely, they discovered that they had been residing only thirty miles apart during the Nazi occupation. Years later, grown tall, dark, and exceedingly handsome, Wolders studied to be an actor, worked in a few European films, and eventually landed in Hollywood under contract to MCA-Universal. His main claim to fame was a season's stint (1966–67) in the NBC-TV series *Laredo*, where he managed a convincing Texas accent as rookie ranger Erik Hunter.

At age thirty-four, he became involved with

fifty-nine-year-old Merle Oberon, by then divorced from producer Alexander Korda and cinematographer Lucien Ballard, and unhappily married to Italian-born, Mexico-based multimillionaire Bruno Pagliai, father of her two children. Passion (and vanity) drove Oberon to emerge from retirement in 1973 to co-star with Wolders in a steamy romance entitled *Interval*, a box-office bomb that she'd financed with several million dollars of her husband's money and which was universally ridiculed by the critics.

But the Oberon-Wolders relationship flourished, turning into marriage in 1975 after Pagliai settled a fortune on her in a divorce. The newlyweds became a conspicuous couple in the international smart set, where Oberon had always been one of its queens. Wolders gave up his modest career to be a full-time husband. Friends say he worshipped Oberon and wanted to do nothing but make her life a happy one. When she died suddenly of a stroke at age sixty-eight in November 1979, he was devastated. Though she left Wolders $2 million, plus their Malibu Beach house and part of her legendary jewel collection, that didn't ease his grief and the lonely void she left in his life.

Oberon also left instructions for Wolders to find another deserving woman to marry so that he didn't spend the rest of his life alone. No doubt Audrey reminded him strongly of Oberon. Though eighteen years younger, she had rare beauty, impeccable fashion sense, and a legitimate claim to being regarded as a classy lady.

404

(Oberon came from the slums of Calcutta but professed to be a Tasmanian aristocrat.)

The initial vibrations between Audrey and Wolders were positive. "We liked each other immediately," he recalled. "It was a normal, friendly kind of contact we had, nothing more. I liked her a lot, and she really did try to put me at ease. Audrey had known Merle and admired her. She understood her death was a great loss to me, and encouraged me to talk about myself."

Audrey once said, "It was certainly friendship at first sight between us. Neither of us was in the frame of mind to fall in love. We had both been through a very difficult and rather sad period. But instantly there was a great friendship and a great deal of understanding."

As the long-distance phone calls became more frequent and tender, another death finally brought Audrey and Wolders together. In October 1980, she received word that her father, about to turn ninety-one in November, was gravely ill. Although she'd been helping him financially since they were reunited in 1964, Joseph Ruston had remained emotionally aloof. He'd never reciprocated her love or expressed any fatherly pride in her accomplishments. Still, Audrey never gave up hope, and she became eager to see him one more time before the end came.

She was also petrified by the prospect of a trip to Dublin. She didn't know what she would encounter there, nor did she feel she could handle it on her own. Not about to ask her estranged husband to accompany her, she immediately thought of Rob Wolders, and he accepted. What transpired after that is unknown, but Ruston died on October 16, three days after Audrey and Wolders arrived. The funeral was carried out in the utmost secrecy. There were no announcements or obituaries in the press. Audrey, and her mother as well, wanted Ruston's fascist leanings and tragic imprisonment buried with him. For the rest of her life, Audrey remained reticent about her father, even with her closest friends. Apparently there was no deathbed repentance on Ruston's part.

In the months that followed, Wolders began visiting Audrey in Tolochenaz—very discreetly at first because Audrey feared the possible consequences. If an intimate relationship did develop with Wolders, she knew there would be difficulties with Andrea, who was still legally her husband and disputing her custodial rights to their ten-year-old son.

Like many men, Andrea Dotti's sense of morality had a double standard. While a husband could philander, his wife and the mother of his children had to be a paragon of fidelity. Even if they divorced, he would be very critical of any relationship she became involved in, especially an unmarried one, because of the damaging effect it might have on the children.

Audrey knew that if she started living with Rob Wolders she would be giving Andrea grounds for having her declared an unfit mother and obtaining full-time custody of Luca. Andrea was already fighting her tooth and nail over that because he didn't approve of Luca spending so much time in Switzerland. He wanted his son to have the same traditional Italian upbringing that he had had.

But love or something prevailed, and Wolders moved in with Audrey at La Paisible in Tolochenaz. Her friends said they'd never seen her happier. Many felt that her two husbands had seemed domineering and calculating. Wolders seemed the exact opposite, almost like an adoring brother, running interference for her but never trying to take the lead. He also probably brought out Audrey's maternal instincts. Despite his surface robustness, he suffered migraine headaches and digestive problems that dated back to malnourishment during World War II. He was only nine when it ended.

Their similar war experiences in Holland gave them an extra bond. Their meeting seemed like the happy ending to a movie about lovers born destined for each other despite impossible odds.

Audrey also sensed that Wolders was a one-woman man. "In her heart, she knew that Robby was her last chance for happiness—a sincere, devoted, faithful man who wouldn't leave her and didn't play around like her two husbands did," a friend said.

But there would be problems. Young Luca took an immediate dislike to Wolders, as he probably would have toward any man who threatened to replace his father, whom he adored. Despite Wolders's efforts to win Luca over, the hostility grew, and Luca began spending more and more time in Rome with Andrea. When Audrey came to visit her son or took him places, Wolders had to stay out of it because the boy would throw tantrums in his presence.

During this period, Audrey also had the disheartening task of caring for her mother, who still lived with her at La Paisible and had been in frail health for several years. Happily, Baroness Ella, now in her eighties, accepted the Dutch-born Wolders as one of the family and didn't resent his being around to help. He carried her back and forth from her bed to the living-room sofa and took her out for airings in her wheelchair whenever weather permitted.

Late one afternoon in mid-November 1981, Audrey received a telephone call from Capucine that William Holden had been found dead in his apartment in Santa Monica, California. Audrey broke down in tears and had to hang up the phone. Though twenty-eight years had elapsed since her romance with Holden, he held a special place in her heart, and they'd always stayed devoted friends. She couldn't reconcile herself to the news, becoming even more depressed and nagged by guilt when it became known that Holden, sixty-three, had died four days before his body was discovered. That the death of such a famous and adored man could go unnoticed so long suggested that he'd been abandoned by his family and friends. He'd apparently been on a solitary drinking spree, tripped on a rug, and cracked his skull on a sharp table edge as he fell.

Capucine, who now resided in Switzerland and had had a tempestuous relationship with Holden for many years, was flying to Los Angeles and wanted Audrey to go with her. Holden had left instructions in his will for cremation and no funeral service, but friends were getting together for a private memorial at the home of his last lover, Stefanie Powers. Audrey had the good taste to decline.

In the years that followed, Audrey had some trying times with Capucine, who, perhaps from guilt over not being more devoted to Holden in his final years, started drinking heavily, phoning friends in the middle of the night, and sometimes threatening suicide. In March 1990, at age fifty-seven, she took her life by jumping out the window of her eighth-floor apartment in Lausanne.

The Dotti divorce was finally granted in 1982, ending a relationship of thirteen years, though the couple had been living apart for the last three. In 1983, Andrea Dotti married the young Italian actress Christiana Borghi. Presumably, Luca could accept a stepmother more easily than a stepfather. In any case, the court seemed to be following Italian tradition by awarding his full-time custody to his father, but Audrey received unlimited visitation rights.

The divorce raised questions about Audrey's relationship with Rob Wolders. Would they marry or just go on living together? Friends believed that a wedding would never take place until Luca outgrew his hostility toward Wolders, which might never happen. Also, Audrey had spent a full half of her life in two unhappy marriages, so that might have seemed enough. Since she was now past the age of bearing children, there was no urgent reason for a marriage license.

But Audrey and Wolders became a highly visible couple, traveling everywhere and making no efforts to conceal their fondness for each other. It may have given Audrey a real thrill just to be able to do that. Such an open affair would have been forbidden when her career was at its zenith in the virtuous 1950s and the early 1960s. But now it was the unbridled 1980s.

Partially by choice and partially for lack of offers, Audrey described herself as a semi-retired actress, but there were frequent demands on her time. Escorted by Rob Wolders, she would fly to Los Angeles for an American Film Institute tribute to Fred Astaire, to New York for a fashion industry testimonial to Hubert de Givenchy, or to Tokyo to open yet another of the film retrospectives that her worshipful Japanese public kept demanding.

There were also sadder trips, some close to home. In July 1983, Audrey lost one of her dearest friends with the death of seventy-four-year-old actor and best-selling memoirist David Niven, whom she'd first met in New York in 1951 while rehearsing for *Gigi*. For the past twenty-five years, Niven had been a Swiss neighbor in Chateau d'Oex, a village near Gstaad. Audrey had visited Niven there many times, sadly watching him waste away from amyotrophic lateral sclerosis (Lou Gehrig's disease). At the funeral service, she was visibly distraught, with tears streaming down her face during the minister's eulogy.

A year later, on August 26, 1984, the inevitable happened with the passing of Baroness Ella van Heemstra at the age of eighty-four at La Paisible in Tolochenaz. Though her mother had been bedridden and heavily medicated for the past three years, Audrey had insisted on taking care of her personally rather than placing her in a hospital or nursing facility.

"I think it's so sad when people have to die away from home. I was very lucky in being able to prevent that," she recalled.

Audrey suffered a severe depression over the death, which had to be expected given the symbiotic relationship she had had with her mother all her life. "I was lost without my mother," she recalled. "She had been my sounding board, my conscience. She was not the most affectionate person—in fact there were times I thought she was cold—but she loved me in her heart, and I knew that all along. I never got that feeling from my father, unfortunately."

It could be said that Audrey Hepburn found herself an orphan at age fifty-five. The deaths of her father at almost ninety-one and her mother at eighty-four seemed to suggest that she had longevity in her genes and could live to a ripe old age herself.

Besides Sean and Luca, Audrey's only surviving blood relation was her half brother, Ian Quarles van Ufford, now at sixty a retired Unilever executive with homes in Lausanne near Audrey and in the South of France. Her older half brother, Alexander, the wartime "diver," had died at age fifty-nine in 1979 in the midst of a long executive career with Shell Oil in Indonesia and Europe.

By the time of her mother's death in 1984, Audrey had not worked in a movie for four years. Offers were still trickling in, but few really appealed to her. The most promising was yet another remake of *The Merry Widow*, this time with Ingmar Bergman or Franco Zeffirelli directing a lavish nonsinging version using Franz Lehar's music only for the background score. The title role would have been Audrey's most glamorous and sumptuously costumed since *My Fair Lady*, but the staggering cost of production and doubts over the movie's mass-audience appeal killed its chances of getting produced.

Yet career was of slight concern to Audrey as she went on with her life, which, for lack of children in residence, now centered around Rob Wolders and her three Jack Russell terriers. She fed the dogs buttered toast for breakfast every morning, which they loved. She eventually bought Wolders a terrier of his own, which they named "Tuppena," or "Tuppy" for short.

"Robbie had never owned a dog, and I thought he should have one," Audrey recalled. "I think an animal, especially a dog, is possibly the purest experience you can have. No person, and few children, unless they're still infants, are as unpremeditated, as undemanding, really. They only ask to survive. They want to eat. They are totally dependent on you, and therefore completely vulnerable. And this complete vulnerability is what enables you to open up your heart completely, which you rarely do to a human being. Except, perhaps, children. Who thinks you're as fantastic as your dog does?"

Audrey often described her life with Wolders in Tolochenaz as "divine" in capital letters. "It is everything I long for," she once said. "All my life, what I wanted to earn money for was to have a house of my own. I dreamed of having a house in the country with a garden and fruit trees. I've lived in Switzerland for more than half my life. I love it. I love the country. I love our little town. The shops. I love going to the market. They have an open market twice a week with all the fruit and vegetables and flowers."

In December 1985, at the age of fifty-six, Audrey became a mother-in-law when eldest son Sean Ferrer, now twenty-five and well over six feet tall, married designer Marina Spadafora, also twenty-five, in California. Thanks to his parental connections, Sean was making excellent progress toward his goal of becoming a producer, working steadily as a junior executive in movies and on TV programs. He was also marrying well, Marina's father being Rudy Spadafora, owner of Spadafora, one of Italy and Europe's leading manufacturers of women's fashions.

Amusingly, the wedding invitations sent out by the bride's parents billed the groom as Sean Hepburn Ferrer, making sure that no one forgot he had a very famous and well-dressed mother.

At the formal wedding at St. Peter's Italian Church in Los Angeles, Audrey, escorted by Rob Wolders, stopped traffic in a bright red long-sleeved silk gown by Givenchy. When Audrey later went over to kiss the new bride, who wore a white pearl-encrusted gown and headdress of her own design, it would have taken Solomon to decide which was the most beautiful woman there.

Mel Ferrer and his wife, Lisa, now married for fourteen years, also attended. At the reception afterwards at the Park Plaza Hotel, everybody applauded when Audrey and Mel got up and danced together as parents of the groom. It was about as close as they'd gotten—or would get—since their divorce of 1968. Except in matters relating to their son, Audrey had chosen to exclude Mel from her life, and he respected that decision.

For a wedding present, Audrey gave Sean and Marina a house in the Hollywood Hills, reportedly valued at $375,000. That was the least she could do for a firstborn son who had seemed a blooming miracle after she'd had so many miscarriages.

In 1987, Audrey finally succumbed to agent Kurt Frings's attempts to persuade her to test the waters of made-for-TV movies. The genre had become a sort of last resort for Living Legends who wanted to go on working but were no longer considered bankable in theatrical features. They had been the salvation of Frings's other major client, Elizabeth Taylor; and everybody from Sophia Loren to Raquel Welch seemed to be doing them.

But unlike Elizabeth Taylor, who always spent her money as fast as she earned it, Audrey had no financial need to work and also wasn't fond of the TV medium, so she kept rejecting the offers.

What made her finally accept ABC-TV's *Love Among Thieves* is anybody's guess, but it may have been just to enable the aging and sickly Frings, who'd been like a father to her all those years, to collect a $75,000 commission on her $750,000 fee.

It may also have been the opportunity to work opposite Robert Wagner. At fifty-seven, he'd long outgrown his pretty-boy phase and seemed to have mellowed even more since the tragic death of wife Natalie Wood in 1981. He was one of the few romantic stars with the charisma of the Cary Grants and Gary Coopers of Audrey's past. If nothing else, the teaming of Audrey Hepburn and Robert Wagner virtually guaranteed a huge Nielsen rating because of her movie following and his popularity from several long-running TV series, especially the 1979–84 *Hart to Hart* with Stefanie Powers.

Love Among Thieves had elements of *Charade*, but this time it was Audrey and not her leading man who just might be the baddie in the romantic thriller. The plot dealt with a kidnapping and stolen jewels, with Audrey as an elegant lady on the run and Wagner as a raffish adventurer she meets while hiding out in the wilds of Mexico. Although it all seemed a bit breathless for two stars past fifty-five, they could probably make it believable with a minimum of close-ups and plenty of Vaseline on the camera lenses.

Produced by Robert Papazian and directed by Roger Young, *Love Among Thieves* was Audrey's first exposure to the world of telemovies, where the working pace was faster and stars received less pampering than they did under the old Hollywood studio system. She didn't enjoy any of it, especially the outdoor location filming in rugged Baja California, where she had to endure hundred-degree heat dressed in ultraglamorous getups by Givenchy.

When broadcast in the autumn of 1987, *Love Among Thieves* received a high audience rating but mostly negative reviews for its uninspired script and the waste of two stars who deserved better. There were also more than a few critics who thought that both Audrey and Robert Wagner had gotten too old for such high jinks and should either retire or restrict themselves to character work in the future.

Audrey seemed to take the advice to heart. She never acted another starring role.

chapter nineteen
ANGEL OF MERCY

With one son married, the other now a teenager living with his father in Rome, and her acting career dormant, Audrey Hepburn needed a new purpose in life. While the liaison with Robert Wolders seemed to be working more serenely than either of her two marriages, at age fifty-eight she was not inclined to take an early retirement in Switzerland. Enticing though it might have seemed when she was younger, she found that life among the Beautiful People could be boring. There were only so many luncheons, dinners, card games, and backgammon tournaments she could take in a week.

Fate took a hand with the death in March 1987 of seventy-four-year-old Danny Kaye, the inimitable comedy star who had spent much of the last twenty years of his life traveling the world as the official Good Will Ambassador for the United Nations Children's Fund (UNICEF). Kaye helped to raise hundreds of millions of dollars for UNICEF's relief work, in 1982 receiving the Academy of Motion Picture Arts and Sciences' prestigious Jean Hersholt Humanitarian Award for his efforts.

UNICEF knew that Danny Kaye would be a hard act to follow but asked Audrey if she'd be

417

interested in taking over some of his work. In the past, she'd often helped them out by appearing at fund-raising galas or promoting the sale of UNICEF Christmas cards. Since Danny Kaye had been a personal friend, and she also felt that she owed the United Nations more than just gratitude for saving her from starvation at the end of the war, how could she refuse?

"My childhood made me more receptive to the ravages of war," she often said. But the examples of Danny Kaye and of her own mother were added motivation: "It's that wonderful old-fashioned idea that others come first and you come second. This was the whole ethic by which I was brought up. Others matter more than you do, so 'don't fuss, dear; get on with it.'"

And Audrey did. Less than a week after enlisting with UNICEF in 1988, she took off, with Rob Wolders as traveling companion and helpmate, for Ethiopia in East Africa, where millions were starving and dying in a tragic collision of drought and civil war. Naturally, representatives of the news media went with her. If her hands couldn't heal, Audrey Hepburn's celebrity could generate instant headlines about places where suffering was taken for granted.

"I'm glad I've got a name, because I'm using it for what it's worth. It's like a bonus that my career has given me," she said later. "My first mission for UNICEF in Ethiopia was just to attract attention, before it was too late, to conditions which threatened the whole country. My role was to inform the world, to make sure that the people of Ethiopia were not forgotten."

Audrey held press conferences and posed for pictures with suffering children in every village and settlement that she visited. "I do not want to see mothers and fathers digging graves for their children," she told a gathering of journalists. "As Gandhi said, 'Wars cannot be won by bullets but only by bleeding hearts.'"

For someone who had always kept her distance from the press, Audrey found it hard to cope with the demands of her new job. "I'd never spoken in public in my life until UNICEF. It scares the wits out of me," she said.

"I wasn't cut out for this job. It doesn't mean that because I was an actress I got over being an introvert. Acting is something different from getting up in front of people over and over again in so many countries. Speaking is something that is terribly important. And having to be responsible. You can't just get up and say, 'Oh, I'm happy to be here, and I love children.' No, it's not enough. It's not enough to know there's been a flood in Bangladesh and seven thousand people lost their lives. *Why* the flood? What is their history? Why are they one of the poorest countries today? How are they going to survive? Are they getting enough help? What are the statistics? What are their problems?"

UNICEF quickly became a full-time job for Audrey. When she wasn't visiting troubled areas, she helped to raise money and support for its causes. "The work that Audrey Hepburn does for UNICEF is imperative for us. It's an absolute necessity," said Lawrence E. Bruce, Jr., president of the United States Committee for UNICEF.

"Many people think that UNICEF gets a slice of the UN pie, which is not the case. The organization has to raise its funds each year, so fundraising is an ongoing effort."

Audrey left no stones unturned. While in New York in the spring of 1989, she addressed 240 children at the private St. Catherine of Siena School on the East Side, telling them, "You are our future. You will make a difference. You will learn from our mistakes, and we have made many." Most of the kids were teary-eyed by the time she finished her ten-minute speech about dying and starving children of the same age.

When Audrey asked for questions, an eight-year-old girl jumped up and wanted to know how she could help. "Send some pennies to UNICEF," Audrey said, "and tell your parents to call the toll-free number, 1-800-FORKIDS, for information about donating money and supplies." When the girl sat down again, she mumbled to herself, "I'm going to do that, to put the pennies in a box or something."

"What was the most challenging event you had to deal with in Sudan?" a twelve-year-old boy asked. "Being there," Audrey replied. "Flying in there safely while a war was going on."

"Yes, I would be afraid, I think," he answered. Turning to the student next to him, he said, "She must be a very brave lady to do something like that."

Audrey also did internal work within UNICEF, helping to recruit volunteers and welcoming new ones to the fold. In her speeches to the volunteers she always cited how her emotional commitment to the organization began with her own suffering in World War II, although her active participation started decades later. "I auditioned for this job for forty-five years, and I finally got it," she would proudly say.

As time went by, Audrey made field trips to many of the 128 countries served by UNICEF, including Bangladesh, the Sudan, El Salvador, and Vietnam. The work was hard, the hours long, the experiences often shocking and upsetting. On several occasions, in Ethiopia and the Sudan, she was in personal danger when meeting with the leaders of both sides in civil wars.

In each country, she learned things that she could use in her fundraising pitches. "Do you know how many street children there are in South America?" she asked in a speech in New York. "All over the world? Even in this country? But especially in South America and India? It's something like a hundred million who live and die in the streets.

"Contaminated water is the biggest killer of children. They die of dehydration caused by diarrhea, which is caused by them drinking the contaminated water. In the last eight years in Bangladesh, we have sunk 250,000 tube wells. They are too poor to have a sanitation system. For a hundred dollars you can pierce a tube well and pump water. It's all done by local labor, but we provide the tubes, the pipes, and everything so that the water can be distributed with the proper sanitation."

The legendary fashion plate learned to travel light. For field expeditions she usually wore sneakers and jeans, topped by sweatshirts or Lacoste pullovers. For fund-raising expeditions throughout the United States, Canada, Europe, and Japan, she restricted herself to two suitcases and a carry-on. She dressed mostly in black and, unstarlike, repeated the same evening gowns. Her jewelry was minimal, too, a good string of pearls and some diamond earrings. In hotels, she pressed her own clothes, did her own hair and makeup, and answered the telephone without disguising her voice or pretending to be a maid.

She still depended on Givenchy for some of her wardrobe. "Audrey knew herself perfectly—the qualities as well as the flaws she perceived herself as having," the designer recalled. "I had not dressed her for a film since she became devoted to UNICEF, but I continued to make some of her evening dresses and day wear. She once told me, 'When I talk about UNICEF in front of the television camera, I am naturally emotional. Wearing your blouse makes me feel protected.' It was one of the most touching compliments she gave me."

Audrey also had become a devotee of American designer Ralph Lauren, whose casual approach suited her globe-trotting. "It's having the best of both worlds, Hubert and Ralph," she once said. "I don't want to compare them. I just want to wear them."

She was often discomposed by the public praise she received for her UNICEF work. "It makes me self-conscious," she told an interviewer. "It's because I'm known, in the limelight, that I'm getting all the gravy, but if you knew, if you saw some of the people who make it possible for UNICEF to help these children to survive. These are the people who do the jobs—the unknowns, whose names you will never know. They give so much of their time. I at least get a dollar a year, but they don't."

Audrey depended on Rob Wolders to help her through. "I could never have worked for UNICEF without Robbie," she said. "Apart from my personal feelings, there's just no way I could do the job by myself. He's on the phone the whole bloody time. He's the one who gets all the flights, for free. UNICEF can't pay for hotels and other things. Robbie's marvelous at it. Sometimes he cajoles airlines for UNICEF needs. He does a million things. When we get to a town where I have to speak the next day, he'll go and check the room and the mike, and he'll listen to what I'm going to say, and he'll tell me, 'No, that isn't right,' or 'It's O.K.,' or whatever. And we have each other to talk to."

Audrey had officially become a Living Legend in 1987 when she belatedly joined the Blackglama mink coat brigade in the long-running "What Becomes a Legend Most?" series of magazine ads. In 1989, she was one of those chosen by Revlon, Inc., for a series of color advertisements honoring "The Most Unforgettable Women in the World," photographed by Richard Avedon.

That year, Audrey turned sixty, a statistic hard to believe about a woman who was still so beautiful and retained the youthful grace of a ballerina. But she also had to face the hard reality that her movie career seemed over, which may explain why she agreed to take a cameo role in director Steven Spielberg's *Always*, figuring it as a valedictory to her almost forty years of film making.

The movie was another of Spielberg's homages, to Hollywood's golden past, this time an updated remake of MGM's 1943 wartime fantasy *A Guy Named Joe*, in which the ghost of fighter pilot Spencer Tracy plays matchmaker between his bereaved sweetheart Irene Dunne and trainee flyer Van Johnson. Amusingly, in the original, Tracy was sent to earth by none other than God himself (called "The General" and portrayed by Lionel Barrymore). But now Audrey would be the dispatcher, a heavenly angel nicknamed "Hap" and garbed in a white sweatshirt and pants. Richard Dreyfuss played the dead pilot (trendily changed to an environmentalist killed while trying to douse a forest fire from the air), with Holly Hunter and Brad Johnson in the Irene Dunne and Van Johnson roles.

Ironically, the original screenplay for *A Guy Named Joe* had been written by Dalton Trumbo, who later scripted *Roman Holiday* under the cloud of the Hollywood blacklist, so Audrey had come full circle in a starring career that started thirty-six years before with that film. Universal Pictures planned to campaign for Audrey for another Oscar, this time for her first supporting role. But *Always* turned out such a dismal rehash of its predecessor that the movie and her performance were forgotten by the time nominations came around.

Perhaps without realizing it, Audrey Hepburn had made her last movie. Starting with *Dutch in 7 Easy Lessons* in 1948, they now numbered twenty-seven, not counting the TV *Mayerling* and *Love Among Thieves*. The total was more than that of a legend like Greta Garbo, who retired from acting at age thirty-six, but considerably less than for others such as Katharine Hepburn, Bette Davis, and Joan Crawford, who were products of the Hollywood factory system and often did two or three pictures a year in their prime.

Since Audrey made only three movies in the 1980s, she was hardly going to miss it, especially with all the work she did for UNICEF. But she did squeeze in one more television appearance hosting the eight-part documentary series *Gardens of the World*, which was syndicated internationally and shown in the United States on the Public Broadcasting System. Serving as a guide to sixteen public and private preserves in England, Europe, the United States, and Japan, Audrey donated her fee to UNICEF.

But there were no views of Audrey's own gardens in Tolochenaz. "She never considered herself a good gardener," said executive producer Janis Blackschleger. "She liked to talk about how good she was at pulling weeds. But that's because she was so modest. . . . We all know Audrey Hepburn is a great legend. But what she was more than that was a great human being. When you were with her you felt prettier, better about yourself and your own possibilities."

Gardens of the World was also expanded into a book, with UNICEF sharing in the proceeds. On publication day in New York City, Audrey agreed to autograph copies that were put up for sale in the flagship store of designer friend Ralph Lauren on the Upper East Side. Potential book buyers were so numerous that the line extended from the corner of Seventy-second Street and Madison Avenue all the way to Park Avenue. Many of the people waiting patiently in the cold weather were unable to get in by closing time.

"I had to leave by a back door because of the crowds," Audrey recalled. "I felt bad because all those people were left standing there in line for so long." The reason for its turtle-like progress was that many fans expected Audrey to sign not only the book but also favorite photographs. "One man handed me a glossy from *Breakfast at Tiffany's*, then another, and another. There used to be a time when you'd just sign the autograph. Now they bring along fifteen pictures for you to sign." She laughed.

Although she'd always shied away from personal glorification, Audrey caved in to requests to participate in testimonials and film retrospectives if UNICEF was the beneficiary. New York's Museum of Modern Art, the Film Society of Lincoln Center, and the U.S.A. Film Festival in Dallas all held galas in her honor.

Afterwards, she described her feelings about the praise: "It's all so—how shall I say it?—it's wonderful, but at the same time you don't know where to put yourself. You just die in a way. I mean, all those compliments. You wish you could spread it over the year. It's like eating too much chocolate cake all at once. And you sort of don't believe any of it, and yet you're terribly grateful."

Audrey's reaction to the incredible excitement

she still caused: "I'm totally surprised. Everything surprises me. I'm surprised that people recognize me on the street. I say to myself, Well, I must still look like myself. I never considered myself as having much talent, or looks, or anything else. I fell into my career. I was unknown, insecure, inexperienced, and skinny. I worked very hard—that I'll take credit for—but I don't understand any of it. At the same time, it warms me. I'm terribly touched by it."

In 1990, Audrey wanted a change from the endless galas she attended for UNICEF and proposed doing "something beautiful with music" that would also raise funds and make better use of her experience as an actress. The result was the *Concerts for Life*, which she put together in collaboration with American composer-conductor Michael Tilson Thomas and which featured readings from the diaries of Anne Frank. They did a five-city tour of Philadelphia, Chicago, Houston, Los Angeles, and New York with the Miami-based New World Symphony Orchestra, followed by a performance in London with the London Symphony Orchestra.

"I'm happy to be able to do this," Audrey said. "Anne Frank and I were the same age, you know. It is a privilege to speak her words. Also, it is a privilege to speak for all of the children who cannot speak for themselves."

Audrey did the narration for an orchestral piece that Thomas entitled "From the Diary of Anne Frank," using musical themes from the Kaddish, the Jewish prayer for the dead. Not long enough to fill a complete evening, it was the centerpiece of a concert that began with Mozart's Symphony Number 35 in D major and ended with Prokofiev's Symphony Number 5.

Audrey gave performances of such mesmerizing dramatic intensity that audiences were reduced to tears. It was the first time she'd emoted onstage in thirty-six years. One can only wonder what she might have achieved if she'd not left the theater for films.

Posterity got one more chance to hear Audrey's melodious voice when she agreed to do some readings of fairy tales for Dove Audio Books for release on cassette and compact disc. Her recordings from "The Carnival of Animals" and "The Mother Goose Suite" turned out to be her last professional endeavor. Given her love of children, Dove expected she would donate her royalties to UNICEF, but instead she assigned them to another organization dear to her heart, the American Society for the Prevention of Cruelty to Animals (ASPCA).

In late April 1990, Audrey flew to Holland to be officially declared a star of the botanical world. It seemed inevitable that two of Holland's leading exports should be consolidated in the Audrey Hepburn Tulip, which has a white flower of exceptional luminosity, a homage to Audrey's work for UNICEF by the Dutch bulb industry.

No better place for its world unveiling than in the gardens of Huis Doorn, once the estate of some of Audrey's kinfolk and now a national museum. The first planting was in full bloom as Audrey and Rob Wolders were given the grand tour prior to a press reception. Joining them was Baroness Jacqueline van Heemstra, Audrey's eighty-seven-year-old maiden aunt and the last surviving of her mother's five siblings. The onetime lady-in-waiting to Crown Princess Juliana was confined to a wheelchair, but that didn't stop her from showing Audrey and Rob places on the grounds where she and Ella had played as children. Afterwards, when Audrey did the ceremonial cutting of her namesake tulip, the first one went to Aunt Jacqui with a hug and a kiss attached.

The world turned a bit out of control in the final months of 1990. When UNICEF teams went into Baghdad in February 1991, even before the cease-fire in the Persian Gulf War, Audrey joined them. While visiting hospital wards and shelters trying to bring hope to the wounded and displaced children, she also appeared in TV news clips that were dispatched worldwide to raise emergency funds. "We brought a convoy of trucks with fifty tons of medical supplies for the children and mothers," she said when she returned. "UNICEF also went there to ascertain the future needs of Iraq and Kuwait. There is no electricity, no water, no sanitation, no heating. The water-purification plants are closed down. The sewage system is backed up. People are both bathing in and drinking from the Tigris River."

Though no one doubted Audrey's sincerity and dedication, the incongruity of that most fashionable of women working tirelessly for the sick and impoverished in the sinkholes of the Third World caused the news media to dub her "Mother

Teresa in designer jeans." Gossip columnist Liz Smith was one of several who also suggested "Saint Audrey."

During World War II, Audrey had never been an eyewitness to the horrors in the Nazi concentration camps, but her UNICEF expeditions into the squalors of the Third World exposed her to sights that were also terrible and singed her heart and mind. Though she tried to put on a brave front, after nearly four years the worry marks were becoming evident. For the first time, she was starting to look her true age, going on sixty-three.

Television talk star Sally Jessy Raphael remembered Audrey coming on her program to talk about UNICEF: "The people who work with me are pretty tough cookies. But during the interview with Audrey these people who've seen it all showed in their eyes such love and such respect. The crew lined up afterwards and she went down the line shaking hands. I've never seen anything like it. Those hardened men and women almost wept. It was as if they knew they would never see her again."

In March 1992, Audrey Hepburn seemed the most logical replacement for Mother Teresa when the latter declined an invitation to attend the annual Academy Awards ceremonies to present an honorary Oscar to India's great director Satyajit Ray. During the worldwide telecast from the Dorothy Chandler Pavilion in Los Angeles, Audrey got a standing ovation as she glided on stage in an appropriately Indian-style one-shouldered rose-red Givenchy, a bold choice given her rawboned thinness. Unfortunately,

Satyajit Ray was too ill to attend, so Audrey introduced a prerecorded acceptance speech from his hospital bed in Calcutta.

It made for one of the saddest moments in Oscar history as the genius of world cinema described the award as "certainly the best achievement of my moviemaking career." Satyajit Ray died a month later. No one knew at the time that it was also the world's last glimpse of Audrey Hepburn as the elegantly dressed movie star.

Four months later, in the summer of 1992, Audrey started experiencing abdominal pain accompanied by colitis, which she dismissed as one of the hazards of traveling under unsanitary conditions in the Third World. Though her doctors in Switzerland wanted to put her in the hospital for tests, she refused to postpone a UNICEF trip to war- and famine-racked Somalia in East Africa.

Accompanied as always by Rob Wolders, Audrey arrived in Somalia looking "exhausted, pale, and very sick," said local UN official Mary Ngigi. "We pleaded with her to rest and not push herself too hard, but she refused. She insisted on taking a grueling twenty-four-hour trip by Land-Rover to a refugee camp at Baydhabo, where hundreds of children had died."

Audrey got there just in time to see some of the corpses being loaded onto trucks for mass burial. "I walked right into a nightmare," she said after returning to the capital city of Mogadishu. "No media report could have prepared me for the unspeakable agony I felt seeing countless little fragile, emaciated children, sitting under the trees waiting to be fed, most of them ill. I'll never forget their huge eyes in tiny faces and the terrible silence."

Pictures taken by a UNICEF photographer of Audrey with starving Somali children were some of the most heartbreaking published since World War II, including one in particular in which she cradled a barely living bundle of skin and bones in her arms. What made it even more poignant was that Audrey herself looked ill and painfully thin, with barely enough strength to lift the emaciated child for longer than the split second needed to snap the photo.

Throughout the African trip and after returning to Tolochenaz, Audrey continued to suffer stomach pain. Doctors still believed it to be an amoebic infection, but at the insistence of eldest son Sean, her Hollywood friend Connie Wald and, of course, Rob Wolders, she finally agreed to fly to Los Angeles to undergo tests at Cedars-Sinai Medical Center. Besides being one of the most advanced and trusted hospitals in the United States, it was also expert at protecting the privacy of the many celebrities seeking treatment there.

On November 2, 1992, three days after being admitted, Audrey underwent surgery for colon cancer. A hospital spokesman told reporters, "There is a strong feeling that surgeons removed all of the malignancy and that none of her organs were compromised."

Before the week was over, gossip tabloids were claiming otherwise. A cover story in *National*

Enquirer said the cancer had spread too far to be effectively treated and that Audrey had been told that she had no more than three months to live.

Longtime friends including Gregory Peck and Roger Moore phoned the Associated Press and other wire services and vehemently denied the reports, which, of course, turned out to be at least partially true. Whether doctors would have been that heartlessly candid with Audrey about her terminal condition seems unlikely, but she was apparently given some hint of its gravity.

"I spoke with her after the operation," Hubert de Givenchy recalled. "She was dumbfounded that she had cancer. She had been convinced that she had contracted a virulent amoebic infection during her work in the Third World. She said to me, 'See, it's thanks to the children that I'm here. If I hadn't believed that I had an infection, I would never have seen a doctor.' Audrey always wanted to see the good side of things. For her, the good side could come only from the children."

Givenchy said that "Audrey wanted to fight, like she had done against famine in Somalia by pleading with world leaders to end the war there. But it turned out that the illness could not be beaten, either by Audrey or the people who tried to help. She was so totally loved that I never stopped hearing from friends—and strangers—who knew of such and such a doctor who could save her. 'Go see him for me, we're all going to fight this together,' they would say."

Luca Dotti, now twenty-two, flew over from Rome to join Sean Ferrer and Rob Wolders at Audrey's bedside. Two weeks after the operation, she was strong enough to be transferred to Connie Wald's house in Beverly Hills. But with the Christmas holidays approaching, she wanted to be taken back to her beloved La Paisible in Tolochenaz, her home now for going on twenty-seven years.

Since Audrey was too frail to travel by commercial airliner, Hubert de Givenchy prevailed on another member of his charmed circle, the super-rich American socialite Bunny Mellon, to loan her private Gulfstream jet. Mellon, who shared Audrey's passion for gardening, filled the plane with flowers—huge bouquets of every species imaginable—to make the long flight to Switzerland more pleasant.

Between the cold, snow, and shortened daylight, December wasn't the best time to enjoy what Audrey liked best about Tolochenaz, but she was sinking fast and probably didn't notice the difference. Unable to keep down solid food, she was being fed intravenously and spent most of the time in bed, her pain alleviated by morphine. When she felt strong enough, her two nurses walked her to the window or, weather permitting, wrapped her in a heavy coat and took her out into the garden. Seeing her breath in the winter air made her feel alive and gave her comfort.

Audrey was also cheered by notification from the White House in Washington, D.C., that she had been chosen as one of the recipients of the Presidential Medal of Freedom for 1992, in recognition of her work for UNICEF. Because of her inability to attend the official ceremonies hosted by President and Mrs. Bush, Audrey's gold medal was personally delivered to her by the U.S. Ambassador to Switzerland.

On Christmas Eve, Audrey gathered her sons and Rob Wolders around her and read them a letter that one of her favorite authors had once written to a grandchild. It said, "If you ever need a helping hand, it's at the end of your arm. As you get older, you must remember that you have a second hand. The first one is to help yourself, the second one is to help others."

Early in January 1993, the Academy of Motion Picture Arts and Sciences announced that Audrey would be given the Jean Hersholt Humanitarian Award for her work with UNICEF at the next Oscar festivities in March (Elizabeth Taylor would also be cited for her AIDS endeavors). Ironically, Hersholt, who died in 1956, had presented Audrey with her Oscar for *Roman Holiday* at the 1953 ceremonies.

A week later, Audrey took what turned out to be her last walk around the gardens of La Paisible. With her dogs at her heels and with Rob Wolders and close friend Doris Brynner supporting her, she stopped at each flower bed and told them exactly what was planted there and what care would be needed when spring came.

Audrey died in her sleep in January 20, 1993. Her passing at age sixty-three (she would have turned sixty-four on May 4) was announced to the world by UNICEF director James Grant, who said, "Children everywhere will feel her death as a painful and irreplaceable loss."

Audrey had survived the operation by seventy-nine days, a shade less than the three months doctors had predicted. Friends claim that she had wasted away to seventy-five pounds but that she never complained once. "It's not that bad," she would say.

But even with medication Audrey experienced terrible pain toward the end and could speak only in a whisper. She could not talk to the acquaintances who kept phoning her from all over the world or even hold the receiver to listen, so Rob Wolders served as intermediary.

In the days following Audrey's death, it seemed as if the whole world had gone into mourning as the news media paid honor to her luminous screen career and her humanitarianism. Most quoted was Elizabeth Taylor's tribute: "Audrey was a lady with an elegance and a charm that was unsurpassed, except by her love for underprivileged children all over the world. God has a most beautiful new angel now that will know just what to do in heaven."

"Farewell Fair Lady" and "We Grew Accustomed to Her Face" turned up with remarkable frequency as the headlines of obituaries and editorials in every language from English and Japanese to Arabic and Hebrew. *Le Soir* in her birthplace of Brussels, Belgium, chose *"Adieu a l'Ange des Enfants."*

While honoring Audrey as "an impassioned ambassador for UNICEF," an editorial in *The New York Times* remembered her for the way she looked: "What a burden she lifted from women! Here was proof that looking good need not be synonymous with looking bimbo. Thanks to their first glimpse of Audrey Hepburn in 'Roman

Holiday,' half a generation of young females stopped stuffing their bras and teetering on stiletto heels.

"Nearly forty years later Audrey Hepburn's face was that of someone who'd squinted into the sun, laughed a few laughs, shed a few tears. The forehead showed some wrinkles, the eyes showed some more, and the strong jawline was softening around the edges.

"As unwilling to fake youth as she had been to fake voluptuousness, she looked like the 63-year-old woman she was. Which is to say, better than any 63-year-old woman who's pretending that she isn't. Would that she were going to be around longer, to teach us all how to grow old."

Audrey's funeral was held at noon on Sunday January 24, in the old Protestant church situated only a few hundred yards from her beloved La Paisible in Tolochenaz. The late morning air was unusually mild and clear as cars delivered floral arrangements sent by absent friends, including Gregory Peck, Elizabeth Taylor, and the Dutch royal family.

Exactly how many friends and relatives were invited is unknown, but about 120 attended, headed by Audrey's two sons, ex-husbands Mel Ferrer and Andrea Dotti, Rob Wolders, half brother Ian Quarles van Ufford, close friends Doris Brynner and Connie Wald, and numerous UNICEF officials. Celebrity mourners included Hubert de Givenchy and actors Roger Moore and Alain Delon, neither of whom had ever made films with Audrey but were her adoring chums for many years.

Givenchy recalled a moment when the group were all assembling at Audrey's house: "Along with the fragrance of the floral tributes, I noticed the fragrance of apples. I had to know where it came from, so I asked a servant. A part of the cellar was filled by the harvest of the previous autumn, which they were preparing to send, at Audrey's wish, as in previous years, to the Salvation Army. Audrey was that way. She thought constantly of others, in all discretion, in all humility. That's what was so marvelous about her and made her someone almost spiritual."

The unpretentiousness of the funeral seemed pure Audrey Hepburn. Her simple pine coffin was carried from La Paisible to the church by Sean and Luca, Andrea Dotti, Rob Wolders, Givenchy, and Ian van Ufford. Mel Ferrer, now seventy-five and looking too frail to share the burden, walked behind them. About seven hundred of the local villagers had gathered to stand outside in respectful silence, listening to the private service on loudspeakers.

Presiding was eighty-three-year-old retired pastor Maurice Eindiguer, who had married Audrey and Mel in 1954 and baptized Sean in 1960. Much more recently, just two hours before Audrey's death, he had given her the last rites. Now, his voice trembling with emotion, he said, "Even in her illness, she visited those children of Somalia. And in their faces was a light reflected from her smile."

Prince Sadruddin Aga Khan, a former head of the United Nations High Commission on Refugees, gave the eulogy, noting that Audrey had chosen to "dedicate herself to humanity. She said that she liked the dangerous places. She was a real trouper. When she went out to the refugee camps, to the squalor of the tents, the mud hovels, think of what she brought to these children. She reached out to them with her smile, her hands and her heart. She was truly what the United Nations is about. She will continue to inspire us. Thank you, Audrey. *Au revoir* and God bless."

Sean Ferrer rose to the pulpit for a few final words about his mother: "She believed love could heal, fix, mend, and make everything fine and good in the end. And it did. She left us with peace, serenity, and her passage was almost devoid of any pain."

After hymns sung by a children's choir from the St. Georges International School in Montreux, the pallbearers, closely followed by the rest of the invited mourners, carried Audrey's coffin the short distance to the village cemetery. Meanwhile, townsfolk milled around reminiscing with reporters about Audrey, remembering how her French became tinged with the local accent, how she had taken pride in her gardens and orchards, and how she had always chatted with passers-by and asked after their children.

"She was a star in France, England, the U.S., Italy," said Mayor Pierre Alain Mercier. "But here she was just another neighbor. I used to see her working on her flowers, like anyone else, and we'd say hello. Everyone knew the same thing about her: She was a person like any other—not at all a star."

The weather had suddenly turned gray and chilly as Audrey's coffin, with a single white namesake tulip on the lid, was lowered into the ground. Her grave, marked by a plain pinewood cross reading "Audrey Hepburn, 1929–1993," sits atop a small knoll overlooking Lake Geneva, with the blue Jura Mountains in the distance. In the other direction is a view of fields and vine-yards, which seems perfect for a woman who was happy whenever she could tend her gardens.

acknowledgments

I suppose I could say that I began this book at age seventeen in 1953, when I saw Audrey Hepburn's first starring movie, *Roman Holiday,* for at least ten times in one week while working as an usher at Loew's Valencia Theatre (now an evangelical church!) in Jamaica, Long Island. Perhaps because we were near contemporaries, she instantly became my favorite movie actress. Over the years, I followed her career and personal life with intense interest, which eventually gave me a head start when I took on this project shortly after her death. I had seen all of her movies in their original release—as they were meant to be seen on the big theater screen—and in the context of the times in which they were produced.

Grateful thanks are extended to all those people who granted interviews and/or assisted in the research. I must start in Breda, Holland, with Mrs. Joke Quarles van Ufford-Snijder, daughter-in-law of Audrey's eldest half-brother, the late Alexander Quarles van Ufford. Over a period of six months, Mrs. Quarles supplied me with bundle after bundle of information from the family archives, including photographs, copies of vital documents (Audrey's birth certificate among them), personal memories, Dutch press clippings covering forty years, as well as a sack of Audrey Hepburn tulip bulbs. I shall never forget her kindness and generosity.

A special medal should also go to another Dutch lady, Nen Roeterdink, a dear friend of mine in Amsterdam for almost twenty-five years. She was not only instrumental in obtaining Mrs. Quarles's cooperation but also provided me with English translations of anything I requested and did valuable research at the Netherlands Film Museum and Archive.

The secrets of Joseph Ruston's past were initially unlocked for me by Lady Diana Mosley, widow of Oswald Mosley, from her home in Orsay, France. In a hand-written letter dated July 3, 1993, she confirmed Ruston's and the Baroness van Heemstra's memberships in the BUF and also referred me for more details to A. W. B. Simpson's then recently published book, *In the Highest Degree Odious: Detention Without Trial in Wartime Britain.*

In a subsequent correspondence that I had with the Oxford-based Professor Simpson, he told me of reports he'd heard of an article written by Baroness Ella for *The Blackshirt*, which I was able to find in the Periodicals Division of the New York Public Library at 42nd Street. I thank him for his tip, which also led to further research at the British War Museum in London, with assistance from my English friend Ron Samuels.

On the other side of the Atlantic, I must also thank Joan Barker of the Historical Section of the Bank of England and Annette Onyn of the Brussels Office of Tourism and Information for helping me to set the record straight on Ruston's employment and the family's residency in Belgium.

Producer Morton Gottlieb, whom Audrey always affectionately called "The man who brought me to America," was a great help on *Gigi* and her residency in New York during that time. I must also commend him for pedaling to the interview on his bicycle, an act of bravery in midtown Manhattan traffic.

Over the years, while working on my previous books, I became friendly with the late Kurt Frings, who often spoke about Audrey with me without either of us realizing that he was providing me with insights for this book. Similarly, the late Edith Head, the late Anita Loos, and the late Margaret (Mrs. William) Wyler were also very enlightening in our conversations.

Grateful thanks are also given to the following for sharing memories and information (and to the others who preferred to remain anonymous): Walter Alford, Alan Arkin, Rona Barrett, the late Sorrell Booke, Alexander Cohen, Richard Crenna, Jean Cummings, Tony Curtis, Dino De Laurentiis, Stanley Donen, Pastor Maurice Eindiguer, Blake Edwards, Eddie Fisher, Joseph Friedman, Radie Harris, Richard Harris, Freddie Heineken, George Kennedy, Leo Lerman, Richard Lester, Henry Mancini, Patricia Neal, Marni Nixon, Jerry Orbach, Henry Rogers, Robert Ullman, Eli Wallach, Martha Hyer Wallis, Nat Weiss, Irene Worth, and Freddie Young.

Poet and writer James Kirkup, who lived and

taught in Japan for many years, provided analysis of the Japanese public's fascination with Audrey Hepburn. His friend and associate, Masako Bamba, did additional research and contact work for me in Tokyo.

In New York, I must thank the staffs of the Performing Arts Library at Lincoln Center and the Film Research Library of the Museum of Modern Art for their assistance. Jerry Silverstein helped with research in Los Angeles at the libraries of the Academy of Motion Picture Arts and Sciences, the American Film Institute, and the University of Southern California.

A further note of gratitude to editor Bob Bender and his assistant, Johanna Li, as well as to my agent, Daniel Strone. Last but not least, hugs and kisses to all the relatives and friends who helped me through, starting with Stella & Russ, Lisa & Brian, Marilyn & Phil, Aunt Ruth & Uncle Steve, Edith & Dave, Yaffa & Jerry, Georgina Hale, Eva Franklin, Florence Wulach, and the Barry Conley circle.

filmography

Dutch in 7 Easy Lessons (Netherlands, 1948). Producer: Hein Josephson. Director: Charles Huguenot van der Linden. Audrey Hepburn made her movie debut in a bit part as an airline hostess in this semi-documentary about a cinematographer (acted by Wam Heskes) given seven days to shoot an aerial travelogue of Holland. B&W, approximately 40 minutes running time. Original Dutch title: *Nederlands in 7 Lessen*.

One Wild Oat (Great Britain, 1951). AH was an uncredited extra in this comedy, which starred Robertson Hare and Stanley Holloway (twelve years later cast as her father, Alfred P. Doolittle, in *My Fair Lady*). B&W, 78 minutes.

Laughter in Paradise (Great Britain, 1951). AH had a bit part as a cigarette girl in a nightclub. Cast: Alastair Sim, Fay Compton, Guy Middleton, George Cole, Joyce Grenfell, Anthony Steel, A. E. Matthews, Beatrice Campbell. Producer-Director: Mario Zampi. Screenplay: Michael Pertwee, Jack Davies. B&W, 95 minutes.

The Lavender Hill Mob (Great Britain, 1951). AH had a bit part as Chiquita in Brazilian airport scene. Cast: Alec Guinness, Stanley Holloway,

Sidney James, Alfie Bass, Marjorie Fielding, John Gregson, Sydney Tafler. Producer: Michael Truman. Director: Charles Crichton. Screenplay: T. E. B. Clarke. B&W, 82 minutes.

Young Wives' Tale (Great Britain, 1951). Cast: Joan Greenwood, Nigel Patrick, Derek Farr, Guy Middleton, Athene Seyler, Helen Cherry, Audrey Hepburn, Fabia Drake, Irene Handl, Joan Sanderson. Producer: Victor Skutezky. Director: Henry Cass. Screenplay: Anne Burnaby, from the stage play by Ronald Jeans. B&W, 78 minutes.

The Secret People (Great Britain, 1952). Cast: Valentina Cortese, Serge Reggiani, Audrey Hepburn, Charles Goldner, Megs Jenkins, Irene Worth, Angela Fouldes, Athene Seyler, Sydney Tafler. Producer: Sidney Cole. Director: Thorold Dickinson. Screenplay: Thorold Dickinson and Wolfgang Wilhelm. B&W, 91 minutes.

Monte Carlo Baby (Great Britain, 1952). Cast: Ray Ventura, Jules Munshin, Cara Williams, Philippe LeMaire, Audrey Hepburn, John Van Dreelan, Marcel Dalio, Russell Collins. Producer: Ray Ventura. Directors: Jean Boyer, Jean Jerrold. Screenplay: Jean Boyer, Jean Jerrold, Alex Jaffe. B&W, 70 minutes. Filmed simultaneously was a French-language version entitled *Nous Irons à Monte Carlo*.

Roman Holiday (Paramount, 1953). Cast: Gregory Peck, Audrey Hepburn, Eddie Albert, Hartley Power, Harcourt Williams, Margaret

Rawlings, Tullio Carminati. Producer-Director: William Wyler. Screenplay: Ian McLellan Hunter, John Dighton (Dalton Trumbo). Cinematographers: Franz Planer, Henri Alekan. Music: Georges Auric. B&W, 119 minutes.

Sabrina (Paramount, 1954). Cast: Humphrey Bogart, Audrey Hepburn, William Holden, Walter Hampden, John Williams, Martha Hyer, Joan Vohs, Marcel Dalio, Marcel Hillaire, Nella Walker, Francis X. Bushman, Ellen Corby, Majorie Bennett, Nancy Kulp, Paul Harvey. Producer-Director: Billy Wilder. Screenplay: Billy Wilder, Samuel Taylor, and Ernest Lehman, based on Taylor's Broadway stage play *Sabrina Fair*. Cinematographer: Charles Lang, Jr. Music: Frederick Hollander. B&W, 113 minutes.

War and Peace (Paramount, Ponti-De Laurentiis, 1956). Cast: Audrey Hepburn, Henry Fonda, Mel Ferrer, John Mills, Herbert Lom, Oscar Homolka, Vittorio Gassman, Anita Ekberg, Helmut Dantine, Barry Jones, Wilfrid Lawson, Jeremy Brett, Milly Vitale. Producers: Carlo Ponti, Dino De Laurentiis. Director: King Vidor. Screenplay: Bridget Boland, Robert Westerby, King Vidor, Mario Camerini, Ennio DeConcini, and Ivo Perelli, from Leo Tolstoy's novel. Cinematographers: Jack Cardiff, Aldo Tonti. Music: Nino Rota. VistaVision, Technicolor, 208 minutes.

Funny Face (Paramount, 1957). Cast: Audrey Hepburn, Fred Astaire, Kay Thompson, Michel

Auclair, Robert Flemyng, Dovima, Virginia Gibson, Suzy Parker, Sue England, Ruta Lee, Alex Gerry, Carole Eastman. Producer: Roger Edens. Director: Stanley Donen. Screenplay: Leonard Gershe, adapted from his unproduced play *Wedding Day*. Cinematographer: Ray June. Music: George and Ira Gershwin, with additional songs by Roger Edens and Leonard Gershe. VistaVision, Technicolor, 103 minutes.

Love in the Afternoon (Allied Artists, 1957). Cast: Gary Cooper, Audrey Hepburn, Maurice Chevalier, John McGiver, Van Doude, Lise Bourdin, Olga Valery, Michael Kokas. Producer-Director: Billy Wilder. Screenplay: Billy Wilder and I. A. L. Diamond, from Claude Anet's novel *Ariane*. Cinematographer: William Mellor. Music: Franz Waxman, except for "Fascination," composed by F. D. Marchetti. B&W, 130 minutes.

The Nun's Story (Warner Brothers, 1959). Cast: Audrey Hepburn, Peter Finch, Edith Evans, Peggy Ashcroft, Dean Jagger, Mildred Dunnock, Patricia Collinge, Beatrice Straight, Rosalie Crutchley, Ruth White, Barbara O'Neill, Margaret Phillips, Colleen Dewhurst, Stephen Murray, Lionel Jeffries, Niall MacGinnis. Producer: Henry Blanke. Director: Fred Zinnemann. Screenplay: Robert Anderson, from the book by Kathryn C. Hulme. Cinematographer: Franz Planer. Music: Franz Waxman. Technicolor, 149 minutes.

Green Mansions (MGM, 1959). Cast: Audrey Hepburn, Anthony Perkins, Lee J. Cobb, Sessue Hayakawa, Henry Silva, Nehemiah Persoff. Producer: Edmund Grainger. Director: Mel Ferrer. Screenplay: Dorothy Kingsley, from the novel by W. H. Hudson. Cinematographer: Joseph Ruttenberg. Music: Bronislau Kaper, incorporating compositions by Hector Villa-Lobos commissioned for the abandoned Vincente Minnelli film. Panavision, MetroColor, 104 minutes. (Though produced after *The Nun's Story*, *Green Mansions* was released theatrically three months earlier.)

The Unforgiven (United Artists, 1960). Cast: Burt Lancaster, Audrey Hepburn, Audie Murphy, Lillian Gish, Charles Bickford, Doug McLure, John Saxon, Joseph Wiseman, Albert Salmi, June Walker. Producer: James Hill, for Hecht-Hill-Lancaster Productions. Director: John Huston. Screenplay: Ben Maddow, from the novel by Alan LeMay. Cinematographer: Franz Planer. Music: Dimitri Tiomkin. Panavision, Technicolor, 125 minutes.

Breakfast at Tiffany's (Paramount, 1961). Cast: Audrey Hepburn, George Peppard, Patricia Neal, Buddy Ebsen, Martin Balsam, John McGiver, Mickey Rooney, Jose-Luis de Villalonga, Gil Lamb, Nicky Blair, Stanley Adams, Joan Staley. Producers: Martin Jurow, Richard Shepherd. Director: Blake Edwards. Screenplay: George Axelrod, from the novella by Truman Capote. Cinematographer: Franz

Planer. Music: Henry Mancini, with lyrics to "Moon River" by Johnny Mercer. Technicolor, 115 minutes.

The Children's Hour (United Artists, 1961). Cast: Audrey Hepburn, Shirley MacLaine, Miriam Hopkins, Fay Bainter, Karen Balkin, Veronica Cartwright, Mimi Gibson, Debbie Moldow, Hope Summers. Producer-Director: William Wyler. Screenplay: John Michael Hayes, from the Broadway stage play by Lillian Hellman. Cinematographer: Franz Planer. Music: Alex North. B&W, 107 minutes. (Released in Great Britain as *The Loudest Whisper*.)

Charade (Universal, 1963). Cast: Cary Grant, Audrey Hepburn, Walter Matthau, James Coburn, George Kennedy, Ned Glass, Jacques Marin, Paul Bonifas, Dominique Minot, Thomas Chelimsky. Producer-Director: Stanley Donen. Screenplay: Peter Stone, from a story, "The Unsuspecting Wife," by Stone and Marc Behm. Cinematographer: Charles Lang, Jr. Music: Henry Mancini, lyrics to title song by Johnny Mercer. Technicolor, 114 minutes. (Produced after *Paris—When It Sizzles* but released theatrically five months earlier.)

Paris When It Sizzles (Paramount, 1964). Cast: William Holden, Audrey Hepburn, Gregoire Aslan, Raymond Bussieres, Christian Duvallex, Thomas Michel, with cameo appearances by Noel Coward, Tony Curtis, Mel Ferrer, Marlene Dietrich. Producers: Richard Quine, George

Axelrod. Director: Richard Quine. Screenplay: George Axelrod, adapted from *Holiday for Henrietta*, by Julien Duvivier and Henri Jeanson. Cinematographer: Charles Lang, Jr. Music: Nelson Riddle. Technicolor, 110 minutes. (Produced prior to *Charade* but released theatrically five months later.)

My Fair Lady (Warner Brothers, 1964). Cast: Audrey Hepburn, Rex Harrison, Stanley Holloway, Wilfred Hyde-White, Gladys Cooper, Jeremy Brett, Theodore Bikel, Isobel Elsom, Mona Washbourne, Walter Burke, John Holland, Henry Daniell, Grady Sutton, Moyna Macgill, Alan Napier, Betty Blythe, Marjorie Bennett, Queenie Leonard, AH singing voice dubbed by Marni Nixon. Producer: Jack L. Warner. Director: George Cukor. Screenplay: Alan Jay Lerner, from his book for the 1956 Broadway musical adapted from George Bernard Shaw's play *Pygmalion*. Cinematographer: Harry Stradling. Music: composed by Frederick Loewe, lyrics by Alan Jay Lerner. Super Panavision 70, Technicolor, 170 minutes.

How to Steal a Million (20th Century-Fox, 1966). Cast: Audrey Hepburn, Peter O'Toole, Charles Boyer, Hugh Griffith, Eli Wallach, Fernand Gravet, Marcel Dalio, Jacques Marin, Moustache, Roger Treville, Eddie Malin, Bert Bertram. Producer: Fred Kohlmar. Director: William Wyler. Screenplay: Harry Kurnitz, from a story by George Bradshaw. Cinematographer:

Charles Lang, Jr. Music: Johnny Williams. Panavision, DeLuxe Color, 127 minutes.

Two for the Road (20th Century-Fox, 1967). Cast: Audrey Hepburn, Albert Finney, Eleanor Bron, William Daniels, Claude Dauphin, Nadia Gray, Libby Morris, Jacqueline Bisset, Judy Cornwell, Georges Descrieres, Gabrielle Middleton, Cathy Jones, Carol Van Dyke, Karyn Balm, Irene Hilda, Mario Verdon, Roger Dann. Producer-Director: Stanley Donen. Screenplay: Frederic Raphael. Cinematographer: Christopher Challis. Music: Henry Mancini, lyrics to title song by Leslie Bricusse. Panavision, DeLuxe Color, 112 minutes.

Wait Until Dark (Warner Brothers, 1967). Cast: Audrey Hepburn, Alan Arkin, Richard Crenna, Efrem Zimbalist, Jr., Jack Weston, Samantha Jones, Julie Herrod, Frank O'Brien. Producer: Mel Ferrer. Director: Terence Young. Screenplay: Robert and Jane Howard-Carrington, from the play by Frederick Knott. Cinematographer: Charles Lang, Jr. Music: Henry Mancini, lyrics to title song by Jay Livingston and Ray Evans. Technicolor, 108 minutes.

Robin and Marian (Columbia, 1976). Cast: Sean Connery, Audrey Hepburn, Robert Shaw, Nicol Williamson, Richard Harris, Denholm Elliott, Ronnie Barker, Kenneth Haigh, Ian Holm, Bill Maynard, Esmond Knight, Veronica Quilligan, Peter Butterworth. Producer: Denis

O'Dell. Director: Richard Lester. Executive Producer for Rastar: Richard Shepherd. Screenplay: James Goldman. Cinematographer: David Watkin. Music: John Barry. Technicolor, 107 minutes.

Sidney Sheldon's Bloodline (Paramount, 1979). Cast: Audrey Hepburn, Ben Gazzara, James Mason, Omar Sharif, Michelle Phillips, Romy Schneider, Claudia Mori, Irene Papas, Maurice Ronet, Beatrice Straight, Gert Frobe, Wolfgang Preiss, Guy Rolfe. Producers: David V. Picker, Sidney Beckerman. Director: Terence Young. Screenplay: Laird Koenig, from the novel by Sidney Sheldon. Cinematographer: Freddie Young. Music: Ennio Morricone. Panavision, color, 116 minutes.

They All Laughed (Time-Life Films, 20th Century–Fox, 1981). Cast: Audrey Hepburn, Ben Gazzara, John Ritter, Colleen Camp, Patti Hansen, Dorothy Stratten, Sean Ferrer, Linda MacEwen, Glenn Scarpelli, Vassily Lambrinos, Elizabeth Pena. Producers: George Morfogen, Blaine Novak. Director: Peter Bogdanovich. Screenplay: Peter Bogdanovich. Cinematographer: Robby Muller. Music: Douglas Dilge, title song by George and Ira Gershwin. Color, 115 minutes.

Always (Universal/United Artists, 1989). Cast: Richard Dreyfuss, Holly Hunter, Brad Johnson, John Goodman, Audrey Hepburn, Roberts Blossom, Keith David, Ed Van Nuys, Marg

Helgenberger, Dale Dye, Brian Haley. Producers: Steven Spielberg, Frank Marshall, Kathleen Kennedy. Director: Steven Spielberg. Screenplay: Jerry Belson; based on *A Guy Named Joe*, script by Dalton Trumbo, original story by Chandler Sprague and David Boehm. Cinematographer: Mikael Salomon. Music: John Williams. Technicolor, 125 minutes.

TELEVISION PRODUCTIONS

Mayerling (NBC, 1957). Cast: Audrey Hepburn, Mel Ferrer, Raymond Massey, Diana Wynyard, Basil Sydney, Judith Evelyn, Lorne Greene, Nehemiah Persoff, Nancy Marchand, Monique Van Vooren, Sorrell Booke, Suzy Parker. Producer: Fred Coe. Director: Anatole Litvak. Teleplay: adapted from 1935 screenplay by Joseph Kessel and J. V. Cube, based on Claude Anet's novel *Idyll's End*. Color, approximately 90 minutes. American premiere broadcast on February 4, 1957, on the *Producers' Showcase* series. Limited theatrical distribution abroad by Paramount Pictures.

Love Among Thieves (ABC, 1987). Cast: Audrey Hepburn, Robert Wagner, Jerry Orbach, Ismael Carlo, Samantha Eggar, Christopher Neame, Patrick Bauchau. Producer: Robert A. Papazian. Director: Roger Young. Teleplay: Stephen Black, Henry Stern, and Sally Robinson. Color, 100 minutes.

BROADWAY STAGE PRODUCTIONS

Gigi (1951). Cast: Audrey Hepburn, Cathleen Nesbitt, Doris Patson, Josephine Brown, Bertha Belmore, Michael Evans, Francis Compton. Producer: Gilbert Miller. Director: Raymond Rouleau. Play in two acts by Anita Loos, based on the novella by Colette. Opened at New York's Fulton Theatre on November 24, 1951, ran for 217 performances.

Ondine (1954). Cast: Audrey Hepburn, Mel Ferrer, John Alexander, Edith King, Alan Hewitt, Marian Seldes, Robert Middleton, Lloyd Gough, Dran and Tani Seitz, Sonia Torgeson, James Lanphier, Peter Brandon, Faith Burwell, William Podmore. Producer: The Playwrights Company (Maxwell Anderson, Robert Anderson, Elmer Rice, Robert E. Sherwood, Roger L. Stevens, John F. Wharton). Director: Alfred Lunt. Play in three acts by Jean Giraudoux, English adaptation by Maurice Valency. Music: Virgil Thomson. Opened at New York's 46th Street Theatre on February 18, 1954, ran for 156 performances.

bibliography

Arce, Hector. *Gary Cooper: An Intimate Biography*. New York: William Morrow & Company, 1979.

Beaton, Cecil. *Self-Portrait With Friends: The Selected Diaries of Cecil Beaton*, 1922–74. New York: Times Books, 1979.

Blyth, Myrna. "Audrey Hepburn at Fifty," *Family Circle* Magazine, June 1979.

Brynner, Rock. *Yul: The Man Who Would Be King*. New York: Simon & Schuster, 1989.

Casper, Joseph A. *Stanley Donen*. Metuchen, N.J.: The Scarecrow Press, 1983.

Clinch, Minty. *Burt Lancaster*. London: Arthur Baker, Ltd., 1984.

Deane-Drummond, Anthony. *Return Ticket*. Philadelphia: Lippincott, 1954.

Dunne, Dominick. "Hepburn Heart," *Vanity Fair* Magazine, May 1991.

Frain, Irene, and Jean-Claude Zana. "Givenchy Remembers Audrey," *Paris Match*, February 4, 1993.

Friedhoff, Herman. *Requiem for the Resistance: The Civilian Struggle Against Nazism in Holland and Germany*. London: Bloomsbury, 1988.

Giles, Sarah. *Fred Astaire: His Friends Talk*. New York: Doubleday, 1988.

Harris, Eleanor. "Audrey Hepburn," *Good Housekeeping* Magazine, August 1959.

Harris, Marlys J. *The Zanucks of Hollywood*. New York: Crown, 1989.

Harris, Radie. *Radie's World*. New York: G. P. Putnam's Sons, 1975.

Harrison, Rex. *A Damned Serious Business*. New York: Bantam Books, 1991.

Higham, Charles, and Roy Moseley. *Princess Merle: The Romantic Life of Merle Oberon*. New York: Coward-McCann & Geoghegan, 1983.

Huston, John. *An Open Book*. New York: Alfred A. Knopf, 1980.

Jong, Louis de. *The Netherlands and Nazi Germany*. Cambridge, Mass.: Harvard University Press, 1990.

Kael, Pauline. *When the Lights Go Down*. New York: Holt, Rinehart and Winston, 1980.

Klein, Edward. "Audrey Hepburn: 'You Can't Love Without the Fear of Losing,'" *Parade Magazine*, March 5, 1989.

Knight, Dennis. *Harvest of Messerschmitts: The Chronicle of a Village at War*. London: F. Warne, 1981.

Lehman, Peter, and William Luhr. *Blake Edwards*. Athens, Ohio: Ohio University Press, 1981.

Leigh, Wendy. *Liza: Born a Star*. New York: E. P. Dutton, 1993.

Loos, Anita. *Cast of Thousands*. New York: Grosset &Dunlap, 1977.

Madsen, Axel. *William Wyler*. New York: Crowell, 1973.

McGilligan, Patrick. *George Cukor: A Double Life*. New York: St. Martin's Press, 1991.

Mosley, Nicholas. *Beyond the Pale: Sir Oswald*

Mosley and Family, 1933–80. London: Secker & Warburg, 1983.

Nelson, Nancy. *Evenings With Cary Grant*. New York: William Morrow & Company, 1991.

Noorbergen, Rene. *Shadow of Terror*. Washington, D.C.: Review and Herald Pub. Association, 1990.

Parker, John. *Sean Connery*. London: Victor Gollancz, 1993.

Payn, Graham, and Sheridan Morley, editors. *The Noel Coward Diaries*. Boston: Little, Brown and Company, 1982.

Pepper, Curtis Bill. "The Return of Audrey Hepburn," *McCall's* Magazine, January 1976.

Reed, Rex. *Valentines & Vitriol*. New York: Delacorte Press, 1977.

Rogers, Henry C. *Walking the Tightrope*. New York: William Morrow & Company, 1980.

Ryan, Cornelius. *A Bridge Too Far*. New York: Simon & Schuster, 1974.

Simpson, A. W. B. *In the Highest Degree Odious*: *Detention Without Trial in Wartime Britain*. New York: Oxford University Press, 1992.

Sinyard, Neil. *The Films of Richard Lester*. London: Croom Helm, 1985.

Stevenson, Burton E. *The Spell of Holland*. Boston: L. C. Page & Company, 1911.

Thomas, Bob. *Golden Boy*: *The Untold Story of William Holden*. New York: St. Martin's Press, 1983.

Van der Zee, Henri. *The Hunger Winter*: *Occupied Holland, 1944–45*. London: J. Norman & Hobhouse, 1982.

Vickers, Hugo. *Cecil Beaton: A Biography*. Boston: Little, Brown and Company, 1985.

Vidor, King. *King Vidor on Film Making*. New York: David McKay Company, 1972.

Wapshott, Nicholas. *Peter O'Toole: A Biography*. New York: Beaufort Books, 1983.

Warner, Jack L., with Dean Jennings. *My First 100 Years in Hollywood*. New York: Random House, 1964.

Wiley, Mason, and Damien Bona. *Inside Oscar: The Unofficial History of the Academy Awards*. New York: Ballantine Books, 1986.

Wood, Tom. *The Bright Side of Billy Wilder, Primarily*. Garden City, N.Y.: Doubleday & Company, 1970.

Woodward, Ian. *Audrey Hepburn*. New York, St. Martin's Press, 1984.

Yule, Andrew. *Picture Shows: The Life and Films of Peter Bogdanovich*. New York: Limelight Editions, 1992.

Zinnemann, Fred. *An Autobiography*. London: Bloomsbury, 1992.

Zolotow, Maurice. *Billy Wilder in Hollywood*. New York: G. P. Putnam's Sons, 1977.

IF YOU HAVE ENJOYED READING THIS
LARGE PRINT BOOK AND YOU WOULD
LIKE MORE INFORMATION ON HOW
TO ORDER A WHEELER LARGE PRINT
BOOK, PLEASE WRITE TO:

WHEELER PUBLISHING, INC.
P.O. BOX 531
ACCORD, MA 02018-0531